Fr. McBride's
GUIDE
TO THE
BIBLE

Fr. McBride's
GUIDE
TO THE
BIBLE

ALFRED McBRIDE, O.Praem.

Our Sunday Visitor Publishing Division
Our Sunday Visitor, Inc.
Huntington, Indiana 46750

Nihil Obstat: Rev. Michael Heintz
Censor Librorum

Imprimatur: ✠ John M. D'Arcy
Bishop of Fort Wayne-South Bend
January 22, 2004

The *Nihil Obstat* and *Imprimatur* are official declarations that a book or pamphlet is free from doctrinal or moral error. It is not implied that those who have granted the *Nihil Obstat* and *Imprimatur* agree with the contents, opinions, or statements expressed.

Unless otherwise noted, Scripture citations are taken from the *The Catholic Edition of the Revised Standard Version of the Bible* (RSV), copyright © 1965, 1966 by the Division of Christian Education of the National Council of Churches of Christ in the United States of America. Used by permission. All rights reserved.

Other Scripture citations, marked with NRSV, are taken from the *The Catholic Edition of the New Revised Standard Version Bible*, copyright © 1989, 1993 Division of Christian Education of the National Council of the Churches of Christ in the United States of America. Used by permission. All rights reserved.

Psalm texts, unless marked otherwise, are taken from *The Psalms: A New Translation*, copyright © The Grail (England) 1963.

The text of this work is based on the teaching of the *Catechism of the Catholic Church*, second edition, for use in the United States of America, copyright © 1994 and 1997, United States Catholic Conference — *Libreria Editrice Vaticana*. Used with permission.

Every reasonable effort has been made to determine copyright holders of excerpted materials and to secure permissions as needed. If any copyrighted materials have been inadvertently used without proper credit being given in one form or another, please notify Our Sunday Visitor in writing so that future editions may be corrected accordingly.

Our Sunday Visitor Publishing Division
Our Sunday Visitor, Inc.
200 Noll Plaza
Huntington, IN 46750

ISBN: 978-1-59276-480-8 (Inventory No. T717)
LCCN: 2008927895

Cover design by Rebecca J. Heaston
Interior design by Sherri L. Hoffman

PRINTED IN THE UNITED STATES OF AMERICA

DEDICATION

I dedicate this book first of all to Father John Bradley who first conceived the idea for a popular companion to the Bible. It was he who edited the original text with his customary genius and his unflagging trust in the value of such books for the spiritual growth of its readers. Thanks, Father John, for a lifetime of friendship and for your passion for the building up of the Catholic Church. I also dedicate this book to Mr. Robert Gallagher, President and CEO of Good Will Publishers. I am grateful to him for releasing the original text, a substantial portion of which appears here. Thank you, Bob, for your missionary spirit in the field of Catholic publishing. Finally I dedicate this book to Greg Erlandson, President and Publisher of Our Sunday Visitor Company. Thank you, Greg, for making this *Guide to the Bible* available for yet another generation.

CONTENTS

Introduction   9

THE OLD TESTAMENT

  1. Creation   15
  2. The Story of Adam and Eve   21
  3. The First Murder   25
  4. God's Constant Concern for Us   30
  5. Abraham Is Our Father in Faith   35
  6. Faith in God Is More Important than Cleverness   40
  7. A Man of Faith and Forgiveness   45
  8. Moses Liberates the Hebrews from Slavery   50
  9. The Israelites' Pilgrimage to Sinai   56
10. The Ten Commandments   61
11. Joshua Conquers the Promised Land   66
12. The Judges: Israel's Charismatic Leaders   71
13. Samuel Creates the Monarchy   76
14. King Saul   81
15. David the King   86
16. The Psalms Are Songs of Faith   91
17. Solomon in All His Grandeur   95
18. Civil War between Israel and Judah   100
19. How the Bible Explains Sin and Salvation   104
20. Elijah: A Fervent and Fiery Prophet   109
21. The Babylonian Exile — Seventy Years of Tears   114
22. Old Testament Prophets — Three Ideas about the Messiah   119
23. Isaiah Sees the Glory   125
24. Jeremiah: The Prophet of Moral Responsibility   130
25. Ezekiel: Reverence the Holiness of God   135
26. Daniel: A Teen Hero   139
27. Amos and Social Justice: A Farmer Urges Social Reform   144
28. Hosea Celebrates God's Loyalty to His Covenant   149

29. The Revelation of Jesus Christ, Son of God and Son of Mary 157
30. St. Matthew's Account of the Birth of Jesus 161
31. St. Luke's Account of the Birth of Christ 167
32. John the Baptist Preaches Conversion 173
33. Jesus Is the Word Made Flesh 178
34. The Wedding Feast of Cana and the Cleansing of the
    Temple: Signs that Manifest Christ's Divinity 183
35. Nicodemus Learns How Much God Loves Us 188
36. Jesus Converts the Samaritan Woman 193
37. Christ Is the Living Bread Come Down from Heaven 198
38. Jesus Is the Living Water and the Light of the World 203
39. Jesus Heals the Man Born Blind 208
40. Jesus Is Our Good Shepherd 213
41. Jesus Raises Lazarus from the Dead 218
42. Jesus Is Tempted 223
43. Christ's Gospel of Love — The Sermon on the Mount 228
44. Jesus Performs Miracles — Signs and Wonders 233
45. Jesus Describes God's Kingdom and Church in Parables 238
46. Jesus Forms His Apostles for Ministry 243
47. Jesus Establishes His Church 248
48. Jesus Defends Two Women 253
49. Jesus Reveals His Glory at the Transfiguration 257
50. Jesus Comments on the Perils of Wealth and Concern
    for the Poor 262
51. Jesus Praises the Prodigal Son and Prodigal Father 266
52. Jesus Describes the Last Judgment 270
53. Jesus Begins His Passion 274
54. Jesus Goes to the Cross 279
55. Jesus Rises from the Dead 285
56. Jesus Sends the Holy Spirit to Us at Pentecost 290
57. Paul Preaches and Witnesses Jesus Christ to the World 295
58. Glory and Praise to You, Lord Jesus Christ 300

INTRODUCTION

All the great religions of the world begin with stories. The reason is that a story is one of the best ways of showing how God is present to every part of life. Originally, most of the Bible was not a written word, but a spoken word. Notable exceptions are the epistles of St. Paul and other New Testament letters. Generally speaking, the Bible was Holy Word before it was Holy Writ. The poets, bards, and minstrels of Israel spoke and sang these ancient stories from generation to generation.

The Story of Our Life with God

Each evening by the firelight the tales of the heroes, saints, kings, prophets, patriarchs, and warriors were told and retold. With each passing age, the narratives grew richer as new sagas of our life with God unfolded. Lest in some way the stories might be lost, they were reverently written down. Eventually they were "canonized" by the Spirit-appointed leaders of God's people as the Holy Word; that is, they really reflected God's intimate love affair with us. They really were God's revealed Word.

This story-telling quality shows why the Bible is best understood when read aloud. The text is rich enough to be tasted, and textured enough to be felt. In the old synagogues of Eastern Europe, they used to celebrate the "Ceremony of God's Sweetness." Very young children were brought to the synagogue for their first introduction to the Bible. A great old Bible was brought out and opened. Some honey was placed on the page and the child was invited to taste of the sweetness. In this way the child's first experience of God's word was pleasant.

The Inspiration of Great Men and Women

The Bible inspires us to live in honest relationship with God and others. Countless great men and women have cited the Bible as their greatest source of light and hope. It is not only the book of saints; it is also the book that helps make saints.

St. Thomas More, in the film, "The Man For All Seasons," says, "I am the king's true subject and [I] pray for him and all the realm. I do none harm.

I say none harm. And if this be not enough to keep a man alive, in good faith, I long not to live." Thomas More knew the spirit power of Scripture in the formation of saints.

Remember Damien who brought the Holy Word to the lepers at Molokai? He felt the spirit of the Bible.

> *"Sooner or later you will catch the disease yourself."*
> *"Yes, I know, but I must go."*
> *"Once you go, you may never be allowed to return."*
> *"I must go to Molokai."*

Getting to Know the Meaning of the Bible

Often we are afraid of something simply because we don't understand it. Too many people are afraid of really trying to get to know the meaning of the Bible because they fear they just won't understand it. Parts of the Bible are strange. However, the purpose of this book is to help you to see that it's really not so strange when you understand it better.

In the Bible you find quarreling brothers, jealous kings, noble patriots, witches, heroic women, prophets, and peaceful men of wisdom. The Bible has its share of wars, dances, revolutions, love, pioneering, and exile. Every major human feeling, failing, and triumph are included in its pages.

No Substitute for the Bible Itself

This is a guide-book to the Bible, and therefore not a substitute for reading actual words of the Bible. This guidebook, then, is intended to lead you to that nourishment that God's Holy Word alone can give you — the divine nourishment through which you will "grow in grace." And this means that as you grow physically in stature, you will also grow "in wisdom and in favor with God and men" (Luke 2:52).

> *For just as from the heavens*
> *the rain and the snow come down*
> *And do not return there*
> *till they have watered the earth,*
> *making it fertile and fruitful,*
> *Giving seed to him who sows*
> *and bread to him who eats,*
> *So shall my word be*
> *that goes forth from my mouth;*
> *It shall not return to me void,*

but shall do my will,
achieving the end for which I sent it.

ISAIAH 55:10-11

The Vision and Method of This Book

In one sense the Bible is quite accessible to a reader. But in another sense one may have difficulty in sensing the progress of the narrative and the coherence of the whole presentation. This is particularly true when reading the Old Testament which spans so many years between the creation of the world, the fall of our first parents, the first aftermath, the call of Abraham and the other patriarchs, the call of Moses, the cycle of the Judges, the chronicles of the kings, the preaching and witness of the prophets and the wisdom writers. In the New Testament the gospels are the clearest expression of God's Word, since it is actually the Son of God, the Word made flesh who is the dazzling center of these unforgettable narratives.

Each of the following lessons centers on God's loving plan to save us from original and actual sin and from the guilt that goes with such sin. Not only does God save us from evil, but the Lord also offers us divine life, grace, and union with the Holy Spirit to make possible a deep union between each of us and the Holy Trinity.

I have selected the major stories found in the Old Testament and laid them out in such a way that you can sense the flow of the history of salvation. I have tried to make this part of the text a coherent presentation of the Old Testament's account of God's revelation of his plan to save us. In the New Testament I have centered on Jesus Christ, our Savior. I begin with the birth stories of Jesus and conclude with the narrative of his passion, death, and resurrection. In between, I place the highlights of Christ's public ministry that began in Galilee and concluded in Judea and Jerusalem.

After every story, you will find a "reflection" designed to help you interiorize the message of the account and apply it to your spiritual and moral behavior. This is followed by clusters of questions for dialogue which you may use for discussion either in your parish or on your own to help you make further applications of God's Word to your life. Every lesson closes with a prayer and a quote taken either from Scripture or from other writers.

It is my hope that you will go on to make your own comparisons and applications to your personal life. Never forget, however, that the Holy Word itself has the most importance. "Let the word of Christ dwell in you richly, as in all wisdom you teach and admonish one another, singing psalms, hymns and spiritual songs with gratitude in your hearts to God" (Colossians 3:16).

THE OLD TESTAMENT

CHAPTER 1

Creation

Genesis 1:1-25; 2:1-4

In the beginning God created the heavens and the earth.

The earth was without form and void, and darkness was upon the face of the deep; and the Spirit of God was moving over the face of the waters.

GENESIS 1:1-2

AND GOD SAID, "THAT'S GOOD"

The Bible's description of creation gives us an earth's eye view of the ordered universe (the cosmos). In the geography of the times, the earth was considered to be flat. It rested on an ocean of water. Seas and rivers were places where this ocean pierced through the earth's surface. The sky was like a solid astrodome neatly fitted to the edges of the earth. Its purpose was to keep out the waters above the sky.

The sun, moon, and stars were like electric lights screwed into the sky-ceiling, which the Bible calls the firmament. In the firmament, also, were trapdoors that God occasionally opened to let down some rain. The people of these ancient times believed that one could fall off the edge of the earth into the great ocean if he walked far enough in a set direction.

People then spoke of three heavens. The first was the atmosphere between earth and sky. The second heaven was the sky itself, conceived of as a solid dome. The third heaven was God's dwelling place above the sky. St. Paul described a vision he had of God in terms of being swept up into the third heaven. "I know a man in Christ who fourteen years ago was caught up into the third heaven" (2 Corinthians 12:2). Numerous biblical passages about heaven picture God's throne to be in a heaven above the skies. Popularly we still think and speak this way, even though we realize God's heaven is not a place in physical terms, but a state of glory and love and unimaginable happiness.

The Spirit Breath of God Drew Order from Disorder

Not having our scientific knowledge, the people of ancient times naturally saw the world this way because that is how it presented itself to them.

To their minds, the basic element was the ocean, a surrounding and terrifying chaos (trackless waste and emptiness). It was out of this chaos that God drew the cosmos. "The earth was without form and void, and darkness was upon the face of the deep [chaos]." Over this formless chaos roamed the creative breath of God, called his Spirit. "And the Spirit of God was moving over the face of the waters" (Genesis 1:2).

Hence, the breath that is God's Holy Spirit hovered over the waters of chaos and drew forth the cosmos. Here we have a theme that will be carried out many times in the Bible — bringing Noah's family out of the chaos of the deluge, saving Lot's family from the chaos of Sodom and Gomorrah as the salt sea surrounded it, rescuing Israel from the chaotic waters of the Red Sea, and drawing Jesus forth from the waters of the Jordan to inaugurate a new creation.

Other Creation Stories

Ever since the explosion of archeological studies, there has been a tendency to see, in the literature of other cultures, comparisons to the stories found in the Bible. Archeologists have found creation stories among the Babylonians that show similarities to the biblical accounts. The Babylonian creation myth, "Enuma Elish," speaks of a titanic battle between the goddess Tiamat and Marduk. *Tiamat* means "chaos." She is slain by Marduk.

Then he, together with another character named Bel, carve up her carcass to make the earth. For biblical studies, the point to be made here is that creation is a process whereby the cosmos is produced out of the chaos. Just doing a little word study enforces the point. Tiamat comes from the word *tehom* meaning chaos. In turn, tehom is a sister word to *tohu*, which is part of the biblical word for chaos.

The beauty of comparing the biblical narrative to the Babylonian one is seen in the restraint and dignity of the biblical text. Gone is the grisly carving scene. The violence of the Babylonian myth gives way to the serene poetry of the biblical text.

The Hebrews Saw Creation as an Ongoing Process

Generally, the question of evolution arises whenever the creation story comes up. What is this matter of the six days? Can we reconcile the theory of evolution with the biblical narrative? As to the six days, we have the matter of the rabbinic teaching about the Sabbath. Hebrew religion stressed that the seventh day should be a time of reflecting on God's gift of creation and the call of humanity to express thanks to God and promise dependence upon the Lord. To reinforce this act of adoration, they described God as a Hebrew laborer who works hard for six days and rests on the seventh day. The faithful Israelite could do no better than imitate the Lord in this regard.

Concerning the matter of evolution, the verb forms used in the creation story are dynamic, not static. In Hebrew, the atmosphere of creation is one of process, not of a finished task. It is not as though creation happened and then is all over with. Rather, creation is something that begins and continues. The process of removing the chaos and bringing about order is a continuous task. God providentially presides over and sustains this process.

God begins the work of creation and fathers forth a world that is to be like a son or daughter to him. But ultimately, he brings forth man and woman who shall be stewards of creation and cooperators with God in the creative task. Certainly, the Hebrew authors were not thinking of the theory of evolution. It was not a problem for them.

These authors used the poetry of the seven days to defend the Sabbath rest. They used dynamic verb forms to show that creation was a process of bringing order out of chaos, and that this was a work common to mankind as imaging the Lord. They didn't do this as a concession to Darwin. It was simply their normal way of understanding the creation event. From a scientific point of view the Bible is a book that shows us how to get to heaven, not a technical work that shows us how the heavens go.

A Note on Evolution: There are varying scientific theories of how the universe evolved. The Church's view is that evolutionary explanations should be understood in the framework of God's original creative act and his providential presence to the process of development. Regarding human beings, the Church maintains that God infuses the human soul at each conception.

God Created Man and Woman in His Own Image

More than likely the creation story as we now have it was written by Israelite clergy. So much of the language used reminds us of the liturgy, which is the central concern of priests. Creation is described in terms of the temple. The word for firmament is borrowed from the word used for the roof of the Jerusalem temple. The words for the sun and stars were taken from the names used for lighting equipment in the temple. God's blessing of creation ("he saw that it was good") is similar to the clerical blessings normally given in the temple.

In other words, the temple was the symbol of the really great temple of creation established by God. Both prophets and priests throughout Israelite history strove to keep the people from idolatry. They insisted that no carved item could be an image of God. They were never totally successful. Images of cherubim were allowed to hold up the Ark of the Covenant. The priestly theologians eventually arrived at the insight that the real image of God is man and woman. No image could be better. "So God created man in his own image" (Genesis 1:27).

What It Means to Be the Image of God

To be the image of God meant three things. First, we are expected to continue the work of creation in cooperation with God. We are to bring life to the earth, develop the potentiality of the universe, and do both of these things for the sake of human concern and the glory of God. God did not lose interest in the world after its creation. He continues to sustain and guide creation by his love, power, and mercy. This is called the providence of God. While he invites us to assume our responsibility for creation, he offers his providential graces to make this possible.

Second, we image God:

- by using our minds to know and apply the truth.
- by directing our wills to love the good and live by it.
- by directing our emotions and passions to serve truth and love.
- by developing our consciences to know what is right and wrong and follow God's will.

As images of God we are blessed with these inner drives to accomplish God's will in creation.

Third, in so acting, we manifest the creative wisdom of God and, therefore, the presence of God. God's presence breaks through in our lives as we imitate God's creative thrust and celebrate his wisdom in the heart of the earth. As we will see, the story of the fall of man and woman and all kinds of sinful behavior became radical obstacles to the proper use of creation. Salvation was needed. Hence a new man had to come.

This new man was Jesus, the most perfect image of God. Indeed Jesus is the Son of God and son of Mary. "He is the image of the invisible God, the first-born of all creation" (Colossians 1:15). Today's Christians should remember their call to image God. They should rejoice that this is made more possible now because Christ has shown us the way and given us the power through Baptism, the other sacraments, above all, the Eucharist.

REFLECTION

In the beginning there was only God. There was nothing side by side with God — no earth, no sky, no material. The term *creation* means that God created the heavens and the earth out of nothing. Everything outside of God must attribute its existence to God. This is the meaning of the first verse of the Bible: "In the beginning, God created the heavens and the earth" (Genesis 1:1).

A human artist or craftsman makes something out of something, a statue out of a block of marble, a wall out of bricks. We tend to call artists creative because their productions seem like God's act of creation. But this is only a comparison. God's act is essentially different. God created all that exists out of nothing. The Genesis narrative uses ancient people's imagination of how this happened.

FOR DIALOGUE

When you hear the words *imagination* and *creation*, what thoughts and images occur to you? Among those you know, who would you consider to be creative? When you look around the natural world, what parts of creation most impress you?

God created the world and ourselves out of love for us. God calls us to be loving stewards of creation. What are three ways you can fulfill this calling? Why is it wrong to misuse the gifts of creation? How does this calling affect our concerns about the environment?

What do we mean by God's providence? How does it link with creation? What are some ways to understand ourselves as images of God? Which aspect of imaging God means the most to you?

PRAYER

Bless the Lord, all you works of the Lord.
Angels of the Lord, bless the Lord.
Sun and moon, bless the Lord.
Holy men and women of humble heart, bless the Lord.
ADAPTED FROM CANTICLE OF DANIEL (DANIEL 3)

In the beginning was the Word, and the Word was with God, and the Word was God... All things came into being through him, and without him not one thing came into being.

JOHN 1: 1-3, NRSV

We believe in one God, the Father, the Almighty, maker of heaven and earth, of all that is seen and unseen.

PROFESSION OF FAITH — THE NICENE CREED

CHAPTER 2

The Story of Adam and Eve

Genesis 1:26-31; 2:5-25; 3:1-24

So God created man in his own image, in the image of God he created him; male and female he created them.... And God saw everything that he had made, and behold, it was very good.

GENESIS 1:27, 31

ADAM VERSUS CHRIST

Probably no Old Testament story has been retold more often than the fascinating story of Adam and Eve. It has been approached in many different ways. Theologians examine it for the impact of original sin and the need for redemption. Biblical scholars wrestle with the comparisons between the old Adam and Christ, the new Adam. Archeologists, historians, and poets are also interested in this story from their own special viewpoints.

The book of Genesis contains two accounts of the way God created man and woman. In the first narrative, God simply speaks and they were made. "Let us make man in our image ... male and female he created them" (Genesis 1:26-27). This version emphasizes the great dignity given to them in being images of God.

In the second account, God makes the man from the clay and breathes life into him. God fashions the woman from the man's rib (cf. Genesis 2:7; 21-22). The man was alone and had no human companion. No animal could be his partner. When the man sees the woman, he cries out with joy that here at last was bone of his bone. He realizes that the woman is another truly human being. They are equal as persons and with human dignity. As male and female they complement one another. In marriage they will form one flesh and transmit human life.

These creation narratives tell in symbolic language truths about the origins of the world and human beings. The Church interprets this symbolic language in the light of the New Testament, teaching us that Adam and Eve were created in a state of original holiness (cf. CCC 375). They lived in harmony with God, each other and creation. God placed them in the garden of paradise — or Eden. From their friendship with God flowed their happiness.

The Fall

Adam and Eve received the gift of freedom. Their joy rested on their free obedience to God. They were told they could eat of the fruits of all trees except the tree of knowledge of good and evil. Obeying this rule, they would admit their dependence on God and the moral laws that determine the right use of reason.

Satan, a fallen angel, tempted Eve to partake of the forbidden fruit. In turn she persuaded Adam to do the same. Scripture proceeds to show the sad consequences of this first sin, what St. Augustine would call original sin.

The couple lost the grace of original holiness. They suddenly found it hard to use their spiritual faculties to control their passions. The harmony between man and woman was replaced by tension. Harmony with creation was severed. Death entered human history.

The next eight chapters of Genesis chronicle the dismal outcome of sin in human history. Cain commits the first murder, killing his brother, Abel. Vanity and pride move men to build a tower right up to heaven. It became known as the Tower of Babel — or babbling, since God caused the builders to lose their understanding of one another's languages. In the Noah story the whole earth is seen as corrupt except for one just family. A flood is needed to wash away the evil. Nonetheless, God's forgiving love is always present as will be seen in his promise of salvation to Adam and Eve.

Garden of Eden Story and Babylonian Gardens

Our first parents were removed from the Garden of Eden. Angels with fiery swords guarded the gates to prevent any return. Archeologists suggest that the pictorial features of the story of the Garden of Eden are taken from Hebrew memories of their life in Babylon during the Exile. Many of them worked as gardeners and landscapers on the vast estates of their Babylonian masters.

Most estates had fruit orchards, and some of the trees were highly cultivated to produce exceptional fruit. These were the masters' favorite trees, and the workers were strictly forbidden to touch such trees or take any of the fruit. If they stole the fruit, they would be fired from the estate.

Around these estates were large walls. At the gates it was common to have decorations. Sometimes, carved on these gates were powerful winged creatures brandishing fiery swords. These figures served as symbolic guardians of the masters' lands. It could be that this situation provided the sacred writer with powerful and memorable material to describe the rebellion of man and woman against God.

Adam and Eve were like Hebrew gardeners on a Babylonian estate. Against strict orders they stole fruit from the favored tree, and so were fired from the garden of happiness. At the gates were the fiery guards forbidding their re-entry into the master's house. Whether or not these were the cultural images used by the sacred writer, it does remind us that he wanted to present a vivid and relevant account of the fall of man in a way the readers would best understand.

God Promises Salvation

Before they leave the garden, Adam and Eve hear a mysterious and reassuring promise from God of a future salvation. The Lord says to the serpent, "I will put enmity between you and the woman, and between your offspring and hers. He will strike at your head, while you strike at his heel" (Genesis 3:15, NRSV). The offspring spoken of here is the future Messiah. The woman will be Mary, the new Eve. The serpent is Satan. Christ the new Adam will triumph over sin and death. Mary will benefit from this saving act. By the merits of her Son she will be preserved from original sin. By a special grace of God she will not commit any sin in her life.

Hence, at the dawn of human history, the Good News of God's loving salvation is revealed even as the first man and woman sin. God's grace will be greater than any sin committed. God's love will be more powerful than any evil performed.

REFLECTION

We all know there is evil in the world. We need God's revelation to clarify the meaning of sin both now and in our origins. Today some see sin simply as a psychological flaw, a mistake, or the result of social pressures. But in the light of God we realize sin is the abuse of our freedom.

Adam and Eve committed a personal sin that affected all humans. This is original sin, the privation of original holiness that is transmitted to all people by propagation. We do not commit this sin, but we inherit it.

Baptism erases original sin and all personal sin and guilt. In imparting to us the life of Christ and his graces, we are restored to God's friendship. Baptism takes away the sin, but not the damage. We retain a tendency to sin and a weakness in the face of evil. To counter this, we need rich infusions of Christ's graces through prayer, the practice of virtues, and the wealth of spiritual powers found in the Eucharist.

FOR DIALOGUE

If you wanted to demonstrate the dignity and equality of Adam and Eve to one another, what Scripture passages would you cite?

Who gave them these gifts?

God also gave them freedom. When we say their joy came from using their freedom to obey God's laws, what do we mean? While freedom includes the possibility of sinning, why do we say that using freedom to do evil reduces our freedom?

Why is it important to note that God immediately introduces the promise of salvation just after the sin of Adam and Eve? Why is it indicated that the sacred author used figurative and symbolic language to narrate the creation event and what occurred in the lives of the first man and woman?

PRAYER

Jesus, renew in us the graces of our Baptism and enrich us with the spiritual powers of the Eucharist. Send us your Spirit to teach us your law and fill us with the strength to resist temptation.

"Being man" or "being woman" is a reality which is good and willed by God.

CCC 369

The London Times once asked some authors to write an essay on the topic, "What's Wrong with the World?" Catholic convert Gilbert Chesterton wrote this brief reply:

Dear Sirs:
I am.

Sincerely yours,
G.K. CHESTERTON

CHAPTER 3

The First Murder

Genesis 4:1-16

By faith Abel offered to God a more acceptable sacrifice than Cain....

HEBREWS 11:4

CAIN AND ABEL

After Adam and Eve were expelled from the Garden of Eden, the effects of their sin were chronicled in Genesis chapters 4-11. These chapters of Genesis contain two narratives that exemplify the spread of evil: Cain's killing of Abel, covered in this lesson, and the account of Noah and the Flood, covered in the next.

The Genesis narrative says that Cain and Abel were children of Adam and Eve. Abel became a shepherd and offered sacrifices pleasing to God. Cain became a farmer and eventually the founder of a town (cf. Genesis 4:17). God did not accept his sacrificial offerings because they were offered without faith, meaning without any sense of a personal relationship with God. Cain was jealous of Abel and angry about Abel's friendship with God. One day he took his brother out to the fields and killed him.

God spoke to Cain and asked him where his brother was. Cain replied that he was not his brother's keeper. God questioned him further stating that the blood of Abel cried out from the earth. God told Cain he must repent of the murder for the rest of his life. But also God put a mark on Cain to protect him from being killed by someone else.

Anyone who has ever had a brother knows the kind of rivalry that can easily grow between brothers. In the Cain and Abel story, this rivalry is carried to its extreme form in Cain's murderous hatred of Abel that ended in Abel's death. This event has acquired applications beyond the account of a murder in the distant mists of history. The Israelites saw in the account three different levels of meaning that concerned: (1) the change from pastoral to city life; (2) the hostility between Israel, the northern kingdom, and Judah the southern kingdom; (3) freedom of worship granted by the Israelites to the neighboring Kenite tribe. We shall consider each of these in turn.

The Change from Pastoral to City Life

In her earliest days, Israel had been a pastoral community wandering from place to place with her sheep. The Israelites associated their nomadic existence in the desert of Sinai with the intense religious experience of the covenant and the giving of the Ten Commandments. Their memory of this life evoked the idealism of the founding fathers and of the unstained purity of real religion.

As they settled into urban life, established a monarchy, and organized their nation, there arose a suspicion and guilt about their new existence. Religious thinkers kept alive the doubt that genuine religion could thrive in the city. They saw the city as basically evil, or at least so immediate an occasion of sin that it did not deserve wholehearted approval.

The city was too secular, leading its residents in a hundred different ways to forget God and indulge in selfishness and idolatry. The sophisticated city dweller had no time for the smells and vulgarity of the shepherds. The technology of the city was superior to the grazing of sheep. Even in our own time, slang puts it this way: the city slicker will put the country hick in his place.

The Cain and Abel story is an image of this conflict. Abel, as the noble shepherd whose sacrifice is pleasing to God, represents the idealism of the pastoral community. Cain, the founder of the first city, is the anxiety-ridden symbol of urban life whose inability to truly worship God leads him to destroy his brother. The original text gave no reason why God preferred Abel's sacrifice to Cain's, but the readers of the original story knew well that it signified the abiding conviction that God could not be worshipped best in the city.

Hostility between Israel and Judah

The story also served as a symbol of the hostility that existed between the northern and southern kingdoms — Israel and Judah. Only for two brief reigns did the Hebrews know political unity. Under David and Solomon, all twelve tribes were united under throne and altar in Jerusalem. But no sooner was Solomon dead than a civil war broke out and the kingdom split apart. From that time on, the hostility between Israel and Judah became a matter of fact.

Judah, the less prosperous nation, considered itself the true religion, and Jerusalem the only true place to offer sacrifice to God. It chose David, the shepherd king, as its patron, and like Abel, was comforted in the thought that God would be pleased with its worship. Israel thrived economically, with its merchant princes making money from wars and natural resources. It entered into treaties with Syria to form a coalition to conquer Judah, and thus kill off its brother.

In the story of the Samaritan woman at the well of Jacob, the woman feels that Jesus would not consider worship at Gerizim, the holy mountain of the northern kingdom, pleasing to God. In other words, Israel was Cain, in the minds of the southern kingdom. Israel was the alienated brother, fat with wealth and poor in faith.

Freedom of Religion Recognized

One of the desert tribes that were neighbors to the people of God was the Kenites. It was traditionally held that they were founded by Cain. In some instances, Kenites lived in the same village with Israelites and were allowed freedom to worship their own god. Again the story of Cain and Abel appeared to be the background for this enlightened religious policy.

After Cain had killed Abel, he wandered "east of Eden." In his conversation with God following the murder, he felt so lost and alone that he thought he himself would be slaughtered by the first man he met. But God told him that any man who would touch him would be avenged by God himself. "'. . . Not so! If anyone slays Cain, vengeance shall be taken on him sevenfold.' And the Lord put a mark on Cain, lest anyone who came upon him should kill him" (Genesis 4:15). So the Kenites and the Israelites lived in religious peace together in the same towns.

Others have seen in the story of Cain and Abel a mystical meaning. Noting that Canon One of the Mass includes the sacrifice of Abel as a foreshadowing of the sacrifice of Jesus, they see, in the shepherd Abel, Jesus the Good Shepherd who not only offered a lamb, but was himself the lamb offered. Abel acted as a priest in presenting the lamb of God. Jesus, too, was the high priest who himself became the lamb offered to the Father.

Many Meanings

It may seem overdone to see all these meanings in this one story. But given the mentality of the people from which the story came, it is not so surprising. The Cain and Abel narrative is but one of a long series of artfully constructed stories that grew out of the centuries of contemplation of the community of faith.

It participates in the quality of great poetry in that it is justly able to be the vehicle for numerous depths of meaning. Growing out of the richness of the life of faith, a poetic narrative is like the ringing of a large bell in which the reverberations continue long after the first strike. It has resonance. This means it resounds many times in many hearts and many situations.

Hence, the original story of a jealous brother is echoed in the rivalry of the brother kingdoms, the sanity of religious tolerance. The Cain and Abel story is strong enough to bear many meanings. It is fair to say that for our own very technical-minded civilization in which the poetic is neglected, such an approach to the Cain and Abel tale will appear unsuitable. But a little honest thinking about it, and a sincere acceptance of the worldview of a culture far different from ours, can make it easier to accept.

REFLECTION

We know that even today brothers and nations rise up against one another with murderous intent. Any newspaper bears testimony to that. The Cain and Abel story reminds us that such hatred is the outgrowth of sin and selfishness. This story also reminds us that we should strive to be our brother's keeper — that is, to have for him the love and concern of Jesus Christ so that we can replace this chaos of hostility in the world with love.

FOR DIALOGUE

Share some stories of sibling rivalry from your experiences. Generally most of these are opportunities for maturing and growing up, but what of cases that become fatal? Why can we legitimately say that inner conflicts sometimes become external ones? Why is it therefore important to resolve inner divisions?

Ancient Israel idealized their years as desert shepherds when their awareness of God was immediate and their faith was strong. They believed that city life eroded such faith. What comparisons could you make today about religion in urban life as contrasted with the faith of people in rural and pastoral settings?

It has been said that wars among nations have grown out of wars between families. How true is this? If not completely accurate, what might be the grain of truth in such an observation?

Dear Lord, when we are tempted by anger and envy to lash out against a member of our family or a neighbor, fill us with the graces we need to calm down, acquire some patience and understanding, and learn to live in peace with others.

O wash me more and more from my guilt
And cleanse me from my sin.

PSALM 51:2

CHAPTER 4

God's Constant Concern for Us

Genesis 6-9

*By faith Noah, warned by God about events as yet unseen, respected
the warning and built an ark to save his household.*

HEBREWS 11:7, NRSV

THE STORY OF NOAH

Many years ago, on a television show the comedian Bill Cosby brought renewed popularity to the old Noah story with his entertaining routine of Noah as a doubter and then as a hard-pressed suburban husband building the ark in his neighbor's driveway. With the true sense of the humorist, Cosby touched the human predicament in which Noah found himself: doubt in the face of the demands of faith, and harassment in trying to do what faith tells us we must do.

Saved by God from the Flood

The biblical narrative tells us that the ultimate consequences of the first sin had now occurred because humans had filled the earth with evil and violence. God would send a flood to remove evil people from the earth. Only Noah was a good man who walked with God. Because he was faithful to God, Noah and his family would be spared the coming destruction.

God instructed Noah to build an ark to house his family and two of every kind of animal. From this nucleus a new creation would be formed. Noah ignored the mocking of his neighbors who thought the flood would never come. He completed the ark because he had faith that God would be true to his word. He must have felt somewhat silly building a ship on dry land with no water nearby. This test of Noah is similar to the one that would face Abraham later on. "By faith Noah, warned by God about events as yet unseen, respected the warning and built an ark to save his household" (Hebrews 11:7).

Noah was allowed to bring unclean animals into the ark, though not so many as the clean ones. In this we can see a rejection of those cults which were alien to God and which used such animals. Then Noah, his family, and the animals entered the ark, and God shut the door after them. Thus God sealed and protected his friends against the coming storm.

The accounts in the Bible about the severity of the flood vary. One account speaks of a forty-day rainstorm. "And rain fell upon the earth forty days and forty nights" (Genesis 7:12). But another account indicates a disastrous worldwide flood. The heavenly ocean above the skies broke through the firmament, and the ancient sea underneath the earth erupted through the land chasms. As a result, creation returned to chaos. "I have determined to make an end of all flesh" (Genesis 6:13).

Not only were men and beasts destroyed, but the very earth itself. But God remembered Noah. God curbed the rush to chaos before Noah and his group were destroyed. And the ark began to find a resting place. The Hebrew word for rest is *nuah,* which, as you can see, is a pun on the name Noah. In the faithful and heroic Noah, rest and peace began to return to the earth as the storm receded.

The Olive Branch, Sign of New Peace

It was a common custom among ancient seamen to send forth birds to test for land sites. Noah had no success with the first bird. It had to return. The second, a dove, was more successful; it brought back an olive branch in its beak. This olive branch of peace signaled the departure of angry judgment and the hope of deliverance. The third, also a dove, was sent forth and did not return. Then Noah knew that he could live again upon the earth.

The first thing Noah did after leaving the ark was offer sacrifice. Hence, the first human act on the liberated earth was an act of worship. This liturgical act celebrated the cleansing of the earth. So awesome was this moment that Noah remained absolutely silent. God "smelled" the sacrifice and was pleased with the sweetness of the gift and with those who offered it.

God Promised to Never Again Destroy the Earth by Water

Then the narrator takes us to the secret thoughts of God. As he had shown a troubled God before the flood, now he notes a new attitude in the mind of the Lord. God is to take a new attitude toward people. This is not directly caused by his pleasure in the sacrifice — the author is always careful to protect the sovereign freedom of the Lord. But at least the sacrifice became the occasion for God's decision never to so punish the earth again.

God knows that we will continue to do evil. It was this that drew forth from him the judgment of the flood. But now this very same condition becomes the occasion of God's grace and providence. He will try now in the face of man's stubborn sinfulness to bring him the saving grace.

God's Covenant with Noah

Chapter 9 of Genesis dwells on the covenant scene between God and Noah. The whole atmosphere was that of a new creation. Once again man was summoned to be fruitful and multiply. He would have control over the animal world and could kill animals for food. But God would retain the sovereign right over human life, though he gave man the right to punish a blood crime. "Whoever sheds the blood of man, by man shall his blood be shed" (Genesis 9:6). In our time the Church maintains that the conditions for capital punishment are so rare that it is virtually impossible to identify a case where it would be justified (CCC 2267).

Then God presented the covenant to Noah. Its purpose was to make clear the relationship that must exist between God and man. There was a difference between this covenant and the ones that would occur later with Abraham and Moses. For them, there was a direct personal call to enter the covenant, and, in a sense, God awaited their free decision. But here nothing was asked of man.

The Rainbow

The rainbow was a covenant sign placed high above the earth. It was wrought out of the colors of the rainbow, a warm and promising assurance that God's grace would never be missing from the earth again. It was a rainbow covenant that kept men looking upward to the peace that comes after a storm, to a constancy that would never fail, to a gracious God who can never forget his world.

> *I will never take back my love:*
> *my truth will never fail.*
> *I will never violate my covenant*
> *nor go back on the word I have spoken.*
>
> PSALM 89:33-34

The Hebrew word from which we take the word "rainbow," ordinarily means a "bow of war." Hence, what the primitive Hebrews understood was that God had pledged to set aside his bow of war and not terrify the creation again with the threat of chaos. The appearance of the rainbow signaled the restoration of the order of nature. As God began to heal the universe, shutting off the ocean from above and the sea from below, he would continue his work of reconciliation in the stormy seas of the human condition.

The whole Bible is just such a story of God's breaking through to our awareness in every way possible, whether by the harmony of colors in the rainbow, the wholesome face of a child, or the broken bodies of the wounded. In countless ways God is always at work reconciling man to himself through his Son, Jesus Christ.

REFLECTION

The first segment of the Bible is finished. Genesis 1-11 comprises the prehistory of God's plan of creation and redemptive purposes. All the great themes of the rest of Scripture are here: creation, the state of holiness and justice for man and woman, the fall from grace, the prophetic promise of a redeemer, the spread of sin in the world, a calamitous judgment of destruction on sinners, mercy on Noah the man of faith and his family, a cosmic covenant, symbolized by the rainbow, a new creation beginning after the chaos of the flood.

We may speak of it as prehistory, a contemplation arising from faith in God's revelation concerning the origins of the earth and of all creatures, especially human beings. The dramatic language is filled with images, symbols, figures, and other poetic devices to fix with ringing authenticity in the minds of God's elected people how the world began, how evil entered human life, and what are the prospects for salvation and hope.

The Genesis account is simple enough to charm a child, sufficiently engaging to absorb a teen, eminently challenging for an adult, a stimulant for a scholar, and a prayer deep enough to feed the heart of a saint. The basic themes of Genesis 1-11 will appear again and again throughout all the rest of Scripture and achieve, with startling and magnificent relevance, the final meaning of the Bible in the life, teachings, death and resurrection of Jesus Christ, Son of God and Son of Mary.

FOR DIALOGUE

Sin is self-destructive. In the Noah story a flood engulfs a corrupted world. What examples can you think of in which sin both harms others as well as causes unhappiness to the self? How would pervasive immorality affect a culture and a society?

The world is never totally bad. There are always good men and women, witnesses of faith in God and compassion for the world. Saints rise up in troubled times. Share some stories of such possibilities you have noticed.

God is always seeking a covenant-love relationship with us. The rainbow is a natural symbol of calm after a storm. God also used it as a sign of everlasting love for us. What ways have you found to maintain a personal faith-relationship with God?

PRAYER

Teach me, Lord, to see your loving and saving presence in the midst of my troubles and the evils of the world. Focus my heart on the light you bring to the world. Let me shine it on others.

CHAPTER 5

Abraham Is Our Father in Faith

Genesis 12-22

Now the Lord said to Abram, "Go from your country and your kindred and your father's house to the land that I will show you."

GENESIS 12:1

THE FAITH OF ABRAHAM

After the prehistory we have just discussed, Scripture begins the history of the patriarchs, the founding fathers of Israel, God's holy and elected people. The patriarchs are Abraham, Isaac, Jacob, and his twelve sons who established the twelve tribes of Israel.

The story of Abraham begins in Ur of the Chaldees. God called Abram, as he was first named in Scripture, to leave his homeland and take his family to a land he would be shown. The Lord promised Abram that he would become the father of a new nation. His descendants would be as numerous as the stars in heaven and the grains of sand by the seashore.

Abram responded with faith and obedience to God's call. He took his family and flocks and embarked on a long journey that would bring him to the lands of Egypt and Canaan. His nephew Lot along with his family joined the journey. Abram encountered a number of challenges to his faith.

One involved a battle with four kings whom he defeated with God's help. After the victory, he met the priest Melchizedek who offered a sacrifice of bread and wine to celebrate the occasion.

In another test of faith he rescued Lot's family from the destruction of Sodom and Gomorrah.

He continued to keep his faith in God's promise of a family, but as yet he had no children, and the prospect was dim since he and his wife were old. One day, three angels in disguise visited Abram. He welcomed them and set before them a fine meal. They told him that his wife would have a son within the year.

Later God told Abram that he was changing his name to Abraham, for he would be the father of many peoples. As sign of this covenant promise

Abraham was to be circumcised. All his male descendants must do the same. Within the year a son was born to Sarah. Eight days after the birth the boy was circumcised and named Isaac. God had begun to fulfill the promises. But now Abraham would be given the greatest test of his faith. God would ask him to sacrifice his teenage son.

The Sacrifice of Isaac

Many a modern dad may become upset with his teenage son because of frustration over the way he dresses, his music, or an obedience problem. But that well-satisfied father, Abraham, had no problems with his son Isaac. Certainly, he would never think of killing Isaac. In fact, nothing could have seemed more absurd. Like the businessman who sees in his only son the hope of carrying on the family name and company ideals, Abraham saw that God's promises to him would be fulfilled through the survival of his son.

Abraham Prepares to Fulfill God's Strange Command

The Bible attempts to relieve the anxiety of the reader by casually noting that this was only a test. Yet somehow the very idea of a father being ordered to kill his son drives the reader to nail-biting. We shall review the facts of the case and then draw some conclusions. (Read Genesis 22.)

In stark, matter-of-fact prose, the Bible describes how God told Abraham to take Isaac to Mount Moriah, and there knife the boy and burn him as a religious sacrifice. With no comment on the disappointment or shock of the father, the text itemizes the preparations, almost as if they were getting ready for a fishing trip. They arise early. The servants are instructed to chop some kindling wood and saddle the pack animal for the journey. A little after sunrise the fated group — father, son, and two servants — sets out on the three-day journey to Mount Moriah.

Abraham and Isaac Arrive at the Place of Sacrifice

Three days later they sight the well-known mountain, and Abraham instructs the servants to go home. The father and son walk on alone in a heavy, embarrassing silence. The boy carries the wood, not knowing it will be used to burn his own young body. The father carries the fire-making equipment and the knife. (The Hebrew noun could be accurately translated "butcher knife.") Only a few words pass between them during that journey. Isaac asks, "Where is the lamb for a burnt offering?" In answer, the old man simply says that God will provide the victim.

Now they arrive at the goal of their journey. The Hebrew text uses verbs here that give the impression of a dream, producing the mood of a robot or a sleepwalker carrying out orders. Abraham piles some stones together in a sort of crude altar bed, upon which he stacks the wood.

A Voice from Heaven Spares Isaac

Then Abraham turns to his son, and ties up the apparently unresisting boy. Placing him on the altar, he raises the butcher knife in midair, ready to destroy his only hope. Only now is the tension broken, when a voice from heaven commands him to spare Isaac. "Do not lay your hand on the boy or do anything to him; for now I know that you fear God, since you have not withheld your son, your only son, from me" (Genesis 22:12, NRSV). At this point Abraham notices a ram snagged by his horns in a nearby bush. He takes this animal and offers it to God in place of his son.

SACRIFICE OF THE FIRSTBORN COMMON IN ANCIENT RELIGIONS

What is the meaning of this strange story, which seems to be cruel enough to scare a young child away from such a God, and to make all of us wonder if this is the sort of bloodthirsty deity to whom we should commit ourselves?

If we were to study other ancient religions, we would note the common practice of pagan rituals that demanded the sacrificial death of firstborn children. We would see in this story God's warning to Israel that he does not want such a practice among them. The Hebrew people were well enough aware of this custom of sacrifice, because it was common among their neighbors. Here are some texts illustrating the point:

"Then he [the king of Moab] took his eldest son who was to reign in his stead, and offered him for a burnt offering upon the wall" (2 Kings 3:27). The men of Sepharvaim immolated their children by fire to their city gods (2 Kings 17:31).

Even Judah itself was guilty of such practices. Ahaz, king of Judah, "even burned his son as an offering, according to the abominable practices of the nations whom the LORD drove out before the people of Israel" (2 Kings 16:3).

THE MEANINGS OF THIS STORY

James Michener, in his novel *The Source*, gives a vivid description of the details and the reasons why the ancients offered human sacrifice. Scientists examining the royal tombs at Ur in Mesopotamia found evidence of the ritual killing of children and substitute kings. But the story of Abraham and Isaac has a deeper meaning than the condemnation of human sacrifice done in the name of religion. Indeed three deeper meanings can be found in this story: (1) God takes a long time to fully accomplish his will; (2) God wills life, not death, for all people; (3) God will provide his Son as the lamb of sacrifice.

Winning one fight does not make a prizefighter. It is rare that an army wins a war in one battle. Abraham's journey to a new country and his patient waiting for Isaac's birth were among the trials to his faith. But these were not enough. The terrible test on Mount Moriah shows the depth of faith needed to accomplish God's plan.

It also shows that his purpose will not be spelled out in one generation. Furthermore, it shows that God is not on the side of death, but wishes life for all men. Prior to Christ's coming, Abraham could only know life after death through the survival of his son and descendants. God's rescue of Isaac from the edge of death is a forecast of the victory Jesus would have over death.

In this story a ram is substituted for Isaac, Abraham's son. In the New Testament, Jesus, God's Son, is the lamb that is sacrificed. It's not hard to see the similarities. In both cases we have the "only son" of the father. Isaac carries the wood up the hill, as Jesus carried the wood of the cross up Calvary. And both stories end with a new lease on life.

REFLECTION

The Bible says that Abraham practiced courageous faith by giving up his homeland to venture forth to a place about which he knew nothing. He heard God's call and responded with obedience and faith. He lived as a stranger and pilgrim in the Promised Land. Holding onto faith in God's promises, Sarah gave birth to Isaac.

By faith Abraham was willing to sacrifice his beloved son. He fulfilled the scriptural definition of faith, "Faith is the assurance of things hoped for, the conviction of things not seen" (Hebrews 11:1). He kept his faith in God throughout all the tests. He is our father in faith. Our mother in faith is the Virgin Mary. She most perfectly embodies the obedience of faith. We praise her with the words of Elizabeth to Mary, "Blessed [are you] who believed" (Luke 1:45). When we need to grow stronger in our faith, we can be inspired by Abraham's perseverance, and we can pray to Mary that she will ask the Spirit to give us deeper faith.

FOR DIALOGUE

Faith is a response to a call from God. You can receive this call from your family and Church and faith-filled friends. How have you received your faith? What are some tests of faith that you have known? How did you respond?

Faith is a gift. Abraham did not make it up. God awakened faith in his life and gave him graces to live by it. What are some ways you can appreciate your faith as a gift from God? When you receive a gift, what is your spontaneous reaction? How could this apply to faith?

Faith leads to understanding God's will for you. It is like love. First you fall in love. Then you must stay in love. This takes work and growth in understanding. How has your faith helped you understand God's will for you?

PRAYER

I believe, Lord Jesus. Help my unbelief. I walk by faith and not by sight. Sometimes I walk in darkness. Be my light. Help me to see the challenges of faith as opportunities to grow in love for you.

Because he was strong in faith, Abraham became the father of all who believe.

CF. CCC 146, ROMANS 4:11

I believe in order to understand.

ST. ANSELM

CHAPTER 6

Faith in God Is More Important than Cleverness

Genesis 25:19-34; 28-33

The blessing... he made to rest on the head of Jacob.

Sirach 44:22-23

JACOB'S STORY

Esau and Jacob are the most famous set of twins in the Bible. Esau was nick-named "Red" because of his complexion, while Jacob was called the "wrestler" for being so aggressive a rival of his brother. They were not identical twins in either their looks or in their likes and dislikes. Esau was an outdoor man, a hunter, and a favorite of his father, Isaac. Jacob, on the other hand, liked being around the house, and was much loved by his mother, Rebekah.

Rebekah Plots to Gain the Inheritance for Jacob

Isaac was growing very old and was making plans to transfer the family farm to Esau, the firstborn of the twins. He would do this at a ceremony called the "blessing." But Rebekah wanted Jacob to inherit the property and leadership of the family. She overheard Isaac discuss the blessing with Esau, and saw him send Esau off to hunt wild game to be used at the dinner preceding the giving of the blessing.

Rebekah, knowing that Isaac was blind and feeble, decided to deceive him. Right after Esau left, she roasted a lamb, using spices to make it taste like a game animal. She persuaded Jacob to wear some of Esau's smelly, old clothes, and she wrapped his neck and hands with animal skins. Then she built up Jacob's confidence so that he would not fear to "play the game," and deceive the old man.

Jacob Gets Isaac's Blessing

It was a nervous Jacob who took the steaming meal into Isaac's room. Tense moments followed as a confused Isaac raised questions. He was surprised that the game had been caught and cooked so fast. Though the boy sounded like Jacob, he had the hairy skin of Esau and the musty smell of sportsmen's clothes. Isaac was satisfied after he had examined his son and had eaten the faked food. He gave Jacob the solemn blessing: "May God give you of the dew of heaven, and of the fatness of the earth, and plenty of grain and wine. Let peoples serve you, and nations bow down to you. Be lord over your brothers, and may your mother's sons bow down to you" (Genesis 27:28-29).

Of course, it was a cruel blow to Esau to discover how he had been cheated out of his inheritance. He knew that the blessing, once given, could not be revoked. He threatened to kill his brother, and so thoroughly frightened him that the smooth-skinned Jacob left home for a few years. (Read Genesis 27:1-28:5.)

The young heir decided to go north and live with his uncle Laban's family. On the way he stopped at the pagan shrine of Bethel. During the night he had a dream about angels traveling to and from heaven on a giant ladder. God told him that his mission was to be like these messengers linking heaven to earth. (Read Genesis 28:10-22.)

Jacob Courts Rachel and Is Tricked by Her Father

The next event in Jacob's life was his meeting with Rachel. He had paused by a well, waiting for someone with a bucket to draw up the water. It was Rachel who came, and when they saw each other, it was a case of love at first sight. It turned out that she was a daughter of Laban, his uncle. She brought Jacob home and there followed a scene of welcome and rejoicing.

Laban hired Jacob to look after his sheep. In time Jacob asked to marry Rachel, promising to work seven years in return for the favor. Laban agreed, but secretly gave Leah, Rachel's ugly sister, to him instead. Her face was so heavily veiled at the wedding that Jacob did not know that this was Leah.

The disappointed bridegroom went to Laban and complained. Laban shrugged the matter off by saying that this was his only chance to palm off the homely girl. Then he shrewdly suggested that for an extra seven years of service Jacob could have Rachel. Jacob grudgingly agreed. (Read Genesis 29:1-30.)

Jacob Outwits Laban

The years passed, and Jacob served Laban well. Now he wanted to return to his own farm and bring his wife and family there. He had quietly begun to prosper during his years in the north as a result of a tricky bargain he had struck with his uncle. They had agreed that Jacob could keep any sheep that had black or spotted pelts. Since these would be so rare, Laban had little to fear. But according to the story Jacob had found a way of breeding that caused an unusual number of such sheep to be born. (Read Genesis 30:25-43.)

So Jacob started home with his family and friends and flocks. He heard news that Esau had become a desert prince over the neighboring tribe of fierce Edomites. What was worse, Esau and four hundred Arabs were riding toward his camp at that very moment — apparently to do him harm. (Read Genesis 32; 33.)

Jacob Wrestles an Angel

That night, Jacob paced the field near the sleeping camp, wondering and worrying about what to do. While he struggled with his fears, a mysterious stranger came up and began to wrestle with him. The battle went on most of the night until Jacob's thigh was thrown out of joint.

The stranger said, "Let me go, for the day is breaking." Jacob answered that he would not do so until he received a blessing. Then the other man said, "Your name shall no longer be called Jacob, but Israel, for you have striven with God and men, and have prevailed." After the stranger left, Jacob said to himself, "I have seen God face to face." (Read Genesis 32:23-32.)

Now he recalled the danger that Esau presented. He sent servants and gifts to calm the oncoming tribesmen. The mission succeeded, and when the two brothers finally met, they embraced each other in forgiveness and love. With that, Jacob happily returned to his homeland and settled with his family and possessions.

GOD'S CHOICE OF LEADERS OFTEN PUZZLES US

This story raises a few puzzling questions. Why did God want the younger Jacob for patriarch instead of Esau? How could the Bible record the deception of Isaac by a future patriarch? What is the moral lesson taught by the cleverness of Jacob?

God chooses all people to receive his blessing. However, he chooses some in a special way, so that through them he can make his love and mercy clearly known to all other people. The privileged person who is chosen in a special way has the obligation of being God's witness in a unique way.

More is expected from the one to whom more has been given. God often picks the unlikely candidate as in the case of Jacob, or in the story of the choice of David as king of Israel. God is free to choose whom he wants. These stories illustrate this freedom.

REFLECTION

It does not seem very flattering to have Jacob cheat Esau out of the blessing, although the ancient peoples loved tales that showed the cleverness of a leader. God obviously did not approve of Jacob's action: He subjected Jacob to a lengthy penance for it at the hands of his uncle Laban.

The long night in which Jacob wrestled with the stranger was the turning point of his life. It was a night in which the conscience of the clever Jacob was purified. He learned that playing it smart is not as important as trusting in God. And so Jacob became Israel, the father of the twelve tribes.

FOR DIALOGUE

In the Jacob narrative there are several stories in which the characters outwit one another. These scriptural tricks were partly humorous ways of describing Jacob as well as reminders that the sainted founder of Israel was an imperfect man. His greatness came from his willingness to believe in God's plan of salvation. How would you compare this way of telling the life of a saint with those you are familiar with? Which way appeals more to you?

In the scene where Jacob wrestles with an angel, what does this tell you about your own faith struggles? Jacob prevails with God. What does this teach you about perseverance in faith?

The scriptural accounts of the life of Jacob highlight his faith and his humanity. Why is it important to stress both aspects of his life?

PRAYER

Heavenly Father, you called Jacob to be the father of twelve sons who became the founders of the twelve tribes of Israel. Your Son, Jesus, selected twelve disciples to be the apostles of your new Israel, the Church. We praise you for your plan to save us. We pray for the kind of faith that Jacob and his sons had as well as the matured faith possessed by the apostles. They were open to the gift of faith. Open our hearts as well.

By faith Jacob, when dying, blessed each of the sons of Joseph, bowing in worship over the head of his staff.

HEBREWS 11:21;
CF. GENESIS 48:8-11

CHAPTER 7

A Man of Faith and Forgiveness

Genesis 37-45

Now Israel loved Joseph more than any other of his children, because he was the son of his old age.

GENESIS 37:3

JOSEPH'S STORY

There is nothing like jealousy to ruin a family. Old Jacob favored his son Joseph, giving him expensive clothes to wear. His brothers stewed in envy because of this. Joseph gained the reputation of being a dreamer. The trouble was that his dreams were about becoming master over his brothers, so his brothers had little love for him.

They had reached such a point of dissatisfaction that they planned to kill him. But one of the brothers, Judah, persuaded them to sell Joseph to a passing caravan of Ishmaelites instead. They dipped his hated cloak in some goat's blood and told Jacob his beloved son was slain by a wild animal. (Read Genesis 37.)

Joseph Enslaved in Egypt

At the age of seventeen Joseph arrived in Egypt where he was sold as a slave to an Egyptian officer named Potiphar. Joseph became manager of this man's estate. Potiphar's wife fell in love with the handsome Joseph, but he would not return her love. This made her angry. One day when Joseph was alone with her in the house, she made one last attempt to entice him.

But Joseph fled from the house, leaving his coat behind. She screamed for help. That night she told her husband: "The Hebrew servant, whom you have brought among us, came in to me to insult me; but as soon as I lifted up my voice and cried, he left his garment with me, and fled out of the house" (Genesis 39:17-18).

So Joseph was jailed. It wasn't long before his leadership talents emerged, and he was put in charge of the other prisoners. One day two important prisoners arrived, the butler and baker of the Pharaoh. They had offended the Pharaoh and were sent to Joseph's prison. At night, wild dreams tore at their sleep and they awoke, puzzled men. Joseph noticed their tense faces and asked the cause. They confided their dreams to him.

The Butler's and Baker's Dreams Interpreted by Joseph

The butler dreamed about a vine with fat grapes. In his dream he had taken the Pharaoh's cup and pressed wine from the grapes and presented it to the Pharaoh. Joseph said: "Within three days Pharaoh will lift up your head and restore you to your office; and you shall place Pharaoh's cup in his hand as formerly, when you were his butler. But remember me, when it is well with you, and do me the kindness, I pray you, to make mention of me to Pharaoh, and so get me out of this house" (Genesis 40:13-14).

The baker dreamed about a platter on his head. Three cakes rested on it. Then birds came and ate the cakes. Joseph hesitated to give the meaning. But the baker pressed him. So Joseph answered: "Within three days Pharaoh will lift up your head — from you! — and hang you on a tree; and the birds will eat the flesh from you" (Genesis 40:19). Three days later the Pharaoh celebrated his birthday. He released his butler and brought him back as cup-bearer. But the body of the baker swayed in the breeze underneath the gallows. The butler, however, did not remember Joseph.

Joseph Interprets the Pharoah's Dreams

Two years passed, and now the Pharaoh had dreams that made him toss in his bed. He stood by the Nile watching seven fat cows grazing in the meadows. Suddenly, seven skinny cows came up and devoured the fat ones. He had a similar dream in which seven thin ears of grain swallowed up seven plump ones. He went to his counselors for an interpretation, but none of them could produce an answer.

Then the butler remembered Joseph who had been so expert in explaining his dream in the prison. Pharaoh sent for Joseph.

The young Hebrew came into the royal court. He listened to the details of the Pharaoh's dream, and then gave his interpretation. "The seven good cows are seven years, and the seven good ears are seven years.... There will come seven years of great plenty throughout all the land of Egypt, but after them there will arise seven years of famine, and all the plenty will be forgotten in the land of Egypt.... And the doubling of Pharaoh's dream means that the thing is fixed by God, and God will shortly bring it to pass" (Genesis 41:26-32).

Pharaoh Appoints Joseph to Prepare for the Famine

The Pharaoh sat there wondering what he should do. Joseph advised him to build warehouses to store extra grain in preparation for the coming famine. He counseled him to appoint a secretary of agriculture to oversee the gathering of the grain and the building of storage warehouses, and to solve the distribution problems for the lean years.

The monarch agreed that this was the best solution. He spoke to Joseph: "Since God has shown you all this... you shall be over my house" (Genesis 41:39-40). He invested Joseph with the proper symbols of his office — the Pharaoh's ring, a linen cloak, a gold neck chain, and a royal chariot.

For the next seven years golden fields of grain greeted the nation's eyes. Workmen built huge granaries to store the wheat. Then sharp winds and hot sun dried up the earth. The famine arrived. Over in Canaan, the family of Jacob saw their supplies of wheat running low, and began to worry. Travelers told them of the grain supplies in Egypt. They held a family council and decided that all the brothers, except Benjamin, the youngest, would go to Egypt to buy grain.

Joseph Reunited with His Family

The law required that those who came from outside Egypt had to check with Joseph for permission to buy grain. His brothers went to Joseph's office. The years had changed him so much, his brothers didn't recognize him. But he knew them right away. He asked them a lot of questions about his father and family. He wanted to know why Benjamin had not come. They said their father feared losing Benjamin as he had lost Joseph years before, due to their jealousy. Joseph demanded to see Benjamin, and held Simeon as a hostage.

They returned home with the grain and the bad news. Jacob grieved, but would not let Benjamin go. In time, however, as food became scarce, they faced the choice of starvation or bringing Benjamin with them. Jacob relented when his son Judah staked his life on saving Benjamin. (Read Genesis, chapters 42, 43.)

Joseph wept when he saw his young brother. He stood up before them and confessed: "Come near to me, I pray you." And they came near. And he said, "I am your brother, Joseph, whom you sold into Egypt. And now do not be distressed, or angry with yourselves, because you sold me here; for God sent me before you to preserve life" (Genesis 45:4-5).

Tears of joy rolled from their eyes as the news sank in. Joseph invited them to come and live in Egypt, bringing with them his father Jacob. The old man received the news with joy, saying "It is enough; Joseph my son is still alive; I will go and see him before I die" (Genesis 45:28).

REFLECTION

Joseph is a colorful and appealing biblical figure. Though he undergoes many trials, rejection by his family, and unjust imprisonment for resisting seduction in the house of Potiphar, he displays a resilient character and positive qualities of leadership.

The episode in the house of Potiphar dramatizes Joseph as a heroic defender of purity and a man faithful to the religion of his fathers. His skill as an interpreter of dreams earns him a major post in the Egyptian government. The reader delights in the test, which makes his brothers uneasy, seeing it as a deserved penalty for their cruelty to him years before. But after making them squirm a bit, he reveals his forgiveness and his desire to bring his family together once again.

In God's plan the Israelites move to Egypt, a rich and powerful civilization. For many years they prospered and multiplied and benefited from the knowledge and skills learned in the most advanced culture of the times. Their identity as a people flourished. The faith of Abraham, Isaac, Jacob, and Joseph molded their beliefs, attitudes, and practices.

But Egypt was not meant to be their homeland. With the passing of time, the government grew hostile and reduced the people to slavery. The next phase of scriptural history deals with the story of Moses and how God made him the liberator of his people. Joseph's story concludes the book of Genesis and leads us onward to the book of Exodus.

FOR DIALOGUE

What are traits in Joseph's behavior that attract you? Why so? What do you admire about the realism of the scriptural narratives? What is the spiritual value of presenting the people with their strengths and weaknesses?

Why does the temptation posed by Potiphar's wife seem so relevant to our own culture? What was there about the character of Joseph that moved him to "just say no" to the seduction?

Scriptural narratives are stories of faith and the challenges to belief. How is this evident in the trials of Joseph — such as the betrayal by his brothers, being sold into slavery, and being imprisoned for unjust cause? Why do we tend to think that our faith life should not be demanding?

PRAYER

Heavenly Father, we are grateful for the inspiring example set for us by Joseph of Egypt. Despite many severe tests, he never forgot the faith of his fathers. He remained true to his covenant with you. We ask for similar courage when faced with challenges to our faith and your will for us.

By faith Joseph, at the end of his life, made mention of the exodus of the Israelites and gave directions concerning his burial.

HEBREWS 11:22;
SEE ALSO GENESIS 50:24-26

CHAPTER 8

Moses Liberates the Hebrews from Slavery

Exodus 2-14

Afterward Moses... went to Pharaoh and said, "Thus says the Lord, the God of Israel, 'Let my people go.'"

Exodus 5:1

Revolutions make the headlines of history. They quicken the patriotism, the energies, and ideals of men, as the history of the American Revolution shows us, and as the struggle of minority groups for equal rights, here and elsewhere throughout the world, amply demonstrates. The Old Testament Hebrew revolt against the Egyptians followed the usual plan of revolutions. Indeed, God knew the sufferings of his people and reached to save them. "The cry of the Israelites has now come to me; I have also seen how the Egyptians oppress them" (Exodus 3:9, NRSV).

REVOLUTION IS BORN FROM A CRISIS OF INJUSTICE

In the centuries after Joseph, the Hebrews were "fruitful and increased greatly" (Exodus 1:7). The new pharaohs forgot Joseph and considered the Hebrews a threat to Egypt. They believed that as the Hebrew population grew, the danger to Egypt increased. The advisers of the Pharaoh Rameses II (1290-1224 B.C.) told him he should (1) use the Hebrews as slave labor; (2) reduce the Hebrew birth rate.

Egypt kept many soldiers on her northern border to fight off invaders coming from the Gaza Strip. But she needed new supply depots closer to the front lines. Hence emerged plans to build the supply cities of Pithom and Rameses. Hebrew men were pressed into slave labor for the work. As for the babies, official Egyptian midwives were ordered to murder all newborn Hebrew boys. (Read Exodus 1.)

God Provides a Leader

God heard the cries of his people, and he raised up a leader to deliver them. Moses was a heroic man: he had a deep religious faith and a sense of justice, and had the courage and prudence needed in a leader who would fight against great odds. Instead of living a life of ease in Pharaoh's court where he had been brought up, he chose to share in the suffering of the people of God. (See Hebrews 11:25.)

He received his official summons to be the freedom leader in a mysterious vocation scene before the burning bush on Mount Horeb. It was an awesome event in which God revealed himself as mighty, consuming as fire, and compassionately interested in the just treatment of people. In revealing his name as I AM to Moses, God disclosed that he was an "I" — a personal God. Later in the revelation brought by Jesus, God would be revealed as a trinity of persons. (Read Exodus 3.)

Aaron the priest was chosen to serve as a spokesman for Moses the prophet. The plan for the revolution was this. First, Moses would rally the people with speeches, stressing that departure from Egypt was the will of the God of their forefathers. Next, they would negotiate with the Pharaoh to seek a peaceful solution. Third, God permitted a series of national calamities to bring the Pharaoh to his knees. (Read Exodus 3-4.)

Aim of the Hebrew Revolution: Freedom and Justice

Now Moses set the plans in motion. He stirred the people and strengthened their desire to be freed from a life of slavery. The negotiations with the Pharaoh failed. Hence began the famed ten plagues to pressure the Pharaoh into submission. (Read Exodus 7-12.)

Many efforts have been made to explain the ten plagues as just plain natural happenings. It is said that the bloody Nile is the result of red slag washed into the river during the spring flood. We are told that flood conditions normally produce swarms of frogs, flies, and lice. And hailstorms and plagues of locusts are not unheard of.

But this is to overlook the real meaning of the story: God is present at the heart of this revolution to bring freedom and justice to his people. These stories are not meant to be fairy tales. They are meant to show us the faith of the Hebrews, through which they knew that they would soon have their freedom as a result of these disasters that were weakening the power of the Pharaoh.

It is the final and most violent plague — the death of the firstborn — that marks a victory for Israel. Pharaoh gives in to Moses. (Read Exodus 12.)

> "Rise up, go forth from among my people . . . and go, serve the LORD, as you have said. Take your flocks and your herds, as you have said, and be gone; and bless me also."
>
> EXODUS 12:31-32

They Owe Their Freedom to the Work of God

The Hebrews had, with God's help, succeeded in throwing off the old order, but this is not enough. The people must understand what kind of new order must come out of the chaos. In human terms, this means the people must now work responsibly to form a new community rooted in justice and freedom. In faith language, this means that people must see the new order as the active presence of God in their midst. They are called to worship, obedience, and surrender to the divine will.

It means they must never forget they owe their freedom to the work of the God of their fathers. It was no simple task to drill this into the people's minds, for even years later they wanted to return to the fleshpots of Egypt. (Read Exodus 13.) In order to keep alive the memory of their deliverance and its meaning, the Hebrews celebrated a paschal meal once a year. During the meal, the events of the escape were recited, God was praised for his concern, and the people reaffirmed their faith in his continuing presence and interest in their needs.

The Need for Faith at the Shores of the Red Sea

The Hebrew revolt against the Pharaoh moved toward success after the tenth and most violent plague — the death of the firstborn. Bearing the bones of the patriarchs, the Hebrews marched toward the Sinai wilderness. The book of Exodus says that God went before them by day in the form of a cloud, and at night in the form of a pillar of fire. In other words, the Hebrew people understood that their true leader was God, glorious in the cloud and radiant in the fire. Not only was he their leader, he was also their defender.

Camped by the Red Sea (also known as the Sea of Reeds) for the night, the Israelites turned in terror to see the Pharaoh's troops coming to bring them back. But the pillar of fire stood between them and the soldiers while Moses prepared the people to get ready to march into the dark sea of death.

The Bible teaches that God wills life and freedom for everyone, but the price he exacts is a trusting surrender to the dark possibility of losing all. Abraham faced the dread of losing his son, and in accepting that risk, he not only saved his son but also became the father of every man who has faith.

This dire night, the Israelites faced the bleak prospect of marching into the waters. Timid and hesitant, they found it hard to move. Moses stirred them to action. "Fear not, stand firm, and see the salvation of the LORD, which he will work for you" (Exodus 14:13). Moses was not just trying to calm their fears. He wanted them to see that this whole event was an appearance of "God's time." In other words, they must see that God is present in this event, and that he is calling on them to have faith in him.

Become a Pilgrim People

Then God announced to Moses the words that have become the motto of the Church in pilgrimage even down to our own times. "Tell the people of Israel to go forward" (Exodus 14:15). With these words God asked Israel (and us) to always be open to the future, to say "yes" to the events that lie before us. God will march before them to reinforce his message that they are to be a pilgrim Church, and that they will find their life and freedom in this way. (Read Exodus 14 and 15.)

In a beautiful Passover hymn, later composed to celebrate this event, Moses describes the astonishing wonders of that night: "At the blast of your nostrils the waters piled up, the floods stood up in a heap... the Israelites walked through the sea on dry ground" (Exodus 15:8, 19). Once the Hebrews arrived safely on the other side, the Egyptian soldiers came across in pursuit. And Moses recalled, "You blew with your wind, the sea covered them; they sank like lead in the mighty waters"(Exodus 15:10, NRSV). Then Miriam, the sister of Moses, picked up a tambourine, and together with the other women began a victory dance by the shores of the Red Sea. Miriam sang to them: "Sing to the LORD, for he has triumphed gloriously; horse and rider he has thrown into the sea" (Exodus 15:21).

Israel's Deliverance Is Marked by the Feast of the Passover

The Israelites were filled with awe and gratitude at the victory that the God of their fathers had achieved for them. They began to celebrate the memory of their deliverance from Egypt every year, and in time this celebration took the form of the Passover festival. This ceremony made present again to the minds of the Israelites the marvelous deliverance that God had accomplished for them in the past.

Here are some details of the meal. The lamb must be perfect, and not more than a year old. The head of the family killed the lamb, pouring its blood into a special hole dug at the door of their tent. In later history the slaying took place at the temple, and the blood was poured at the base of the altar — a symbol of the doorway to God's house. This was done just before sundown.

Instructions called for roasting the lamb. Bitter herbs, made of lettuce, chickory, peppermint, snakeroot, and dandelion, were part of the menu. They symbolized the sufferings of Israel. Bread at the meal was dipped into a sauce, called haroseth, made of pounded nuts and fruit, sprinkled with vinegar.

The recital of the events of the night they escaped from Egypt was a revered memory that strengthened the people's sense of God's saving presence in their own time and situation. The father of the family related the exodus event to the present situation of his own family, reminding them that God is always ready to bring deliverance to his faithful people. The idea of a word service being linked to the Passover meal has been carried over into our own Eucharist today in which a series of readings and prayers precede the sacrificial meal.

So we see in the Red Sea story an event and a Passover meal. The event was Israel's march to freedom. In time, the Passover meal took the form of a festival that would help Israel remember the Holy Night, and share in the dynamic power of God, manifested then and throughout all their history. In Christian times this event is the death and resurrection of Jesus. The Eucharist is the new and definitive Passover meal.

REFLECTION

Amazing Grace, how sweet the sound,
That saved a wretch like me.
I once was lost but now I'm found,
Was blind but now I see.

This section of Scripture is packed with mighty themes of suffering, slavery, the need for a savior, the process by which God brings about salvation for his people. It involves the call of a powerful leader, Moses, who embodies God's saving design for the Israelites. We are taught that God is just as much interested as we are in the need for justice and freedom when tyranny and cruelty oppress people.

In our American history the African American slaves found courage and inspiration and hope for freedom in these texts from the book of Exodus. Their spirituals echoed the great cry of Moses, "Let My People Go!" Important as political and human freedom are, Scripture raises our sights to a deeper type of freedom behind all these other forms, and that is freedom from sin and guilt. Political and economic evils are rooted in the sinfulness of the human soul.

The greatest form of liberation is the delivery from sin, guilt, and evil. Christ's redeeming work had no immediate political or economic consequences. Jesus led no rebellions. His first purpose was to free us from sin and offer us divine life and the kingdom of love, mercy, and justice. Once we are thus redeemed, then peace, justice, and other communal values should follow and be implemented in human life and society.

The most fundamental rebellion is the one against the corruption of sin. As the biblical story unfolds, this is always the principal message. The excitement generated by the drama of Israel's political liberation from Egypt will be followed by the greater and deeper process of a pilgrimage to Sinai and the Promised Land where themes of covenant and moral reform take center stage.

FOR DIALOGUE

As you look around your world today, what are situations of political and economic injustice that oppress people? What kind of leadership is needed to address this? What inspiration can you draw from the Moses story?

Why is it fascinating to note that Scripture portrays God as the first one interested in liberating Israel? Why is it wrong for political leaders to invoke God's name in oppressing people? Lincoln once said, "We should be careful in claiming that God is on our side. Better to find out if we are on God's side." What do you think of this?

Scripture moves us to realize that the greatest form of rebellion is the struggle against our sinfulness and guilt. Why didn't Jesus mount a political rebellion? Why is his focus on our personal redemption from sin and the offer of divine life?

PRAYER

Father in heaven, you sent your Son to redeem us from sin and guilt by the life, death, and resurrection of your Son, Jesus Christ. Send us your Spirit to remind us of this most important of all the truths of faith. Thank you.

Thy right hand, O LORD, glorious in power,
thy right hand, O LORD, shatters the enemy.

EXODUS 15:6

CHAPTER 9

The Israelites' Pilgrimage to Sinai

Exodus 15:22-27; 16-18

I rejoiced because they said to me,
We will go up to the house of the LORD.

PSALM 122:1

Freedom doesn't automatically make us mature. The magic age of twenty-one with its legal freedoms is not a guarantee that we have a responsible person on our hands. Freedom makes it possible for a person to gain maturity. The victory at the Red Sea brought the Hebrews freedom, but they still needed to grow up and find themselves as a people.

WOULD THE HEBREWS' FAITH GROW DEEPER?

The pilgrimage to Sinai, on which the Hebrews set out after their escape from Egypt, was a maturing process. It took faith to bring the people to an exodus triumph. But life must go on, and God wanted to see whether their faith would grow deeper. The writer of the book of Exodus does not concentrate on the historical and geographical details. Like an artist brushing in the bold strokes on the canvas, the author cites a few of the stops on the way to Sinai.

He chooses to dwell on the faith development of these people. The harshness is mentioned, but the details are few. Everything is streamlined to make the point: the saved Israelites were still subject to the same kind of struggle that all people meet in history. The big difference here is that revelation from God gives the real meaning of the struggle.

The desert pilgrimage, with its fears and crises, conveys the teaching that Israel's faith, begun at the Red Sea, needs much deepening before final fulfillment. Hence, Israel must live responsibly in history. God saved Israel, but hunger, thirst, and enemies still abide. God tested them to see whether they would live by the faith that had brought them this far.

The Sour Waters of Marah

Water becomes all-important to desert travelers. Occasionally some of the desert springs turn sour for any number of reasons. The people complained to Moses that the wells of Marah were bitter. He dropped some wood into the water, following an old Bedouin solution to this problem. In so doing he was successful in sweetening the water. Moses taught the people that God was the healer of Israel, that the sweetening of the water was a sign of this. He reminded them that this was but the beginning of the challenges God would address to their faith. (Read Exodus 15:22-26.)

Their Confidence Weakens

Israel journeyed onward past the wells of Marah, coming next to the lush oasis of Elim, sheltered and cooled by seventy palm trees. The road over which Israel marched has been identified by modern scholars as an ancient highway built by the Egyptians for the purpose of easy communication between Egypt and the copper mines of the Sinai peninsula. Refreshed by the stop at Elim, the people picked up again, moving into a territory known as the Wilderness of Sin.

Weeks passed, and a heavy boredom set in. Bare rocks, bland food, and a dull sameness began to eat away the already frail self-confidence of the people. Their memories drifted back to Egypt's gardens, to the village markets crowded with meats and spices and fruits, to evening meals that filled the air with flavor. Their present problem was the more painful because they were tempted to a certain hopelessness. After all, where were they going? Was there really a goal to achieve? What kind of God would do this to them?

The Gift of Manna

They came to Moses and laid their cards on the table. They made it clear that their morale was low, that the situation was worsening, and suggested that it might be better to return to the "fleshpots" of Egypt rather than rot away in despair. Moses took the matter to God in prayer. God's answer was the gift of manna. Underneath the tamarisk trees the people would find manna, a sweet breadlike substance that would remove the blandness of their diet and serve as a sign of the divine presence. "Each morning you shall see my glory in the appearance of the manna." The word "glory" in the Bible usually means striking evidence of the divine presence.

Manna, then, marks the presence of God. Its new arrival each day taught the people a growing trust in the divine leadership. In later centuries the book of Wisdom, recalling the manna story, taught that divine wisdom, like manna, brings pleasure to the human heart. "You gave your people food of angels, and without their toil you supplied them from heaven with bread ready to eat" (Wisdom 16:20, NRSV).

In chapter 6 of the gospel of John, Jesus speaks about the Eucharist as being the ultimate meaning of what was foreshadowed in the books of Exodus and Wisdom. And in the Lord's Prayer we say: "Give us this day our daily bread." This manna-wisdom teaching is remembered in every benediction of the Blessed Sacrament ceremony by the following versicle and response: "He has given us bread from heaven. Containing in itself all sweetness."

The Quail

Coupled with the manna story is the narrative about the gift of quail, migratory birds from East Africa that used the Sinai peninsula as a landing strip for rest after their exhausting trip. "And there went forth a wind from the LORD, and it brought quails from the sea, and let them fall beside the camp.... The people ... gathered the quails" (Numbers 11:31-32).

It is curious, however, that the eleventh chapter of Numbers considers the quail incident a curse and not a blessing. "While the meat was yet between their teeth, before it was consumed, the anger of the LORD was kindled against the people, and the LORD smote the people with a very great plague" (Numbers 11:33). Some of the people died and were buried at that spot. The Bible's moral judgment is that their craving was unreasonable, and that such undisciplined desire can lead only to one's destruction. (Read Exodus 16.)

Water from the Rock

The Israelites came to the oasis of Rephidim only to find the water supply had failed. Once again, the frayed nerves of the people showed how much maturing they needed and how thin was their trust in God. Their complaint was loud. God, like an exasperated father, advised Moses to strike a rock called Horeb. Out of it came a fresh stream of water. But the depth of the people's bitterness and the shallowness of their faith made Horeb's rock a monument to human fickleness and a testimony to God's fidelity.

It was at this spot that Joshua and a band of guerilla fighters had to ward off the attack of a Bedouin tribe led by a man named Amalek. The Bible notes that Moses kept his arms upraised in prayer, and that it was through his prayers that God awarded Israel the victory. (Read Exodus 17.)

These are but a few instances of the trials of Israel that somehow developed their faith and contributed to their maturity. They were a pilgrim people in quest of a deepening faith and a growing awareness of God's presence. Their pilgrimage has goals: first to Sinai for a covenant and commandment experience, then onward to the Promised Land that will become a symbol of the Kingdom of Heaven proclaimed by Jesus.

REFLECTION

While Scripture at this point dwells on the human frailty of the people, it also stresses the fact that they are on a journey, actually a pilgrimage. It may be termed a pilgrimage since it is more than a psychological trip; it is also a spiritual passage. Scripture is always concerned about the dialogue between God's call and our faith response. While it necessarily has a human component, it always retains a faith dimension.

We are not simply humans, isolated from God. In the Lord, we live and move and have our being. Divine providence is never absent from our daily development. We may have difficulty remembering the presence of God. On the other hand, God never has any problem remembering our presence. This is not watchdog behavior on the part of God. It rather is like the loving maternal presence of a mother, ever attentive to our needs and ready with the graces that will minister to our human and spiritual growth.

The pilgrimage image perfectly suits our calling. We never stand still. Either we march forward or lag behind. There is nothing static about our existence. We may be annoyed by the weakness of the Israelites in the biblical narrative, but that is because it so accurately becomes our story, a history of complaints and pettiness and human weakness.

Instead of being discouraged, we should rejoice that God stays the course with us, sending us graces, symbolized by the scriptural water from a rock, manna from a tree, and quail from the warm winds. Let us get on with our pilgrimage and praise God for the gifts of the journey. We march to the goal of covenant, commandment, and kingdom, with an earthly component and a final one in heaven.

FOR DIALOGUE

Do you sense that you are "on the move" in your life? What are some goals that motivate you to look forward? Why do we associate growth and maturing with a life journey?

At the same time you have an interesting journey model in the pilgrimage of the Israelites. As you examine your faith journey from your baptism, first confession, first communion, Confirmation, your prayer life, and your moral development, how could the image of a pilgrimage of faith affect your self-understanding and spiritual future?

How could you find a certain comfort in the ways the Israelites reacted to the discomforts of their pilgrimage? Why is there no painless way to grow up whether in human or in spiritual ways?

PRAYER

Dear God, you marched with the Israelites in their pilgrimage to Sinai and the Promised Land, challenging them and carrying them forward with your graces. Please walk with us in our pilgrimage that the experience may bring us closer to you and to the Kingdom.

I lift up my eyes to the hills —
from where will my help come?
My help comes from the LORD,
who made heaven and earth.

PSALM 121:1, NRSV

CHAPTER 10

The Ten Commandments

Exodus 19-20

Give me understanding, that I may keep thy law and observe it with my whole heart.

PSALM 119:34

Friends are not won easily. Friendship cannot be achieved overnight. God had set out to make friends with Israel. He began by demonstrating his saving power in Egypt. He took his people safely through the Red Sea. He provided them with signs of love and care during their pilgrimage to maturity. God now brings Israel to Sinai for what the Bible calls a covenant event.

COVENANT: A HANDSHAKE OF TRUE FRIENDSHIP

A covenant is like the right hand of friendship, a clasp that cements relations. Today we would use the word covenant to describe a treaty or an agreement. The ancient world knew of two kinds of covenants. There was the covenant that took place between a powerful overlord and a relatively small and helpless neighbor. The powerful chief promised protection and other such benefits in return for loyalty, and perhaps a tax. There was also the covenant that took place between two kings of equal strength who imposed upon themselves mutual obligations.

The covenant at Sinai was like the one between the overlord and the small and helpless neighbor. God was the powerful overlord who had delivered Israel from her enemies, who had lifted her up and helped her toward a sense of identity, and put in her the hope of becoming a holy nation and a kingdom of priests.

As a holy nation she would experience a certain separateness from other peoples. As a kingdom of priests she would have the mission of bringing the meaning of God to all the world. Israel's later history proved that she was unable to hold this balance of the holy and the priestly. On the one hand, she became insufferably ingrown and nationalistic. On the other hand, she went out to welcome the false gods of other nations and fell into the grossest forms of idolatry. Later, St. Peter, in one of his letters, told the new Christian Church that it, too, should be holy and priestly, and hence should not repeat the error of Israel (cf. 1 Peter 2:9-10).

The Covenant as a Contract

Ancient covenants followed a special literary style. They opened with a passage that named the parties involved. This was followed by a historical prologue, which stated the advantages received by the lesser power from the overlord, such as military protection and financial assistance. This element is clearly seen in the following passage:

> *Thus you shall say to the house of Jacob, and tell the people of Israel: You have seen what I did to the Egyptians, and how I bore you on eagles' wings and brought you to myself.*
>
> EXODUS 19:3-4

The next element of the covenant was the obligations placed on the underling by the overlord. Again the Bible follows this pattern.

> *Now therefore, if you will obey my voice and keep my covenant, you shall be my own possession among all peoples; for all the earth is mine, and you shall be to me a kingdom of priests and a holy nation.*
>
> EXODUS 19:5-6

This text illustrates not only an obligation of Israel, but advantages she will enjoy should she choose to respond. The terms of her obligations will be expressed mainly in the famed Ten Commandments.

Ancient covenants, then, always recalled the favors bestowed on the underling by the overlord, and then went on to lay down what the underling must do in return. In like manner, the covenant at Sinai recalled the favors God had in the past bestowed on Israel, and then laid down what the Israelites must do in return: mainly, they must keep the Ten Commandments. Keeping the commandments, then, is really a gracious way of accepting God's favors. Thus, living a moral life would not be a burdensome task; it would be a sensible and reasonable reply to God's goodness.

It should be noticed that God saved Israel before asking her to keep the commandments. The word "saved" here refers to God graciously liberating them from slavery. Israel knew salvation before agreeing to keep the law of God. We often hear that we must keep the commandments in order to be saved. But we must be careful not to think that we earn salvation by keeping the commandments. God first gives us the gift of salvation, and we then respond by keeping the commandments as a sign of our gratitude.

We are first saved from our sins at baptism, which is symbolized by the redemption of the Israelites at the Red Sea. This salvation was actually achieved for us by the death and resurrection of Jesus.

We keep the commandments, moreover, as a sign of our resolution to remain in the process of salvation.

Salvation at the Red Sea was not enough. The march to Sinai was not enough. For, even after the giving of the covenant and the agreement to live up to it, there still lay ahead of the Hebrews the journey to the Promised Land. Even after this, life went on, and Israel was expected to live up to the high standards agreed to at Sinai.

Our Salvation Is the Work of a Lifetime

For us, too, though salvation begins at baptism, it does not stop there. It is a process that develops over an entire lifetime. Keeping the commandments, then, is a covenant entered into at baptism, deepened by the renewal of the covenant in every Mass, and brought to a climax at the moment of our own death, in which we most perfectly identify with Christ's cross.

The Hebrew text calls the commandments the "Ten Words" of God. In the Bible, God's word is first presented to us as something creative. The opening chapter of Genesis shows God fathering all things into existence by his word. At Sinai, God speaks his ten words in order to bring into being a fresh creation, namely, his people. By his ten words, he forms them into a holy and priestly nation. His words describe the quality of the relationship they are to have with him.

They are to be a people who do not worship false gods, or kill or steal or offend God in any other way. These words of God resound in the minds of Israel and soak like oil into their bones. The prophet Hosea would describe this later on in terms of a lover speaking to the heart of his beloved (Hosea 2:14-15). In the New Testament, the ten words would find their fullest meaning when Jesus required that love be the basic motivation of all law.

REFLECTION

We can never stress enough that the covenant with God comes first and only after that the commandments. Although we have described the covenant in the cultural terms of ancient times — an overlord's agreement with an underling — the actual covenant with God was more like a union of love. It was more than a legal contract; it was an exchange of vows to remain in love with one another forever. God always remained faithful to his vow. Israel often broke the vow, repented, and renewed the union of love. Christians, too, have embraced the Christ-covenant. Christ never breaks the vow. Christians, sadly, do sin and break the covenant and need repentance and renewal.

Covenant is the context for understanding the commandments. Though love is essential, it is too global and even too mysterious to be a guide in particular behavior. That is why we need concrete commandments to notice how love takes a practical shape in human life. The romantic person enthuses, "Love is all you need." In a general sense this is true. But people need direction about how love should be demonstrated in everyday affairs.

In the Sermon on the Mount (see Matthew 5-7) Jesus comments on the Ten Commandments. He has established the context for obeying them by teaching that the greatest commandments are love of God and love of neighbor as we love ourselves — which is another way of speaking of covenant. Then he introduces the need to probe our inner attitudes as part of keeping God's laws. Murder is bad, but so also is the anger that leads to it. Adultery is evil, but so also is the inner lust that causes it. Of course Christ's vision of covenant really begins with his plan to save us from sin and guilt through his life, death, resurrection, and sending of the Holy Spirit. Divine covenants always begin with divine salvation. Godly covenant begins with absolute Love. Only then do discussions about commandments begin.

FOR DIALOGUE

How would you compare your view of covenant first and then commandments as ways to implement covenant with what Scripture actually teaches on this matter? Why does God begin the covenant proposal with expressions of salvation done out of love for people?

If you heard someone say, "Love is all you need," what would your response be? What is the value of rules and laws in our relationships with one another? What would be wrong with a relationship that rested only on rules and laws and was exclusive of love?

Even though God never breaks his offer of love in the covenant, humans often depart from their vows and promises. What then is the role of guilt, repentance, and atonement?

PRAYER

Loving Father, thank you for your loving covenant with us. We also appreciate the gift of your commandments that guide us to see how we can stay in love with you. It was a beautiful experience to fall in love with you. We pray for the graces we need to stay in love.

Public opinion is stronger than the legislature, and nearly as strong as the Ten Commandments.

CHARLES DUDLEY WARNER

CHAPTER 11

Joshua Conquers the Promised Land

Joshua 1-24

Joshua fit the battle of Jericho.

AFRICAN-AMERICAN SPIRITUAL

It is one of the ironies of history that the greatest Hebrew of the Old Testament never entered the Promised Land. Moses, who had been the fiery freedom fighter for Israel, died before he could set foot on the land promised to his people. But his old eyes were privileged to see the new land beyond the Jordan. On the eve of his death, his friends carried him to the summit of Mount Nebo from which he gazed on the hoped-for land of promise.

It was with this memory and this hope that Moses died, leaving the leadership to his trusted lieutenant, Joshua. "And Joshua the son of Nun was full of the spirit of wisdom, for Moses had laid his hands upon him; so the people of Israel obeyed him, and did as the LORD had commanded Moses" (Deuteronomy 34:9).

ISRAELITES HAD TO FIGHT FOR THE PROMISED LAND

It is generally thought that God simply handed over the land of Canaan to the Israelites. After all, he promised it to them. But as it turned out, the terms of the promise involved the personal bravery and skill of the people. They had to invade the country and conquer it. The books of Joshua and Judges are documents that preserve the accounts of the military conquest of the land of Canaan.

Sometimes it is hard to realize why they were so insistent on having land. The reason is that the Hebrews wanted to form themselves into a coherent nation. Without a land upon which they could settle and call their own, they would have had great difficulty in achieving identity and a place in history. Land gives stability to a people. Unless the Jews had this land, there would not be an Israel. Hence they saw in their successful conquest of Canaan the blessing of God allowing them this good earth as a gift.

Joshua the General

Joshua emerges not so much as a prophet, but as a general. One of his first decisions was to send spies across the Jordan to scout the area around Jericho. They slipped into the city, took note of the defenses, and paused for a night in the house of a woman named Rahab whose rooms were joined to the walls of the city. During the night, police raided her place looking for the spies, because someone had alerted the king about the strangers.

Rahab hid the spies and sent the police away. When they were gone, she made a deal with the spies that if their soldiers were successful in taking the city, they would spare her and her family. The spies assured her that she would be protected. They advised her to hang a red banner from her window so that in the heat of battle the soldiers could identify her house and not harm it. Rahab is honored in Scripture by being mentioned in the family tree of Jesus as recorded by St. Matthew. (Read Joshua 2.)

After the spies returned, Joshua gathered the people for the crossing of the Jordan. They solemnly formed into ranks and marched to the banks of the Jordan. The priests walked ahead of them carrying the Ark of the Covenant on their shoulders. As their feet touched the water, the experience of the Red Sea was repeated. The waters parted, and the people crossed in comfort.

Joshua called for the building of twelve memorial stones to celebrate the long-awaited moment when the Israelites would set foot on the land promised to Abraham. As the paschal meal commemorated the liberation from Egypt, so these stones commemorated the liberation from the sufferings of the desert. At the paschal meal the children asked, "What does it mean?" And Joshua said to the people of Israel, "When your children ask their fathers in time to come, 'What do these stones mean?' then you shall let your children know, 'Israel passed over this Jordan on dry ground.' For the LORD your God dried up the waters of the Jordan for you until you passed over, as the LORD your God did to the Red Sea, which he dried up for us until we passed over, so that all the peoples of the earth may know that the hand of the LORD is mighty; that you may fear the LORD your God for ever" (Joshua 4:21-24).

The Taking of Jericho

Joshua's first and most famous conquest was the taking of the city of Jericho. The strategy was strange by almost any standard. Every day for seven days, the army, led by the clergy carrying the Ark of the Covenant, walked around and around the city in absolute silence. This silent mob endlessly circling the city must surely have been an unnerving sight to the inhabitants of Jericho. On the seventh day, to the accompaniment of the bone-piercing noise of the rams' horns, the walls came tumbling down, and Joshua's soldiers entered the city. As had been arranged, the family of Rahab was spared.

Kathleen Kenyon, a British archeologist, has uncovered most of the ruins of the city of Jericho. She has concluded that it is one of the oldest cities in the world, probably founded about seven thousand years before the birth of Christ. One of the levels of Jericho uncovered, which dates from the time of Joshua (around 1200 B.C.), seems to show evidence of an earthquake. As a result of these findings, some scholars have tried to connect the earthquake with the tumbling walls of Joshua. Whatever happened, the old ballad singers of Israel remembered the important fact that Joshua took the city, and did so with the aid of God. (Read Joshua 6.)

Brutal Treatment of Enemies

There is a serious moral problem raised in the books of Joshua and Judges. It can be illustrated by this passage: "Then they utterly destroyed all in the city, both men and women, young and old, oxen, sheep, and asses, with the edge of the sword" (Joshua 6:21). This utterly brutal way of dealing with enemies has puzzled commentators through the ages. How could someone blessed by God do such a thing?

What we must recall is that Joshua and the people were creatures of their times, held to the customs that prevailed in morality and warfare then.

Their barbaric views and primitive approaches to war are not meant to be an example to us. We cannot argue this was God's will. At most we can say that those people believed mistakenly that it was God's will. Joshua acted in the light of primitive ideas of what was right or wrong in warfare.

In one sense humanity has progressed since then, and morality of what is permissible in war has developed with it. But if one looks at the record of twentieth-century wars with carpet bombing of civilians, the atomic bombing of Hiroshima and Nagasaki by various combatants, as well as the genocide of the Armenians, the holocaust of the Jews, the Communist slaughter of Christians and subject peoples, and the ethnic cleansing in the Balkans, it makes one wonder if indeed we, as a presumed enlightened human community, have satisfactorily improved our warlike behavior as much as we should since the days of Joshua.

One other text that has plagued interpreters is the one concerning the day the sun stood still. "And the sun stood still, and the moon stayed, until the nation took vengeance on their enemies" (Joshua 10:13). Not realizing that this was simply a fragment of poetry from an old soldier's ballad romantically idealizing the victory, never meant to be literally interpreted, some commentators have futilely racked their brains looking for eclipses and so on.

The final chapters of the book of Joshua describe the dividing of the land for the twelve tribes. In chapter 24 there is a covenant scene similar to that at Sinai. As you read these old stories, keep in mind the mentality of the people of those days. In this way, the book of Joshua can have much inspirational and religious interest for us today.

REFLECTION

In the Liturgy of the Hours, the Church assigns the reading of the book of Joshua for the tenth week Ordinary Time. For the second reading, the Church selects the letter to the Romans by St. Ignatius of Antioch. This is an intriguing choice since the letter dwells on the saint's reflection about the martyrdom that he would face when he arrived in Rome. After reading about the killing involved by Joshua's conquest of Canaan, it is fascinating to ponder the story of a man who bravely sails to Rome to give up his life for his witness to Christ. One kills; the other offers his body to be killed.

Ignatius eagerly sought the crown of martyrdom in the spirit of St. Paul: "For to me to live is Christ, and to die is gain... I am hard pressed between the two. My desire is to depart and be with Christ, for that is far better" (Philippians 1:21-22). Ignatius compared his forthcoming martyrdom to the wheat that is ground to become the bread of the Eucharist. He begs his friends not to try to bar him from the grace of dying for Christ:

> *"I am glad to die for God, provided you do not hinder me. I beg you not to show me a misplaced kindness. Let me be the food of beasts that I may come to God. I am his wheat, and I shall be ground by the teeth of beasts, that I may become Christ's pure bread."*

Here then we have two figures involved in God's unfolding plan of salvation. The soldier Joshua is a warrior who claims the Promised Land. In thinking about what he had to do, we may recall St. Augustine's comment that "There are some things we must do in a mournful mood." Maybe it is better to say that Joshua acted within the limits of what was known and understood in his day.

On the other hand we have Ignatius, one of the greatest bishops of the early Church, deliberately seeking martyrdom and cautioning his followers not to prevent this possibility. He understood all too well St. Paul's insight into Christ's will that our participation in the Cross would be a sharing in his saving work for the Church:

Now I rejoice in my sufferings for your sake, and in my flesh I complete what is lacking in Christ's afflictions for the sake of his body, that is, the church. . . .

COLOSSIANS 1:24

FOR DIALOGUE

Why is it important to do all we can to prevent war? Why should we join those who work strenuously to reduce the impact of war on civilians and prisoners of war? How can we support the Church's position that nuclear war must never happen?

If you were asked to die for your beliefs, what would be your response? What stories of martyrs have had an influence on you? What do you think of the violent deaths of Ghandi and Martin Luther King? When Christ asks you to carry your cross as the price of being his disciple, what do you think he had in mind?

Share stories of heroic people whom you admire. What are the qualities they witness that you wish you possessed?

PRAYER

Teach us, Lord, to be witnesses of peace in our relationships and our participation in the life of our nation. Grant us the graces of courage and heroism in practicing your call to faith, hope, love, and humility.

The blood of martyrs is the seed of Christians.

TERTULLIAN

CHAPTER 12

The Judges:
Israel's Charismatic Leaders

Judges 4-5; 14-16

Whenever the LORD raised up judges for them, the LORD was with the judge, and he saved them from the hand of their enemies all the days of the judge; for the LORD was moved to pity by their groaning because of those who afflicted and oppressed them. But whenever the judge died, they turned back....

JUDGES 2:18-19

Judges is a book that has little to do with judges in our sense — men and women who preside in a courtroom. A better description of them would be charismatic military leaders sent by God to liberate their people from various forms of oppression. They filled the leadership roles between the time of Joshua and the creation of the monarchy. The theme of this book is the matter of Israel's fidelity to the covenant and commandments of God. Things went well when they were faithful. Matters fell apart when they were not. When they repented, God raised up a judge to save them.

The judges emerge as the heroes of ancient days, closely tied to the period of conquest begun by Joshua. Generally, scholars speak of six major Judges and six minor Judges. To get the flavor of the book, it is probably best to concentrate on two of them and make a passing reference to some of the others.

A RELIGIOUS MESSAGE: ISRAEL NEEDS A SAVIOR

Aside from the personalities that dominate the book, there is a noticeable religious message leaping out from every page. It runs in the form of a repeatable cycle. Israel finds herself in a state of moral decline. As a result, her enemies move in and conquer her, making slaves of the people. At this, she cries out for deliverance. God hears her plea and sends a judge-savior to bring her to freedom. Hence Israel identified her defeats on the plains of battle with her moral decay.

Deborah the Prophetess

Out of the various colorful characters, we choose Deborah and Samson to illustrate the work of the Judges. Deborah is like an Old Testament Joan of Arc. She first appears as a wise old prophetess, uttering her oracles under a sacred tree. Israel has fallen under the power of her enemies, and Deborah is approached for guidance as to what to do. Caught by the Spirit of God she says it is time to fight back. She chooses Barak as her general and plans to meet the enemy on the plains of Esdraelon, just below Mount Tabor, where years later the Lord would be transfigured before the apostles.

As is often the case in biblical battles, the Israelites seem hopelessly outclassed. The enemy plans to use chariots with great blades curling out from the sides, so that when the rushing horses bring the chariots into the thin ranks of the Israelites, the effect will be that of a farmer's scythe cutting down a field of grain. Furthermore, the chariots are made of iron, and the soldiers are well-armored. And against these are the ill-trained, ill-equipped soldiers of Israel. They have no horses, no chariots; their spears have stone tips. Yet Deborah says they must fight and have confidence.

A Hebrew Victory

On the day appointed for the battle, as the troops got into position, a violent rainstorm broke out. The River Kishon roared over the banks in a flash flood and the field of Esdraelon was transformed into a bed of mud. The chariots were stuck in the mire; the horses reared in panic with every clap of thunder and arrow of lightning. The heavy-armored enemy weaved clumsily through the storm, unable to withstand the light-footed Hebrews.

The captain of the enemy, a man named Sisera, fled from the battlefield. He went to the tent of a Hebrew woman called Jael and asked for refuge and food. She gave him some warm milk and soothed him to sleep. Then, with a fierce look and purpose, Jael took a tent peg and drove it through the sleeping general's head.

The fifth chapter of Judges records a song that Deborah is said to have sung at the victory celebration. Of the storm she chanted: "From heaven fought the stars, from their courses they fought against Sisera. The torrent Kishon swept them away...." And of the deed of Jael: "He asked water and she gave him milk, she brought him curds in a lordly bowl. She put her hand to the tent peg and her right hand to the workmen's mallet; she struck Sisera a blow, she crushed his head, she shattered and pierced his temple. He sank, he fell, he lay still at her feet; at her feet he sank, he fell; where he sank, there he fell dead" (Judges 5:20-21; 25-26).

Samson

Even more colorful and beloved is the story of Samson. Born of a family in the tribe of Dan, Samson grew up into a man of tremendous strength. His parents enrolled him in the fraternity of the Nazirites. The Nazirites were a group noted for their special dedication to the cause of God. They symbolized their dedication by never cutting their hair or taking a strong drink. According to the story, Samson's strength lay in the great seven locks of hair that flowed from his head.

The accounts of Samson illustrate both his sense of loyalty to God and a human weakness that made his strength count for nothing. He entered into a mixed marriage with a pagan woman from Timnah, Delilah, only to find grief for his infidelity. Her wedding guests mocked his peasant ways and his inability to make up riddles. When he finally did make up a riddle, out of his experience of finding honey in the carcass of the lion he slew, his wife betrayed him.

The marvelous exploits, which show Samson burning a Philistine harvest with torches attached to three hundred foxes' tails, slaying a thousand men with the jawbone of an ass, and single-handedly breaking down the gate of the city of Gaza, are stories recalling how the Hebrews completed the conquest of Canaan.

Samson's affair with Delilah has caught the imagination of poets, artists, and filmmakers. This account, wisely noting that even the most powerful can fall victim to temptation, stands out as a uniquely human story. The loss of his hair signifies the loss of something much more important. He has been unfaithful to God. Samson resolves to make atonement for this. The return of his hair and his power accompanies the renewal of his faith. His destruction of the temple of Dagon, along with hundreds of people, symbolizes God's power, a power that can crush the false gods of Canaan. (Read Judges 13-16.)

The Judges Are Inspired Leaders

The Bible describes the choice of judges in spiritual terms in which the judge is called by God for a mission and guided by God's Spirit. Some other judges who achieved fame are Gideon, noted for his skill as a leader in conquering the Midianites, and Jephthah, who made a foolish vow to kill the first living creature he saw after a victorious battle: he planned to offer the victim as a thanksgiving sacrifice. Unfortunately, it was his daughter he met.

These epic sagas breathe of pioneer days. It is a time of battles and brutality. The judges are leaders, inspired by the Spirit of God, who earned the respect of the tribes. In a sense, the whole state of the Hebrews at this time is somewhat freewheeling and bordering on complete disorder. It is precisely because of this sense of approaching anarchy that the people eventually make known their desire for a king, to get greater discipline and unity.

REFLECTION

One way of appreciating the problem facing God's people during the era of the judges was their attraction to the false gods (the "baals") of their military enemies. While they did not want to be ruled by others, they did find the religion of their enemies easier to swallow and less demanding than the God of their fathers. The baals seemed more friendly and much more in tune with the people's sensual desires. The purification of Israel's religious commitment required both the conquest of the Philistines and an internal resistance to the seduction of the idols.

In our own times our religion is challenged by a secularized culture, even a culture of disbelief. Secularity is far less demanding than the commandments of our God. The sensual lure of the present culture seems to make our faith a joyless affair. The "baals" today are the seductive celebrities in business and entertainment whose external beauty, greed, and amoral lives seem more to be preferred than the tough demands of the gospel.

We need new "Deborahs" and "Samsons" to rise up and shake us out of the trances and enchantments mediated to us by the media-driven narcissism and the futile preoccupation with self. Genuine happiness in the long run can only be gained by a covenant love with the true God and observance of the commandments that illustrate the way to love. The Israel of the judges would have collapsed and disappeared had God not come and delivered them from the illusion of the baals. We pray that in our times holy men and women will come to us and lead us to more wholesome and holy lives.

FOR DIALOGUE

As you contemplate the pull of the culture and your faith requirements, what would you say are some of the conflicts you experience because of these opposing demands? What has been your usual way of handling these challenges?

In your life, who would be some public figures that influence you to question your religious commitment? What is so appealing about them? Where would you turn within the Church to find responses to these approaches and support for your faith?

When raising your children, what would you do to strengthen them for the "spiritual combat" that a secularized culture will present to them?

PRAYER

God of strength and spiritual power, come to us and fill us with your Holy Spirit of courage and commitment. Cleanse our sight that we may see the weakness of a world without you. Open our hearts to your ever-faithful love.

Superstition, idolatry, and hypocrisy have ample wages, while truth goes a-begging.

MARTIN LUTHER

CHAPTER 13

Samuel Creates the Monarchy

1 Samuel 8-10

The people said, "We will have a king over us!"

1 SAMUEL 8:20

Every great nation has its cast of heroes. The book of Judges preserves the thrilling story of the Israelites' dramatic rise to power. The period was a time of inspired leaders, a time of freewheeling chieftains, warlords, and soldiers ready to fight for what they could get out of it. It is a textbook of wars aimed at illustrating a religious idea. The trouble was, however, that the independent chiefs seemed to have no sense of the need to unite more firmly. They did not realize that unless they united, total disorder would be the result.

SAMUEL'S PROBLEM

It was the last and greatest of the judges who had the wisdom to notice the danger, and had the courage to take a painful step to do something about it. As a Spirit-filled judge, Samuel was well aware that God had entrusted to him the destiny of the people. He was long familiar with the need to be sensitive to the divine presence. He was literally raised in a sanctuary, sleeping and dreaming each night beside the Ark of the Covenant.

During his early manhood, Samuel was engaged in military exploits like the other judges before him. When he reached his declining years, he thought to make his sons serve as successors. But the elders of Israel felt that something more than the system of judges was needed to keep the tribes from falling apart. "Behold, you are old and your sons do not walk in your ways; now appoint for us a king to govern us like all the nations" (1 Samuel 8:5).

This was the origin of Samuel's problem. It was not that he was so attached to pushing his own sons into the leadership. Rather, it was his lack of certainty. He was not sure whether it was a good thing for Israel to have a king. He knew that kings could bring much injustice in their time. And kings would naturally limit the freedom of the people.

Samuel's Courageous Decision

Samuel warned the people that the king would take the Israelites' sons and make them his horsemen; take their daughters to be perfumers and cooks and bakers; take a tenth of their flocks; make the people his slaves. Then Samuel told them, "And in that day you will cry out because of your king, whom you have chosen for yourselves; but the LORD will not answer you in that day" (1 Samuel 8:18).

Kings would take away their freedom and make them forget God. In a kingdom the tendency to idolatry would be great. With judges they would probably not forget God, and anyhow after a time judges would probably disappear. Get a king and lose God. Keep the judges and lose the nation. What was Samuel to do?

Against his feelings urging him to save the old way, Samuel chose the kingdom. The Bible does not describe the problem as clearly as we put it here. The biblical method is to place contrasting stories side by side. One story shows Samuel fighting to save the system of the judges. Then another story describes him defending the need for the new kingdom and the efforts everyone must make to save the nation from falling apart.

The Spirit of the Lord Comes Upon Saul

In chapters 9 and 10 of the first book of Samuel, you will find the description of the process whereby Saul is chosen as king and the part Samuel played in this. You should note that Samuel speaks of the special action of the Spirit of God. He tells Saul that he will meet a band of prophets. "Then the spirit of the LORD will come mightily upon you, and you shall prophesy with them and be turned into another man" (1 Samuel 10:6). The reason for Saul's anointing of the Spirit is to show the people that he is truly one who represents God among them.

The people had become accustomed to having Spirit-filled men as their leaders. Hence, for the sake of a smoother crossing over from judges to kings, this presence of the Spirit would be expected. Revolutionary as the new order would be, it would not dispense with the obvious requirement that the leader should display the imprint of God. Not only was there an invisible anointing of the new king by the inrush of God's Spirit, there was also the visible anointing with oil.

Samuel Chose What God Wanted — Not What He Wanted

It is interesting that in chapter 11 of the first book of Samuel there is a different account of Saul having been chosen as king. Rather than being chosen by the Spirit of God or the wisdom of Samuel, Saul is chosen by the people because he has shown such courage and bravery in war, especially in the struggle with the Ammonites. This is a story preserved, not to sell short the work of Samuel, but to satisfy an understandable pride of a people who would naturally want to think their first king was a brave and worthy man.

The beauty of Samuel's solution to his problem is that he, an old man, broke away from the old way, which he himself preferred, and supported a new way of life for Israel because he loved her so much, and because he sensed it was what God really wanted.

REFLECTION

Interpreters of culture tell us that stable societies create institutions to ensure continuity and the capacity to serve people's needs. They use the axiom that charisma needs institution. By charisma they refer to a quality of some people who are gifted with personal charm, creativity, and magnetic attractiveness. The person with charisma has a talent and an insight useful for the common good. Normally such a person does not have a method for conserving the gift. At this point men and women who have organizational skills enter the scene and create structures to contain and perpetuate the gift of the charismatic leader.

This dynamic is behind the Samuel-Saul story. The history of the judges is a record of twelve charismatic leaders, endowed with courage, creativity, and responsiveness to God. They were tribal leaders who maintained the faith of Israel when the people were bewitched by the fertility gods of Canaan. The judges sustained a reservoir of living and effective faith partly by the strength of their personalities and partly by their skills in winning a number of little wars. But God's revelation and the people's faith needed a firmer foundation than the charismatic personalities could provide.

If the religion of Israel hoped to survive, it needed a structure, an institution to incorporate it and make it last. The solution was the adopting of a king and a kingdom model. Though it would also have its shortcomings, it did provide a national and religious identity that has lasted actually to this present day. As we will see, the kingdom itself eventually withered and died, but by then its vision was achieved and its usefulness reached its conclusion.

Our Church is a reasonable reflection of this development. It has a "charismatic" aspect in that it is a mystery of God, a reality sustained by the Holy Spirit, a communion of believers formed and fed by the Eucharist. At the same time it is an institution with pope, bishops, priests, religious, hundreds of millions of laity organized into a central government at the Vatican along with dioceses, parishes, monasteries, convents, and mission stations worldwide. Samuel's insight has come a long way!

[The use of the terms charisma and charismatic in this reflection are strictly drawn from an anthropological and sociological analysis. It is not derived from the spirituality movement of charismatic renewal, though it obviously has a relationship to that reality in the sense that the renewal provides vitality for the institutional Church.]

FOR DIALOGUE

As you reflect on your own personal development, what might you characterize as the free-spirited "charismatic" period of your life? What might be described as the "institutional" side of your life? Why are both helpful for you?

What is your experience of religious leaders with "charisma"?

What are some examples you could share about the transition from charisma to institution either from your own experience or from your study of Church history?

Scripture frequently describes the appointment of religious leaders such as judges, kings, and prophets in terms of a calling from God along with a visible presence of God's Spirit in the person's life. What are some stories of such events in the Church today?

PRAYER

Lord, thank you for calling me to holiness in my baptism and the repetition of that call when I made my first confession and first communion and received confirmation. Abide with me each moment of each day that I never fail to hear your call and never cease to say yes to you in word and deed.

And the LORD called Samuel again the third time. And he arose and went to Eli, and said, "Here I am, for you called me." Then Eli perceived that the LORD was calling the boy. Therefore Eli said to Samuel, "Go, lie down; and if he calls you, you shall say, 'Speak, LORD, for thy servant hears.'"

1 SAMUEL 3:8-9

CHAPTER 14

King Saul

1 Samuel 10-15

*Then Samuel took a vial of oil and poured it on his head, and kissed him
and said, "The LORD has anointed you to be prince over his heritage."*

1 SAMUEL 10:1

FORGETTING GOD IN THE DRIVE FOR WORLDLY SUCCESS

Saul, the first king of Israel, soon discovered that it isn't necessarily fun to be king. Samuel, the last of the judges, never quite reconciled himself to the new order of things, even though he somehow knew this was the way things had to be. The Saul stories deal on the one hand with his military campaigns against the Philistines, and on the other with the problem of religion in a time of rapid social change.

The Challenge Facing Saul

Saul knew he had to break the Philistines' control over the mining and production of iron. Not only did they reap the financial benefits from iron production, they also had a strong military dominance over significant amounts of territory. Saul knew that to overcome the Philistines, he must train his men to be skilled troops.

At the same time, Saul was faced with the problem of religion in the new world he was creating. He was bringing Israel from the simple life of the shepherd to the complicated life of the town dweller. Now his people's uncomplicated faith was exposed to the exotic and erotic religious practices of the Philistines. God was aware of these problems and sent the holy man Samuel to be the watchman of Israel during these troubled years of change.

Saul Condemned by Samuel for Offering Sacrifice

After his anointing, Saul's first big campaign was against the Philistines at Michmash. Saul was expected to make a sacrificial offering before going into battle so that he would have God's blessing. However, the rite of sacrifice was reserved to Samuel. Saul, under pressure of the advance of the enemy, decided to offer the sacrifice himself. Samuel arrived at this moment and angrily condemned Saul for not waiting. "Obedience is better than sacrifice," declared the old judge.

As the battle began, Saul commanded the soldiers to eat nothing until sundown. But his son, Jonathan, needed energy. He saw some honey and ate it. Saul heard of this toward evening and considered punishing Jonathan with death for his disobedience. Fortunately, Jonathan was bailed out by the soldiers who assured Saul that he had no need to be so strict.

Obedience Is Better Than Sacrifice

The Bible goes on to recount the second campaign of Saul against the Amalekites. Because this was to a certain extent a "holy war," Saul was expected to wipe out the city and every living thing in it. "Now go and smite Amalek, and utterly destroy all that they have; do not spare them, but kill both man and woman, infant and suckling, ox and sheep, camel and ass" (1 Samuel 15:3).

This biblical equivalent of Hiroshima, an extreme of brutality difficult for us to understand, was technically a religious holocaust. The Hebrew word for holocaust is *olah*. In religious services, the *olah* implied that the entire offering be consumed by fire and hence ascend in smoke to God. This is in contrast to the communion offering, in which part of the animal was saved and eaten by the people making the offering.

Saul did defeat the Amalekites. "But Saul and the people spared Agag, and the best of the sheep and of the oxen and of the fatlings, and the lambs, and all that was good, and would not utterly destroy them; all that was despised and worthless they utterly destroyed" (1 Samuel 15:9). So Samuel came again to rebuke Saul. The king defended himself by saying that he planned to use the good animals for a great sacrificial service of thanksgiving. Samuel, never one to miss a dramatic possibility, broke out into a poetic chant:

> *Has the LORD as great delight in burnt offerings and sacrifices, as in obeying the voice of the LORD? Behold, to obey is better than sacrifice, and to hearken than the fat of rams.*
>
> 1 SAMUEL 15:22

Reducing a Religious Service to Magic

The point at issue here, as in the incident at Michmash, is a religious problem. It doesn't mean that sacrifice is unimportant, but the inward disposition of obedience to God's will must be present. Always turn your heart to God when you offer sacrifice. King Saul, under the pressures of unifying the tribes, building a nation, and breaking the Philistines' control over the mining of iron, was reducing liturgy to magic.

This is all the more significant since Samuel's second condemnation takes place at Saul's encampment at the pagan shrine city of Gilgal. The Philistines had established several well-known shrine cities where elaborate sanctuaries were built to practice idolatry. Some of the best known were Bethel, Hebron, Shechem, Mizpah, and Gilgal. The fact that Saul was planning to make a sacrifice almost as a formality, in a pagan sanctuary that had not yet been replaced and purified by Israelite religion, partly accounts for the almost excessive hostility of Samuel.

Samuel's religious theory was this: one must have a holocaust of the heart before he can offer a liturgical holocaust. So strongly did Samuel believe this, that he resorted to the extreme measure of taking the kingship away from Saul's family: no son of his would ever sit on the throne of Israel. The situation seems unusually severe to us in the light of Saul's deeply humble efforts at repentance and his plea for forgiveness.

"Now therefore I pray, pardon my sin and return with me, that I may worship the LORD" (1 Samuel 15:25). Saul desperately clung to the robe of Samuel and even tore a piece from it. Samuel, however, was unmoved. He looked at the piece of cloth in Saul's hand and told him this was a sign that the kingdom would be torn from his family.

A Broken and Tragic King

After this, Saul's career spiraled downward. Samuel anointed David to be his successor. This brilliant young lieutenant achieved striking military victories and charmed all the people to his side. Saul's final years were filled with deep depression and black moods. He was jealous of David, and felt deeply the ingratitude of a people who gave him little credit for the breakthrough he made against the Philistines.

Saul was better on the field of battle than he was by the lamps of the sanctuary. As happens to many men, he allowed his drive to get things done to obscure his religious principles. He produced an efficient war machine, but compromised his God in the process. He died a broken and tragic king.

Fortunately, David was not blind to Saul's greatness, and lamented him saying:

Saul and Jonathan, beloved and lovely! In life and in death they were not divided; they were swifter than eagles, they were stronger than lions.

2 SAMUEL 1:23

REFLECTION

Power corrupts. Absolute power corrupts absolutely. Pride and power ruined the career of King Saul. He had many military and political victories. He began the unification of the twelve tribes of Israel into a political and cultural identity. He rescued them from their insular, nomadic shepherd ways and led them into the customs and benefits of a stable society. By constructing an army out of all the tribesmen, he showed them how to win wars and exert the power that comes from victories. As Samuel had predicted, Israel was becoming "like the nations," that is, God's people were being transformed into a royal, military, political, and economic nation.

The price to be paid was the loss of a religious focus. The original intent was to institutionalize the spirituality of the wandering shepherd communities, lest the call of the covenant LORD be forgotten. Saul won a nation, but lost the faith purpose for making it happen. That is really what was behind the anger of Samuel against Saul's empty sacrifices and refusal to obey the ban regarding the extermination of defeated peoples.

This may seem very alien to us. Yet do we not often mindlessly attend Mass? Do we not babble prayers without putting our hearts into them? Yes we do not approve of exterminating enemies, yet seldom raise little objection about the so-called "surgical" strikes in which the deaths of enemies are called "collateral damage." The quest for purity in our religion is always a challenge. Pride and power can corrupt us just as well as it did Saul. His story is instructive. We pray that ours will have a different ending.

FOR DIALOGUE

Share stories about the destructive effects of pride and power on public leaders. What do you learn from such narratives? Why does power corrupt people? What is the spiritual antidote to power?

It would seem that humility is what people need. Why do the saints tell us that humility is the baseline for practicing the virtues? How would you distinguish humility from timidity, shyness, and bashful natures? Why is being humble different from being a doormat?

How can leaders in any area of power retain their faith focus? What are some examples you know about where someone in power converted from being "power hungry" to using authority to serve others?

Jesus, you asked us to learn your attitudes of being humble of heart. Give us the grace to avoid any addiction to power and to absorb from you the gift of a humble heart.

You will find fishing to be like the virtue of humility, which has a calmness of spirit and a world of other blessings attending upon it.

IZAAK WALTON

CHAPTER 15

David the King

1 Samuel 16-17; 2 Samuel 5-7; 11-12

"Has not the Scripture said that the Christ is descended from David,
and comes from Bethlehem, the village where David was?"

JOHN 7:42

Almost any nation would be proud to include David in the list of its leading public figures. He was a shepherd, a poet, a warrior, a statesman, a lover, a sinner, a saint. He was grateful and perceptive enough to know that his wide-ranging success depended a great deal on the spadework of Saul, from whom he inherited a disciplined army and people, and a clearer idea of the role of religion in the new nation.

DAVID'S FIRST TASKS

After his anointing at the shrine city of Hebron, David understood that his main missions were: to overcome a few who, with the help of Saul's family, still opposed him; to search for a neutral city to serve as a capital; and to establish a shrine around which could be built the religious fervor of the people.

Chapters 3 and 4 of the second book of Samuel preserve the accounts of David's unhappy task of overcoming the remaining opposition of the house of Saul. The followers of Saul centered their hopes in the son of Saul, Ishbosheth, who was a hapless and ineffective leader. Ultimately he was beheaded by two assassins as he lay in his bed. They, in turn, were executed by David. This may seem gross ingratitude to us, but we must remember that Saul's son shared in the privileges granted to those whom the Lord had anointed. Only God could punish them for wrongdoing. David always kept this in mind in his treatment of anointed men of the Lord.

The fifth chapter describes how David took the Jebusite stronghold of Jerusalem. This mountain fortress seemed so safe from all attack that its defenders taunted outsiders with the remark: "All we need are the blind and the lame to ward you off." But David was a shrewd general, not easily put off by smooth walls and remarks such as this.

He discovered that the water supply for the city was hoisted from a tunnel deep in the mountain. David calculated: "Whoever would strike down the Jebusites, let him get up the water shaft to attack..." (2 Samuel 5:8, NRSV). By sending his soldiers into the tunnel and up the water shaft, David took the city.

In selecting the neutral city of Jerusalem, David avoided causing jealousy among the tribes. By moving the government offices away from Hebron, he gained a certain independence from the lobbying of any one tribe.

The Ark of the Covenant Brought to Jerusalem

Now David had a religious problem to solve. Samuel had warned the people that the coming kingdom would make them "like all the nations." But Israel was supposed to be different from the nations, for they were the elected Community of God, called to be a people of faith, abiding in his strength rather than in a totally human endeavor. Israel had a mission to be holy and priestly, not to be just another oriental kingdom.

In the days of the judges, the religious ardor of the nation was sustained by the abiding glory of God that rested on the Ark of the Covenant. Wherever they went, the Ark of the Covenant went with them, impressing on them the supreme importance of their religion. But now that their nation had achieved stability, it was necessary to find a new way to centralize and make effective the rulership of God in Israel.

David's solution is found in the sixth chapter of the second book of Samuel. He reasoned that since he had established a political center in Jerusalem, why not have a shrine to crown the work of the state? He would bring the ark to the city and there build a permanent temple to house it. State and Church would stand side by side in friendly partnership. The kingdom would be served and God given his due glory.

The journey bringing the ark to Jerusalem was marred by the sudden death of Uzzah, who put out his hand to save the falling ark when the oxen pulling the wagon stumbled. Seen in context, his death was a way of instructing people in the need to preserve a reverential distance from the awesome God. In our age, when awe and wonder are no longer so closely connected with the divine and in which God is rarely associated with revenge, this story may have less meaning. Nevertheless, it should serve to remind us that this sense of awe and wonder should be preserved in every age even though the method for this should be one that resonates with our culture.

David Dances before the Ark

A second scene that captures our attention is the dance of David before the ark. It is hard for people today to link dancing with liturgy, but this was not the case in biblical times. It was only natural to take one's whole body and leap and sway with it rhythmically to praise the living God.

Some Bible commentators have seen in the procession of the ark a model of the procession of Mary to the house of Elizabeth. Mary, as the New Testament expression of the Ark of the Covenant, stayed three months in the house of Elizabeth, just as the old ark rested in the home of Obededom. As God rested upon the ark, so his Son rested within Mary.

The Israelites Thought of David as Their Shepherd

David solved the basic challenges of his life by establishing a centralized government crowned by the Church through the presence of the ark. His son, Solomon, would build the temple. Many colorful stories surround the figure of David, for instance, his struggle with Goliath (1 Samuel 17:32-49) and his historic friendship with Jonathan (1 Samuel 18-20).

He was not without his sins and flaws as exhibited in his adultery with Bathsheba, resulting in deceit and causing her husband to die. His repentance is remembered at morning-prayer every Friday in the Liturgy of the Hours when the Church prays David's psalm 51. He was a sinner who acknowledged his sin, confessed it, did penance for it, and changed his ways. These and other stories about David in the Bible show him to be one of history's great and appealing human beings.

The Israelites liked to think of David as their shepherd. Israel remembered the days when they were a tent community, enjoying the freedom of being on the move, experiencing the deepening of their relationships, and sustained in hope by the glory of God always marching before them. It seemed to them to be a time of original innocence. It was seen through the idealized mists of nostalgia for a time when they felt God's presence as a friend and treated one another with the care they gave to the lambs. This is something David understood well since he himself had been a shepherd before entering public life. The New Testament sees the life of David as a preparation for the Messiah who would be born of the family of David and would establish God's authentic kingdom of love, justice, and mercy.

REFLECTION

Some people concentrate on life as a process. Important as this is, its pitfall causes many to forget goals, especially the final goals of our life of faith. Some say the "process is the product." Others claim, "Life is a journey, not a destination." Such a preoccupation with process is as old as the ancient Greek philosopher Heraclitus who taught that life is like a moving river, always changing. He said, "You never swim in the same water twice." This is a half-truth. There is constant change, but there is also stability. Life is a rock as well as a river. The process is not the product. The product is the product. The process is not the goal. The goal is the goal.

One of the reasons why King David was so effective was his clear-headed focus on his goals: disarm the opposition; choose a neutral city for a capital; make the shrine of the Ark of the Covenant the spiritual basis of the nation. It was his goals that stirred his imagination and released his phenomenal energies. St. Thomas says that the goal is the first thing we should think of, even though it is the last matter to be achieved.

When the goal burns brightly in our hearts then we move off the dime. Despite his faults and sins, David loved God with passion. God was as real to him as the night sky he scanned for so many years as a young shepherd. He never forgot the holy presence when history drew him into world affairs. His mighty repentance was due to his robust love for God. His final goal was God. He set the goal first and then found a process to reach it. He knew where he was going before he found the way to get there. David offers us the excitement of recovering our sense of a final goal on our spiritual journey. Then our process of going there is truly an adventure.

FOR DIALOGUE

What would you say are three goals you have in mind for your life? Which of the three seems the most important to you? How clearly do you visualize your goals? What is there about your life that has made you choose such goals?

What methods and processes have you chosen for reaching these goals? How is it possible to become so wrapped up in the means to achieve your goals that they drain your energies to the point you actually forget where you are going?

Even if one of your goals is a spiritual one, why is it possible that your journey becomes more important than the goal? What might you do to establish a balance between setting your goals and the process to reach them?

Lord God, you alone satisfy the longings of my heart. You alone are worthy of my hopes. Inspire me to seek a union of love with you and to choose the right ways to achieve this, always realizing that your grace is what makes this happen.

Well, I do not run aimlessly, I do not box as one beating the air. . . .
1 CORINTHIANS 9:26

I have fought the good fight, I have finished the race, I have kept the faith.
2 TIMOTHY 4:7

CHAPTER 16

The Psalms Are Songs of Faith

Psalms 1-150

Sing to the LORD a new song.

PSALM 96:1

For some reason, we don't ordinarily picture a soldier writing Church poetry. But that is exactly what the warrior King David did. He did not write all of the 150 psalms, but so great was his influence on the composition of psalms, that the book of Psalms has borne his name as the author ever since. The psalms are prayers, but people today sometimes find it hard to really think of them that way. Here are some considerations that might be helpful in understanding the psalms.

HE WHO SINGS PRAYS TWICE

St. Augustine says that he who sings prays twice. It is too bad that most people regard the psalms as a text to be read silently. The psalms are the "songs" of faith: war chants, victory songs, enthronement anthems, hymns about nature. In the shadow of the temple, fraternities of musicians gathered to compose melodies for the psalms.

There has been a revival in psalm singing, prompted by the work of Father Joseph Gelineau and Father Lucien Deiss, French priest-musicians and many other composers. The popularity of the guitar has an impact on the singing of psalms, not just because David used a stringed instrument, but because it suits the vigorous rhythm of the words and the excitement of the situation.

Israelite Poetry

The poetry of the Israelites is somewhat different from our ordinary idea of what poetry should be. There is no rhyme nor fixed rhythm in the sense we would normally expect. It's true that the free verse movement has given us a broad idea of what poetry can be. Israelite poetry might be summed up in the saying: never say anything once that you can say twice, and better still, three times. The rhythm of the psalms is a rhythm of ideas. The psalms rhyme thoughts. In the following examples see how the second line parallels the idea of the first:

> *May God be gracious to us and bless us*
> *and make his face to shine upon us.*
>
> PSALM 67:1

> *Thy solemn processions are seen, O God*
> *the processions of my God, my King, into the sanctuary.*
>
> PSALM 68:24

> *How long, O LORD? Wilt thou be angry forever?*
> *Will thy jealous wrath burn like fire?*
>
> PSALM 79:5

The rhythm of the poetry of the psalms is a rhythm (and rhyming) of ideas. An idea is stated and then repeated with different shades of meaning. It is the balanced drumming of a declaration that arises from the heart of one who has known the miracle of God and now speaks out of the ecstasy of response. Some psalms are the result of the experience of miracle and ecstasy. By miracle we mean the appearance of a mighty act of God, such as the Red Sea victory; by ecstasy we refer to the joyous, human faith-experience of God's work. Other psalms reflect the quiet presence of God experienced by a solitary shepherd, a religious experience then applied to God as the shepherd who protects us from harm even when we are in the valley of the shadow of death.

The Psalms Celebrate Events as Mighty Acts of God

It is true that we in the Western world love to reason, but this love need not exclude poetic experience. The psalms indeed revel in such vivid images as: mountains that dance, seas that howl like animals, clouds that ride in the sky as noble horsemen of God, and lightning that writes like a pencil God's presence into the hollows of the earth. When we can admit that these descriptions are real and not just fanciful ways of talking about God, we can accept the message of the psalms.

It was characteristic of the Israelites to find the presence of God in nature and history. It was the unique privilege of the Israelites to see and know that God was really doing something in this world. It has, after all, always been his world, but it takes a long time for many to admit it.

We owe a tribute to Israel for being perceptive enough to know that the events of nature and history are not just simple happenings, but the very acts of God. In the psalms we see that the Israelites had the original insight into God's presence in the movement of history. Put in another way, it was the Israelites who really were the first ones to see the divine purpose in history. As they saw the unfolding of historical events, they came to understand their history as salvation history. They learned to attribute these events to the presence of God.

The Psalms Are the Central Prayers of the Church

The psalms hold a privileged position in the history of prayer. They serve to show us how to pray. As part of sacred Scripture the psalms are God's revealed prayers sung by faith-drenched poets and saints. The Church has chosen the psalms as the centerpiece of the Liturgy of the Hours and having an honored place in every Mass as seen in the "responsorial psalms." For over fifteen centuries monks and nuns in monasteries have made the psalms the central prayer of their lives. In the psalms, God has revealed prayer.

Psalms show us that in singing our prayer we are totally involved in it and yet lifted out of ourselves. They help us see that poetry and symbols in prayer lead to the throne of God. Finally, they remind us that all prayer reflects real life both on earth and in the heavenly realms. The psalms are rooted in the shouts, tears, smiles, and noises of a real world. Psalms are a theological commentary on the life of the people who sang them.

REFLECTION

Faith becomes especially evident when people assemble for worship. The worship experience assumes faith. Our words for those who gather for worship are "the assembly of believers." Psalms achieve their ultimate richness when sung by the community of believers. No one person exhausts the wealth of a psalm, nor does any psalm exhaust the wealth of a faith community.

When Christians gather together to sing the psalms, they realize the significance of the Church and witness their faith to the world. These "faith hymns" are not only a glad sound for the world, which may stand back in open-mouthed disbelief. By the power of the Spirit these songs forge deeper belief in the hearts of the singers.

It is the will of Jesus that the attitudes of the psalms will penetrate the hearts of the singers and move them to witness their faith to others. Psalm singing is not meant to be an esthetic pastime for the esoteric, nor a mere emotional jag. The psalms stand on the plains of battle. They are more than sweet sounds to charm the heavens, or emotional releases for the indiscriminate. The psalms serve as a battle cry to stir the heart of the Christian offering Christ's love and mercy to a reluctant world.

FOR DIALOGUE

What has been your experience with the psalms? When you participate in the responsorial psalms at Mass, what impact do they have on you? How much do you experience the psalms as prayer?

What is your favorite form of prayer? How do the psalms compare to it? What would you like to know about the psalms?

Since the psalms are a revealed form of prayer, why might they be a special source of faith for you? If you love the psalms, which ones are your favorites and why?

PRAYER

Lord, show me how to pray your psalms with a fervent heart and a willing mind. Remind me that Jesus and Mary regularly prayed the psalms. Open their treasures of prayer to me.

The book of Psalms is a complete gymnasium for the soul, a stadium for all the virtues. All who read it aloud may find the cure for their own individual failings.

ST. AMBROSE

CHAPTER 17

Solomon in All His Grandeur

1 Kings 3; 6; 8; 10

"Consider the lilies of the field, how they grow; they neither toil nor spin; yet I tell you, even Solomon in all his glory was not arrayed like one of these."

MATTHEW 6:28-29

SOLOMON: HIGH PRIEST AND KING

If Rome gloried in the memory of Caesar, Israel rejoiced even more in the memory of Solomon. He was Israel's ancient equivalent to Louis XIV, France's "Sun King," though in many ways nobler and wiser. His father, David, was the romantic poet and warrior, while he emerges as the shrewd administrator and wise man. Palace plotting almost kept him from the throne, but the prompt intervention of his mother, Bathsheba, saved the day.

Solomon's Practical Wisdom

Solomon's first decrees swept away all major pockets of opposition to his rule. The priest, Abiathar, who had supported forces hostile to Solomon, was put under house arrest in the sleepy, clergy town of Anathoth several miles north of Jerusalem. With no remorse, Solomon had General Joab executed right at the altar of sacrifice. It was Solomon's opinion that Joab's brutal and uncalled-for murder of Abner was deserving of capital punishment. (Read 1 Kings 2:28-35.)

Having pretty well cleaned house, Solomon turned his attention to the problems of organizing the nation. In his early years he was a deeply religious man. This was fairly well manifested by his prayer for wisdom and the energy he devoted to the building of the temple. He quickly saw that no oriental monarch could survive without a large fund of practical wisdom. Life in the palace and the nation had a much better chance of survival if it took advantage of the heritage of accumulated wisdom that circulated in the courts of Egypt, Babylon, Syria, and Phoenicia.

It was Solomon's particular genius to combine his study of such wisdom with his faith and obedience to God. His prayer for wisdom shows he believed that the greatest wisdom of all was that which led men to godly devotion. (Read 1 Kings 3:1-9.)

The Transition to Town and City Culture

Solomon's greatest achievement was the building of the temple, or as the Bible puts it: establishing the name of the Lord. The decision to build the temple was no light matter from either a religious or a technical point of view. For Israel, God was never in any fixed place. He moved with his people. As a pilgrim people, Israel was always moving forward to richer pastures and a better future. And God marched with them into that future.

Those who were caught up in this religious view of the divine presence feared that fixing a permanent abode for the Ark of the Covenant would take the power and movement out of their religion. Religion to them had overtones of a church on the move. Israel would always think of its nomadic days in the desert as the ideal time.

The Israelites had the uneasy suspicion that once they settled down into town life, they would somehow be stained by urban living. They had, at first, a basic mistrust of the city, feeling that it promoted sinful living. It took away their sense of change, movement, and adventure, which they had known in their desert wanderings. Their previous contact with cities introduced them to the immoral religious practices of the Canaanites. Actually, the story of Cain and Abel reflected this opposition between the pastoral Abel and the founder of the first city, Cain.

The Temple Symbolizes the Covenant with God

Now the fixed temple and the stabilized shrine of the covenant both stilled the mood of change and adventure, and reminded them of the civic shrines of the Gentiles. Solomon, however, wanted to show them another way of looking at the temple. He knew that, in time, they would become accustomed to city life and learn to celebrate the creative possibilities that such a life has to offer.

As a shrine the temple would illuminate the sense of covenant that God had established with David and his successors. Moreover, the temple stood at the top of Mount Zion (or Sion) as a prophetic purifier of the state. Not that the temple itself could purify, but its very existence was a solid reminder that the divine presence brooded over the city and the nation. It was God who truly ruled the nation from Mount Zion and who raised up prophets to stand before the kings and governors and the wealthy, to call them to deal justly with the people and support a high standard of morality. (Read Isaiah 1:10-17.)

The architecture of the temple was an occasion of concern for the conservative and devout Israelite. Building fashions at the time were set by the commercial cities of Tyre and Sidon on the coast of Phoenicia. Solomon hired Phoenician architects and construction engineers to handle the building of the temple. Many a devout old Jew looked with puzzlement and wonder at the top of Mount Zion where he saw a building styled like the pagan sanctuaries used by the Canaanites. It seemed at first too secular, too profane, and not at all worthy of their God. But in time they came to accept it and eventually to glory in it.

The Temple Is Dedicated

Solomon's prayer at the dedication of the temple (1 Kings 8) parallels his prayer for wisdom, and implicitly offers a few ideas for the understanding of public worship:

- Liturgy begins with the official arrival and presence of God's glory.
- The gathered community is called by God.
- Their high priest and king recites the mighty works of God.
- In a litany of intercession he gathers up their prayers.
- The liturgy is climaxed by a sacrificial meal that celebrates the works of God and the faith of the people, and opens them in hope to the future.

After the clergy had placed the ark in the temple, the cloud-radiance of God's presence came and filled the temple. It was so awesome that the priests could not stay within the temple walls. This is a way of showing that liturgy officially is begun by God. The people who gathered around the building are called *qahal* in Hebrew. This is a word that indicates they are a "community called by God." They stand at the place of worship because they have a vocation to do so from God himself. The worshipping community is one that is both summoned and formed by God.

Solomon: High Priest and King

Solomon, as high priest and king, assumes the role of the old patriarchs who were accustomed to preserving and reciting the splendid works that God had performed for his people. As king, Solomon summarized and announced the memory of the community. This was designed both to reinforce the people's sense of identity and to sustain an attitude of straightforward gratitude in them. The litany of intercession expressed the abiding dependence of the Israelites on God and a renewal of their trust in the covenant.

The sacrificial event proclaimed the people's desire to praise God, to live in total dedication to God as shown by the holocaust of the lamb, and to have new hope in the future as they ate of the holy food. These elements of presence, recital, litany, gathered community, and sacrifice are themes that govern our own liturgy today. Read the story of the dedication of the temple (1 Kings 8) to renew and refresh your understanding of liturgy. In this event Solomon reached a summit of spiritual grandeur.

REFLECTION

Religion is the nursery of nations. Nothing illustrates this more vividly than the Solomon story. Scripture remembers him as a wise king who built a temple that served as the spiritual heart of the nation. He acts as both a priest and a king. Religion is like the father. The state is like the child. But children grow up and require a life and independence of their own. So also does the state.

In ancient cultures the state rarely escapes the brooding presence of the god. An uneasy relationship between religion and the government always emerges. We do not see it yet in the Solomon narrative. It will become evident upon his death. Still through most of history religion and the state will be tightly intertwined. In Israel's history the kings will soon look for other gods who are less demanding. This will give rise to prophets who courageously face the powers that be and challenge them to return to the ancient faith.

Multiple lessons will be drawn from these tensions. Here we are at the dawn of the kingdom. The king is grand and wise, but already toying with false gods. "For when Solomon was old his wives turned away his heart after other gods" (1 Kings 11:4). Nonetheless, the two substantial memories we retain of Solomon was his being a student of wisdom and the builder of a magnificent temple for the glory of God and the spiritual touchstone of the nation. His commitment to wisdom became the seed of a rich spirituality in Scripture, encompassed by the title of the "wisdom literature." Its unique value partly lies in its dialogue with the wisdom of other ancient cultures, drawing from them guidelines consistent with the covenant goals of Israel.

Solomon's other achievement, the temple, established so powerful a symbol of the people's religion that its destruction never eliminated the temple dream, so much so that it was rebuilt in an even grander style by Herod. The destruction of the second temple by the Romans has never daunted the people of the Hebrew covenant in their commitment to their ancient faith.

FOR DIALOGUE

Solomon's wisdom draws your attention to its necessity in your lives. Why do you think that people generally distinguish knowledge of facts from wisdom? What is the difference? You need to know facts, yet how do you acquire wisdom? Solomon prayed for wisdom. The Holy Spirit can give you the gift of wisdom. What will that mean for you?

Solomon's temple penetrated the self-consciousness of the state. Why do you think your parish church plays a local role in the faith awareness of you and your family? What are a number of values a church building signifies?

Solomon, Saul, and David faced social change in their time, the major move away from nomadic existence to life on farms, towns, and cities. How might a move from a remote small farm in a rural area to the heart of a major modern city affect the faith life of a family?

PRAYER

Holy Spirit of Wisdom, we ask you for the gift of wisdom so that our faith may grow stronger amid our fast-changing type of world. May your wise ways guide us to prayer and thoughtfulness in all we do.

Knowledge is proud that he has learned so much;
Wisdom is humble that he knows no more.

WILLIAM COWPER

CHAPTER 18

Civil War between Israel and Judah

1 Kings 11-12

Cry "Havoc!" and let slip the dogs of war.
WILLIAM SHAKESPEARE'S *JULIUS CAESAR*

Apparently even the wisest of men can make the most absurd errors. Solomon's early career was a brilliant mixture of practical administration and devoted service to God. He built a splendid temple to illustrate his conviction that real religion should unify the spirit and thought of a nation. At the height of his career, his counseling talents were sought by world leaders. The queen of Sheba graded Solomon as the wisest man in the world.

THE STAGE IS SET FOR TROUBLE

But into this paradise of wisdom crept the old temptation — to use human wisdom, not as a stairway to the stars, but as a means of satisfying our desires. Solomon found it was no simple matter to have an ambitious building program. He needed vast sums of money and a large labor force to build the temple and all the government offices now needed. Therefore, he taxed the people heavily. It is true that he took in great sums of money from foreign trade; but, since this was not enough, he resorted to slave labor. This practice was quite common in Mesopotamia and Egypt, but was fiercely resented by the Israelites.

Nothing in the Bible texts seems to indicate that Solomon imposed any new taxes on his own people of Judah, but this is because the tax and slave labor policy more than likely had been introduced in Judah by his father, David. This is indicated both by the census David took, and by the rebellion of Absalom who represented the dislike of the people for this system.

Solomon organized the northern tribes into districts for taxation and the draft. The twelve tax districts of Solomon did not correspond to tribal lines; in fact, Solomon deliberately tried to dissolve the old tribal ties in order to attach the people directly to the throne. He failed in this. The discontent that this caused contributed much to the civil war that followed his death.

Solomon's Marriages and Idolatry

We shall now consider Solomon's second mistake. The Bible tells us that King Solomon loved many foreign women. "He had seven hundred wives, princesses and three hundred concubines" (1 Kings 11: 3). This is probably an exaggeration, but it does offer a clue to the grand style in which he lived. That he was able to marry an Egyptian princess showed both to what height Israel had ascended and to what a state of weakness Egypt had descended.

Solomon's marriages eventually led him to the support of idolatry. "For when Solomon was old his wives turned away his heart after other gods.... For Solomon went after Ashtoreth the goddess of the Sidonians, and after Milcom the abomination of the Ammonites. So Solomon did what was evil in the sight of the LORD.... Then Solomon built a high place for Chemosh the abomination of Moab, and for Molech the abomination of the Ammonites, on the mountain east of Jerusalem. And so he did for all his foreign wives.

"And the LORD was angry with Solomon" (1 Kings 11:4-9).

After Solomon's Death, the Crisis Grows

Even before Solomon's death the signs of coming trouble were apparent. Hadad, the prince of Edom, was hired by the Egyptian pharaoh to make life difficult for the aging king. The desert brigand Rezon established an independent kingdom at Damascus that became in time a serious threat to the kingdom of Israel. A group of prophets persuaded Jeroboam to initiate a rebellion against Solomon's slave policies. It was not a successful attempt, and Jeroboam was exiled to Egypt.

Idolatry, burdensome taxation, and a humiliating slave policy marked the corruption of Solomon's last days and fostered the kind of unrest that led to civil war after his death. Speaking of his death, the Bible notes simply: "And Solomon slept with his fathers, and was buried in the city of David his father; and Rehoboam his son reigned in his stead" (1 Kings 11:43).

With Solomon dead, the crisis of disunity in the kingdom surfaced. The enthronement of the new king, Rehoboam, was to take place at the old sanctuary of Shechem. The leaders of the northern tribes summoned Jeroboam back from Egypt to represent their grievances to the new king. "Your father made our yoke heavy. Now therefore lighten the hard service of your father and his heavy yoke upon us, and we will serve you" (1 Kings 12:4). King Rehoboam asked for three days to study the problem before he would reply. He went into conference with the elders, who knew his father well. They counseled moderation, a mild answer, and the promise to live as a servant of the people.

Rehoboam Insulted the North: A New Kingdom Is Formed

Then Rehoboam had a meeting with a council of ambitious young men who had grown up with him. They urged the king to take a hard line: rather than cut back on taxes and slavery, increase them. Rehoboam decided to follow the advice of the young hard-liners. Three days later, at a meeting with Jeroboam and the northerners, this harsh statement was made by Rehoboam: "My father made your yoke heavy, but I will add to your yoke; my father chastised you with whips, but I will chastise you with scorpions" (1 Kings 12:14). At that, the northern tribes angrily left the conference, and declared that they would break off from the south and form a new kingdom to be called Israel. From then on, the southern kingdom would be named Judah.

The political break between the north and the south was accompanied by a religious one as well. The northerners set up a center of worship on Mount Gerizim to rival the sanctuary in Jerusalem. Centuries later, at the well of Jacob, Jesus talked about these two sanctuaries with the Samaritan woman. The civil war tore the nation apart both politically and religiously. Since few things are more likely to divide people than religion and politics, it is easy to see why the Jews and Samaritans hated each other with a passion. It is also why Christ's story about the good Samaritan was so challenging to his Jewish listeners later on.

For our own day, the religious schism between Israel and Judah is a painful reminder of the division between Christians in our own time. Israel and Judah knew the tragedy of religious disunity, and yet there was the shining light of prophecy in both churches. But further, their religious quarrel turned them in upon themselves, and they thus lost their sense of mission to the Gentiles. Today's search for unity among the Christian churches provides a healthy contrast to the story of the fighting of brothers in the book of Kings.

REFLECTION

Pope John XXIII taught that justice is needed in order to have peace. The decision of Rehoboam to follow the unseasoned and blind advice of his youthful advisers led him not only to maintain the injustices of his father's regime, but to make them worse. The injustice led to civil war. The kingdoms of Israel and Judah were formed. Political and religious rivalry ensued and broke the fragile unity so long sought for by Saul, David, and Solomon. The days of glory were brief.

In our times a glance at the world's troubled spots soon leads us to see seething injustices beneath the surface that cause anger, violence, and death. The injustices usually are about dehumanizing poverty, deprivation of freedom and human rights, oppression, and a despair based on lack of opportunity for self-improvement. Petty tyrants are as numerous as ever. As a line from a song puts it, "When will they ever learn?"

Difficult as it may seem to solve these problems, we must never give up doing what we can to address these issues and use whatever practical means we have at hand to remove all injustices wherever they may be found. While it is proper to employ political pressures, financial assistance, and public opinion to change such situations, we should also be involved in personal spiritual growth, communal prayer, and trust in the divine power to change hearts. The old axiom still secures our attention: Act as if all depended on ourselves. Pray as if all depended upon God.

FOR DIALOGUE

As you survey the world, which trouble spots engage your attention? What do you believe are the causes of the strife? What injustices appear to be at the root of the problem? What international efforts have been used to heal the divisions?

In your own family and community, what trouble spots could you identify? What injustices might be the source of the discord? Who are the healers and reconcilers who could bring peace? How would they do it?

In your moments of self-reflection what turmoil do you find in your own heart? What do you think has caused such an assault on your peace of heart? What spiritual and moral means can you use to put yourself at ease once more?

PRAYER

Lord God of peace and justice, look with mercy on your divided children. Inspire courage in the men and women who can help warring peoples to eradicate the causes of strife and reach peaceful solutions.

I believe that religious duties consist in doing justice, loving mercy and endeavoring to make our fellow creatures happy.

THOMAS PAINE

CHAPTER 19

How the Bible Explains Sin and Salvation

Genesis 3; John 3:16-18; Hebrews 9:11-18

Ah, sinful nation, a people laden with iniquity.... They have forsaken the Holy One of Israel, they are utterly estranged.

ISAIAH 1:4

The Hebrews, once one nation, were now divided into the northern kingdom of Israel and the southern kingdom of Judah. The books of Kings tell how each of these kingdoms became sinful nations, abandoning God, practicing idolatry, and sinking into total decline. The Bible writers make it clear that sin directly caused the disorder and decline in which these kingdoms ultimately found themselves. At this time it would be helpful to review some of the notions that are included in the Old Testament idea of sin and salvation.

Sin Is a Personal Matter

Scripture sees sin as a personal matter as well as the breaking of an abstract rule such as one of the commandments. Scripture often stresses that sin is a breaking of a personal relationship with God, usually through pride and disobedience. The Lord confronts Adam about eating fruit from the forbidden tree in the Garden of Eden. God summons Cain to the bar of judgment for murdering his brother, Abel. God sends the prophet Nathan to King David to point a nagging finger at the monarch, accusing David of adultery.

God Wants to Save Us from Sin

Sin narratives often conclude with redemption symbols or savior figures. After the sin of Adam comes the seed of the promise of a savior. Cain is saved from despair by God, who protects him by means of a mark on his forehead. The dread waters of the deluge that washed away the world's sin give way to the optimistic rainbow that signifies God's intent not to harm the earth again.

The exodus and Calvary events are the ideal saving moments in sacred history. Samuel, David, and Isaiah are among the savior figures that abound in the Bible. This emphasis on salvation all through the Bible keeps us from viewing sin in a purely negative way — something for which we are bound to be damned. God's grace is greater than any sin. God's love surpasses all the world's evils. Of course it is the revelation of Jesus Christ, Son of God and Son of Mary, as the Messiah and Savior that makes sense of all the salvation symbols and saviors that went before. Jesus alone makes ultimate sense of history.

Sin Also Refuses to Accept the Salvation God Gives Us

The books of the prophets commented on the sins of the people as recounted in the books of Kings. Whereas Deuteronomy concentrated on the collective sinfulness of the nation, the prophets shifted attention to the individual guilt of each person, inferring that sin lies in the hearts of people — men and women who are free and responsible human beings.

The main conclusion of these writers is that sin is a refusal to accept God's saving work, and that this is seen in Israel's failure to measure up to the covenant standards set by God, and to which the chosen people had pledged themselves.

These ideas are helpful for seeing the meaning of sin. They make us recall the personal character of sin. They broaden our outlook, enabling us to see sin in the cycle of grace, fall, cry for mercy, and redemption. They put sin on both a collective and an individual basis, relating it to a refusal of redemption and a failure to measure up to the divine standards to which we freely commit ourselves.

The Bible's History of Sin

The biblical history of sin can be seen in two broad patterns. The first is the Adam pattern as seen in the primitive history given in chapters 1 to 11 of Genesis. The pattern is repeated in the story of the formation of Israel from the time of Abraham to the exile. The Adam cycle includes the fateful event of Adam and Eve, the story of Cain's murder, the savagery of Lamech, and the account of Noah and the deluge. The story of Adam and Eve shows that sin is a break in mankind's relation to God. Within this account of the Garden of Eden is found God's initial offer of love and grace to men. Sin is the refusal to accept this gift and its gracious Giver.

The account of Cain's murder illustrates that sin also breaks the relationship between people. It not only affects the divine-human contact, but puts us out of touch with one another. Hence sin has disastrous consequences in the social order. Sin also spoils our control of the earth and our management of the land. Adam will no longer till the earth in comfort and confidence. He must sweat over it. The earth will be resistant to man unless he uses it for the sake of others. "Now the earth was corrupt in God's sight, and the earth was filled with violence" (Genesis 6:11).

The rest of the Genesis story tells of the gradual decline of the world. Men begin to deal with one another ruthlessly, as indicated by the savage chant of Lamech: "have slain a man for wounding me, a young man for striking me. If Cain is avenged sevenfold, truly Lamech seventy-sevenfold" (Genesis 4:23-24).

Sin has consequences that affect our relationship to God, to one another, and to the earth itself. Sin projects all peoples into a hopeless loneliness that wrings from each one an anguished cry of despair:

"My punishment is greater than I can bear. Behold, thou hast driven me this day away from the ground; and from thy face I shall be hidden; and I shall be a fugitive and a wanderer on the earth, and whoever finds me will slay me" (Genesis 4:13-14). These words of Cain present a powerful interpretation of the effect of sin.

God's ultimate weapon against sin is twofold. By the deluge, he will destroy all those who do not measure up to his plan. By the ark, he saves the family of Noah, the only just group on the earth. This salvation-damnation movement is found all through the Bible. After the deluge, God begins a new creation, calling men and animals forth from the ark to start a new way of life.

God's Grace Can Overcome Sin

The original sin of the first man and woman shows its effects in the sins of Israel. God graciously delivers the Israelites from the darkness of Egypt, and brings them into the symbolic Garden of Eden of the desert, where bread falls from heaven and waters spring forth from the rock. He gathers his people at Sinai for the covenant event, only to find that they forget him and worship the golden calf. As Adam refused God's love symbolized by Eden, so now Israel rejects his love typified by the saving exodus and the gifts of the desert. Chaos and deluge followed the sin of Adam, and the same happens to Israel.

The story of the judges illustrates Israel's problem with idolatry. The history of the monarchy demonstrates the progressive worldliness of Israel amid tales of murder, civil war, strife, adultery, diplomatic intrigue. This history ends with the fall of the monarchy, the slaughter of the people, the burning of their cities, and the enslavement of the remnant in the Babylonian exile.

Still, God kept alive the promise of redemption. Savior-figures crowd the pages of Israel's history: Moses, Joshua, Samuel, David, Josiah, and Isaiah.

The Babylonian exile is like the deluge in the days of Noah, but the faithful remnant live together as in an ark, sustained by the hopeful sermons of Ezekiel and the other prophets until Cyrus pronounces the joyful deliverance and return to the Promised Land.

Though sin crouches at our door, God's grace is greater. This is the encouraging and optimistic teaching of the Bible and the corrective to the tragic decline of the two kingdoms.

REFLECTION

One way of seeing the dominant themes of Scripture is simply to summarize them in three acts: (1) God's creative grace, (2) Human sinfulness and repentance, (3) God's forgiving grace. God's loving graces enfold human beings on all sides. The Bible begins with paradise, proceeds to tell the stories of human sinfulness and the narratives of those who repent, concludes with redeeming acts that peak with the supreme saving act of Jesus Christ. Since this is so, it is curious that a number of religious-minded people seem so skittish about the reality of sin.

Despite the plain-spoken lines of Scripture that speak of sin in endless detail, it makes one wonder how anyone could miss the point.

From the original sin in Eden to all its abundant effects and multiple ways that people have found to sin, Scripture is a lengthy record of the history of evil. But, at the same time God's salvation is everywhere to be found in the Bible. St. Paul emphasizes the victory of grace no matter how widespread sin flourished:

Where sin increased, grace abounded all the more.
ROMANS 5:20

Sin must always be seen in the light of the salvation brought by Christ. From the moment that the shadow of sin first occurred in creation, God was swift to announce that salvation from it was offered and that the evil power of the serpent (Satan) would be definitively overcome by the seed (Christ) of the woman (Mary, the New Eve). All the sin-salvation stories that crowd the pages of the Old Testament are dress rehearsals for the powerful revelation of Jesus Christ as the merciful and loving Savior of the world. "For

God sent the Son into the world, not to condemn the world, but that the world might be saved through him" (John 3:17).

FOR DIALOGUE

What would happen to your faith if the entire concentration were on your sins? Why is such a one-sided approach unhelpful? What support would there be for this approach in the Bible?

But suppose you seldom heard about your sinfulness, what impact would that have on your faith? What is contradictory about emphasizing salvation, yet rarely or never alluding to sin?

What is assuring and heartening about the authentic biblical teaching about sin and salvation? What has been your experience of homilies and religion classes regarding sin and salvation? What kind of balance is needed on this issue?

PRAYER

O Lord, be merciful to me a sinner. Call me to confess my sins in a humble and sincere manner. Remind me that you are a welcoming and forgiving God.

She feared no danger, for she knew no sin.

JOHN DRYDEN

CHAPTER 20

Elijah: A Fervent and Fiery Prophet

1 Kings 17-19; 2 Kings 2:1-12

Elijah the prophet came near and said, "O LORD, God of Abraham, Isaac, and Israel, let it be known this day that thou art God in Israel, and that I am thy servant."

1 KINGS 18:36

THE PROPHET ELIJAH

It has been said that history is written by the victors. It is also often true that history is the account of kings and their court intrigues. In the light of this, it is refreshing to see in the books of Kings a dramatic biography devoted to a local hero, the rugged and fiery prophet Elijah.

Elijah crashes onto the biblical stage like a bolt of lightning and exits in a fiery chariot. The only other prophetic figure who might outmatch Elijah is the venerable Moses himself. In the series of Elijah stories the colors are bright, the emotions volcanic, and the noise like the shouting at a spirited football game.

Elijah Is Called to Purify Israel

Following the death of Solomon, the Hebrew people broke apart into the kingdoms of Israel in the north and Judah in the south. Both nations progressively declined into political and religious anarchy. Elijah entered Israel's history at the time when Ahab ascended the throne. Ahab married a pagan girl from Sidon, named Jezebel, built a temple of Baal for her in Samaria, and allowed her to install a community of four hundred pagan clergy in the capital city. "Ahab did more to provoke the Lord, the God of Israel, to anger than all the kings of Israel who were before him" (1 Kings 16:33). And God called Elijah to purify the kingdom.

Elijah Brings a Drought to Punish King Ahab

Elijah stormed into the palace of Ahab and announced that for the next three years no rain would fall in Israel. The drought was designed to touch the conscience of the king and bring him to repentance. The prophet retired to the brook Cherith beyond the Jordan. It was by that fast disappearing stream that the series of legendary wonders that surrounded Elijah's career began. To satisfy his hunger, God sent ravens every morning and evening with meat and bread for the prophet.

When the stream dried up, Elijah went to the village of Zarephath where he obtained lodging with an old widow and her young son by paying rent with a miraculous supply of oil and meal. "'The jar of meal shall not be spent, and the cruse of oil shall not fail, until the day the LORD sends rain upon the earth'" (1 Kings 17:14). Some weeks later the little boy died, but Elijah raised him from the dead after receiving a proper scolding from the widow: "'What have you against me, O man of God? You have come… to cause the death of my son!'" (1 Kings 17:18).

When the three years of drought were up, Elijah returned to King Ahab and demanded to meet with the priests of Baal. The terms of this contest are worthy of the publicity stunts of a Hollywood press agent. Elijah and the priests were each to take a bull, put it on an altar, then pray that their respective god would send down fire to consume the animal. The scene of this strange encounter would be on the beach near Mount Carmel. To the victor would be given the "privilege" of slaughtering the defeated.

God's Power Is Tested in a Strange Challenge

The scene that day must have been like a sports event, with the spectators lining the hills as though in a grandstand. Elijah insisted that the priests of Baal have the first try. All morning long they filled the air with magic chants and psalms. Their bodies became more and more frenzied as they did one ritual dance after another around the animal offering. By noon they were barely limping. Elijah began to mock them: "Cry aloud, for he is a god; either he is musing, or he has gone aside, or he is on a journey, or perhaps he is asleep and must be awakened.' And they cried aloud, and cut themselves with swords and lances… until the blood gushed out upon them… they raved on… but there was no voice… no one heeded" (1 Kings 18: 27-29).

Then it was Elijah's turn. He ordered an altar built of twelve stones, representing the number of the Hebrew tribes. Next he demanded that a huge trench be dug around the altar. Wood was placed on the altar and the animal offering was laid carefully upon the wood. And there were spectacular details. Elijah instructed the people: "… Fill four jars with water, and pour it on the burnt offering, and on the wood…. And the water ran round about the altar, and filled the trench…" (1 Kings 18:33, 35).

The Almighty God Appears as a Consuming Fire

Then with superb dignity, summoning up in himself all the faith of Israel, Elijah prayed: "O LORD, God of Abraham, Isaac, and Israel, let it be known this day that you are God in Israel.... Answer me, O LORD, answer me!" (1 Kings 18:36-37). With that, a great fire came from heaven and consumed the burnt offering, the wood, the stones, and the dust, and licked up the water that was in the trench. This brought the crowd to their knees with the fearful chant: "The LORD, he is God; The LORD, he is God." But Elijah wasted no time. He shouted: "Seize the prophets of Baal!" And they were captured and executed. (Read 1 Kings 18:39-40.)

But these extraordinary events were not enough to change the heart of Queen Jezebel. She promptly sent out the royal police to arrest Elijah. Disgusted, frustrated, and disappointed, the prophet went away to the wilderness and sank in despair under a broom tree. His comment rose from an empty heart: "It is enough; now, O Lord, take away my life; for I am no better than my fathers" (1 Kings 19:4). He sank into a merciful sleep. On awakening, he found a loaf of bread and a jug of water by his side. He refreshed himself and looked up and saw an angel who commanded him to go forth and meet the Lord at Mount Horeb. And for forty days and forty nights he marched, sustained by the bread of God he had eaten under the broom tree.

The Voice of God Again Shows Elijah the Way

Elijah climbed the mountain and waited. Soon a hurricane wind shook the hills. This was followed by an earthquake. Then came a fire that baked the rock. But the Bible notes that none of these violent happenings manifested the presence of God. It was in the gentle breeze that followed these events that the voice of God was heard.

The Lord spoke to Elijah and directed him to anoint Hazael as king of Damascus, Jehu as the king of Israel, and Elisha to be Elijah's personal successor as prophet. This appearance of God at Mount Horeb, which is sometimes called Sinai, restored the prophet's strength. He went forth and did what he was told. He foretold the downfall of Ahab and Jezebel, especially condemning their unjust stoning of Naboth and the stealing of his vineyard. (Read 1 Kings 19:13-21; 21.)

Elijah's career ended with the passage of his cloak to Elisha and his ascension into heaven in a fiery chariot. Elijah's great vocation was to restore the purity of the covenant. This is why so many details of the life of Moses, the great covenant figure, surround the history of Elijah. The ravens that fed Elijah in the desert are like the manna in the exodus account. The conquest of the prophets of Baal recalls Moses' single-handed attack on the worshippers of the golden calf. The restoration of Elijah's strength at Mount Horeb (Sinai) recalls the covenant mediated by Moses at Sinai. But it is interesting to note that Moses saw God amid the thunders of Mount Sinai, whereas Elijah met God in a gentle breeze on the same mountain.

Elijah's Fervor Heartened Generations to Come

Figures as heroic as Elijah deserve more space than can be given here. May it suffice to note that Elijah loved Israel and attempted to save the kingdom, realizing that religious and moral corruption would dissolve the nation. He had temporary success, and his fervor sustained the faithful among the chosen people for generations afterward.

REFLECTION

The impact of Elijah was felt throughout the history of Israel up to New Testament times. The gospel accounts of the ministry of John the Baptist echoed the courage of Elijah; each man stood up to the kings of their day. When Jesus asked the apostles about people's opinion of him, they replied that they thought he was another Elijah.

The gift of moral and spiritual courage, when acted out at the highest levels of a given society, may seem beyond our reach. But such stories are not meant to imply that all of us could be called to scary encounters with the leaders of nations. There are simpler challenges that we may face in the everyday experiences of our lives.

Maybe we will be asked to be a whistle-blower against an injustice in our workplace, or called to resist improper sexual advances from others, or to act firmly when someone tempts us to falter regarding a deeply held religious belief.

Heroic stories of courage are not designed to demand unrealistic imitation from a rational point of view, rather they remind us that God gives each of us the graces we need at whatever level we are called to function.

FOR DIALOGUE

It has been said that the role of a prophet is to comfort the afflicted and afflict the comfortable. Elijah afflicted Ahab and comforted the widow of Zarephath. Why is it important that prophets keep both parts of their calling in mind?

Elijah fasted in the desert as part of his spiritual discipline. What is the advantage of fasting for spiritual growth and discernment? Who are some people today who discipline their food intake for spiritual reasons? What is the difference between a diet and fasting for spiritual reasons?

Elijah confronted King Ahab and Queen Jezebel for their infidelities to God. He also contested the false prophets at Mount Carmel for their idolatry. It required exceptional courage to act against the powers that be. How is such courage acquired? How are you planning to have similar moral courage today?

PRAYER

Come, Holy Spirit, with your gift of courage, that I may serve you with a cheerful heart this day. Strengthen me when my fears arise and threaten to keep me from performing my duty. Show me how to prepare for the challenges of faith and love that I will have to face.

"A prophet is not without honor except in his own country and in his own house."

MATTHEW 13:57

CHAPTER 21

The Babylonian Exile — Seventy Years of Tears

2 Kings 24:18–25:21; 2 Chronicles 36:5-8

By the waters of Babylon, there we sat down and wept.

PSALM 137:1

The seeds of destruction planted by the follies of Solomon and the division of the nation that followed his death eventually resulted in the fall of the kingdoms of Israel and Judah. Great prophets like Elijah tried to save the northern kingdom, but his efforts ended in a disastrous loss of hope.

The great prophets, Isaiah and Jeremiah, strained to bring Judah to repentance, but their sermons went unheeded. It is true that there was a temporary reform under good king Josiah, but it was too little and too late. The powerful forces of the Babylonian king, Nebuchadnezzar, were gathering as God's avenging arm against his faithless people.

WHY JUDAH WAS DESTROYED

The Bible assigns a religious reason for the destruction of Judah. "Surely this came upon Judah at the command of the Lord, to remove them out of his sight" (2 Kings 24:3). Jeremiah, in his famed temple sermon, outlines God's indictment against his people. He accuses them of theft, murder, and adultery, while hypocritically coming to worship at the temple. They rob defenseless widows, throw orphans into the streets, greedily grub for land, and then piously shroud their injustice with incense before the altar of holocausts. "The children gather wood, their fathers light the fire, and the women knead the dough to make cakes for the queen of heaven [an idol], while libations are poured out to strange gods in order to hurt me" (Jeremiah 7:18).

Over the mountain of Topheth, they threw their firstborn sons and daughters into the fire to placate a false god. Immorality, hypocrisy, and idolatry were common among the covenant people. Jeremiah literally shouts: "Be appalled, O heavens, at this, be shocked, be utterly desolate, says the LORD, for my people have committed two evils: they have forsaken me, the fountain of living waters, and hewed out cisterns for themselves, broken cisterns, that can hold no water" (Jeremiah 2:12-13).

Isaiah's Call to Repent Goes Unheeded

Isaiah repeated the same ideas in his biting speech about liturgy in the first chapter of his prophecy. He comments on the great crowds that flock to the temple offering huge numbers of sacrificial animals, faithfully attending the festivals at the time of the new moon. Isaiah claims that God hates all this. He will not look when they spread out their hands to him, nor will he listen to the multitude of their prayers, "Your hands are full of blood" (Isaiah 1:15). Unless they cease to do evil, seek justice, correct oppression, they will be devoured by the sword (see Isaiah 1:17, 20). A hypocritical liturgy offered by a wicked people is a sign of the end fast approaching Judah.

But the people's ears were deaf, and their hearts were corrupt. So in the reign of King Zedekiah, Nebuchadnezzar, the king of Babylon, came and laid siege to Jerusalem. Zedekiah and his men fled the city but were caught by the enemy and slaughtered. Then Nebuzaradan, the captain of the king of Babylon's bodyguard, began the systematic destruction of the city of Jerusalem.

The Babylonians burned the temple, razed the palaces, and tore down the city walls. They took the bronze and gold of the temple and melted it down as part of the booty to be taken to Babylon. All Jews who were capable of any kind of skilled labor were chained and taken captive to Babylon. "But the captain of the guard left some of the poorest of the land to be vinedressers and plowmen" (2 Kings 25:12).

Jeremiah Mourns for the City

The fall of the holy city signaled the end of an era. It was a tragedy that was especially heartrending to a great prophet like Jeremiah. He loved his city and his land with the emotion of a patriot and the heart of a saint. He captured the mood of his own and the national grief in the mourning poems known as the lamentations. "How like a widow she has become, she that was great among the nations... a princess among the provinces has been made vassal.... My groans are many and my heart is faint" (Lamentations 1:1, 22).

It may seem strange that a prophet who was so fiercely critical of Jerusalem should now mourn so deeply over the city's destruction, until we remember that his criticism flowed from a genuine love for his people. The lament of Jeremiah is similar to the feeling expressed by Jesus about the holy city when he predicted its coming judgment.

"O Jerusalem, Jerusalem, killing the prophets and stoning those who are sent to you! How often would I have gathered your children together as a hen gathers her brood under her wings, and you would not!" (Matthew 23:37)

Exiled to Babylon

The seventy years of Babylonian exile was a time of purification. As Samuel had foretold, the monarchy would be a way of life that would turn the people away from honoring God as their true king. The monarchy did, however, serve the useful purpose of creating a national unity that was not possible under the tribal confederacy. Prior to the monarchy, the tribes tended to be independent of one another and could have dissolved into chaos without the unifying factors brought to bear by the political possibilities of a monarchy.

But, in turn, there was a weakness in the monarchy in that the prosperity it brought and the idolatrous influence of other nations dimmed the people's memory of the covenant and turned their hearts to other gods. Their prosperity was often achieved by injustice to the weak. Their idolatry arose from fascination with the gods of other nations. Babylon was the fire that would purge out corruption and idolatry.

The prophets, however, strove to keep alive the exiles' hopes for the future. Jeremiah wrote a letter to the exiles that is astonishing, both for its practical advice and its optimism. "Build houses and live in them; plant gardens and eat their produce. Take wives and have sons and daughters.... Seek the welfare of the city where I have sent you into exile, and pray to the LORD on its behalf, for in its welfare you will find your welfare.... I will... gather you from all the nations and all the places where I have driven you, says the LORD, and I will bring you back to the place from which I sent you into exile" (Jeremiah 29:5-7, 14).

The Babylonian exile makes it clear that God will bring destructive judgment upon the sinful. There is no sentimentality here. Evil men will be punished. But there is always the hope of Noah's rainbow that God will not forget the promise that he made to Abraham and to his seed. This is the hope that sustained the Babylonian exiles. It is the same hope that must hearten our Church today.

REFLECTION

It is humbling for all ages of faith to read the sad account of the fall and exile of God's people in the Old Testament. It shows that none of us in today's Church should look back on our faith ancestors with any kind of smugness. Our own Church history is filled with stories of failure to keep the vision of Christ alive, of sins of greed and lust very much like those of the biblical people we read about in the books of Kings and the sermons of the great prophets.

It is not the sins or the punishments that ought to occupy our attention so much as the abiding mercy of God that characterizes every account of human wickedness. While the prophets rail against evil, they only do so for medicinal purposes. They want to cure, not to kill. They roar with colorful language in order to wake up human conscience. They try to help people be aware that sin is self-destructive.

Immoral behavior wreaks its own vengeance on the sinner. In today's terms this is like the warnings about smoking or eating an unhealthy diet. The cancer that ruins the lungs as a result of smoking or the cholesterol that clogs the blood due to poor eating habits is not caused by God, but rather by our foolish choices. It is the same with sin. Immorality is as harmful to the soul as unhealthy choices are to the body. It is not God who causes corruption of the soul. We have no one to blame but ourselves. If we wind up in a contemporary version of Babylon — a life of addiction to evil and its consequences, we must always remember that the saving graces of Jesus Christ are available to us for our redemption.

We cannot save ourselves by any kind of exertion or forms of will power. This is a condition from which we must be saved by the grace of Christ. In biblical times God kept sending holy prophets and saints to arouse consciences and open hearts to God's mercy. It is the same today. The words of the Bible ring with the loving call of God. "Come home. I love you. I want to make you happy. I want to give you peace." Stop and listen to these saving words.

FOR DIALOGUE

What goes on in your mind when you read about the lack of faith among God's people in earlier times? Why did they fail to see that God's will was better for them than the choices they made? What are the root causes of evil?

When it is said that sin is self-destructive, what examples of this teaching occur to you? Why is it correct to say that the unfortunate consequences of sin are not so much the punishments of God (though in one sense they are) so much as the logical outcome of our immoral behavior?

Why do people resist being saved when it is obviously the best solution to their misery? Even when the love of Christ is so compassionately shown, why do some people reject it? What may be some examples of your own inability to accept the helping hand of Christ when it is offered to you?

PRAYER

Dear God, help me to learn about your mercy as I read the biblical accounts of exile. Wake up my conscience to see my own need of the salvation you so generously offer.

To an exile, his friends are everything.

WILLA CATHER

CHAPTER 22

Old Testament Prophets —
Three Ideas about the Messiah

Isaiah 11; 42; 49; 50; 53

In the wilderness prepare the way of the LORD, make straight in the desert a highway for our God.

ISAIAH 40:3

Old Testament prophets were busy men. They hastened between royal court and temple pulpit; they attended closed-door briefings on foreign affairs; and, they had their moments of repose alone with God. They had the unpleasant role of being professional critics of the state and religion. Yet they possessed the personal joy of divinely supported insight into the meaning of the public affairs of their day. Their hearts were anchored in the assurance that they were God's mouthpieces for the community of faith.

THE PROPHET'S FUNCTION

The name prophet comes from the Hebrew word *nabi* that means something like "mouthpiece." A prophet was God's voice trumpeted throughout the hills and cities of Israel. Prophets summoned kings and peasants to repentance, cursed politicians who led Israel into idolatrous alliances with foreign powers, and blessed the people with the hope of a messianic "day of the Lord."

While the prophets' main task was the religious interpretation of the contemporary events of history and the purification of the consciences of the people, they also made pronouncements about the future. It is as foretellers of the future that prophets are generally remembered, even though this was really a small part of their task. It is easy to understand how this attitude came about.

The early Christian Church was faced with the problem of urging the Jewish community to accept Christ. It was clear to the apostles and early Church fathers that Christ was the center of history. Jesus fulfilled the meaning and yearning of all the hopes of God's people. The life, teachings, and redemptive death and resurrection of Jesus cast a brilliant light backwards on the texts of Old Testament Scripture. What was dimly seen then became obvious in Christ.

Hence, some of their theological thinking centered around material showing how Jesus was the Messiah foretold by the prophets. It is not so much that the old texts give meaning to Christ. It is Jesus who gives meaning to the old texts. Jesus IS the full revelation of God's plan for the world. This is why the theologians of the apostolic age mined the prophetic writings for every kind of text that demonstrated the messianic mission in Christ's life. And, admittedly, the life of Jesus finds remarkable prophetic resonance. The writings of the prophets are rich with material that identifies the characteristics of the messianic age and the Messiah himself. But this only becomes clear when Christ appears and reveals the divine plan of salvation in its fullness.

The Idea of a Messiah

The idea of a Messiah grew out of the dissatisfaction of the prophets and the people with the given state of affairs. Present sorrow nudged them to a hope of better things to come. From the time of King David until Christ, three major messianic pictures emerge. Some saw the Messiah as a king, others as a suffering servant, and, finally, a few envisioned him as a man from heaven with a divine mission.

The idea that the Messiah would be a king was popular during the times of the monarchy. God had made a covenant with King David, promising him that his throne would never die out (cf. 2 Samuel 7:4-17). As the years passed, with Judah experiencing one bad king after another, good men yearned for another King David, a messianic figure who would set things right.

Toward the end of the monarchic period, Judah did have two fine kings, Hezekiah and Josiah, but it soon became clear that neither measured up to the stature of a Messiah. Isaiah's famous prophecy of the Messiah being born of a virgin (Isaiah 7:14) was in the context of a Messiah seen as a king. The same is true of his poem about a Messiah who would rise out of the root of Jesse (Isaiah 11).

The Suffering Servant

However, after the fall of the monarchy, the numerous sorrows that attended the Babylonian exile, and the miseries experienced after the exile caused a sadness that Judaism found difficult to shake. Thoroughly disenchanted with the monarchy, the nation licked its wounds caused by the selfishness of its kings. It was no easy matter to revive the idea of a royal Messiah.

This vast, national sadness offered the prophets the opportunity to face up to the problem of suffering and its relationship to covenant and redemption.

Their long thoughts came to a peak in the now famous "servant poems" found in chapters 42, 49, 50, 52, and 53 of Isaiah. No longer does a triumphant, royal messianic king hold the center of the stage. Now, it is the servant of Yahweh, called by the Spirit, entrusted with the vocation to bring justice to the nations, who solves the riddle of suffering by giving it value in the form of salvation.

Salvation is accomplished through the voluntary acceptance of suffering by the anointed servant of the Lord: "Surely he has borne our griefs and carried our sorrows; yet we esteemed him stricken, smitten by God, and afflicted. But he was wounded for our transgressions, he was bruised for our iniquities; upon him was the chastisement that made us whole, and with his stripes we are healed" (Isaiah 53:4-5).

New Testament writers found in Jesus the perfect realization of this messianic insight, especially in the light of his agony and crucifixion. The earliest preaching of the apostolic Church often used the servant theme for Jesus (see Acts 8:30-35). St. Peter included the idea in his letters: "He himself bore our sins in his body on the tree, that we might die to sin and live to righteousness. By his wounds you have been healed" (1 Peter 2:24). It must be noted that the idea of a suffering Messiah was little appreciated until Christ the Messiah actually did suffer and die for us. It was the Christ of the Cross who conferred meaning on the ancient prophetic insight.

The Son of Man

Toward the end of the Old Testament period a third theme appears, that of the man from heaven, or the "Son of Man," as found in the prophecy of Daniel. In Daniel's seventh chapter, he relates a nightmarish dream in which stormy winds bring forth four monsters from a black lake. These monsters gain control of the earth and tyrannize its peoples. What this really means is that the first creation went awry and people did not fulfill their destiny as true images of God serving the world out of love and concern.

The dream continues with a white-bearded, fiery-eyed judge, called the "Ancient of Days," setting up a throne of judgment against a sinful people. He takes away from sinful nations the control of the earth. At that moment, a glorious sky figure, called the "Son of Man," journeys across the heavens, his face totally fixed on the Ancient of Days. In the Garden of Eden, the old Adam had turned his face away from the Lord and had hid himself from his gaze. Daniel sees this new heavenly Adam as a messianic figure. To this glorious sky figure the Ancient of Days gives dominion over the earth.

King, Suffering Servant, Son of Man

It is not hard to see how these three ideas about the Messiah (king, suffering servant, Son of Man) found their way into the gospel accounts. Popular piety was naturally interested in the royal Messiah, because of the stirring memories of the glories of King David and the humiliation of a subjected people. The common people plainly wanted a political liberator.

But those who lived on a deeper level of faith realized that a spiritual salvation was also required. Thus, they were sympathetic to the religious teaching about the Messiah seen as a suffering servant.

Jesus was not unwilling to be identified with the Davidic and servant titles. But he is often best remembered for taking as his own the title of Son of Man. In this way, he was showing that his messianic destiny included the founding of a new mankind, a new creation wherein he would take charge of the earth.

He would become the Lord of the universe and would share this rule of the earth with the Church that he intended to found. In this light, the Church becomes a messianic community bent on ordering the earth to the glory of God and the love of people. It was Jesus himself who took the rich prophetic vision of a Messiah as a king like David, as a suffering servant, and as a Son of Man. He showed all of us what these titles really mean. As the real Messiah Jesus gave us the royal kingdom of God's love, justice, and mercy. He underwent the passion and the sufferings of the Cross to show us what great discipleship would require. As the real Son of Man, he gave us a glimpse of the final resolution of history when all the puzzles, riddles, and mysteries of life will finally be made clear at the Last Judgment.

The Old Testament prophets uttered more than they knew about the Messiah. Jesus alone clarified what they spoke in mystery. The prophecies could never be truly understood until the One prophesied came and showed us what the words meant.

REFLECTION

When dealing with Old Testament prophets, two mistakes are often made. One error looks at them as somewhat magical figures staring into a crystal ball and predicting in great detail the life and meaning of the Messiah. Related to this is the view of the gospel writers as literary detectives searching the texts of the Bible to prove that Jesus was the Messiah.

We have insisted that it was Jesus who revealed who the Messiah was. After all, he was the Messiah. The prophets certainly had a Spirit-inspired insight that a savior figure would come one day to rescue God's people. They variously spoke of the Messiah as a king, a suffering servant, or a Son of Man. These were generalized meditations. The prophets looked into the future, not with the certainty of a movie documentary, but with the faith conviction that somehow God would not abandon his people.

Similarly, the gospel writers were either apostles who had known and experienced Jesus or disciples of those who did. They basked in the full glow of Christ's glorious self-revelation. They saw the glory. The magnificent light of Christ illuminated the dark shadows of earlier revelation. The gospel writers realized that the Old Testament's holy words shone with the meaning they could not have had until Christ appeared. The conversation about the Messiah and prophecy took place in this environment of revelation and faith.

The reason for stressing this point is that we can never shortchange the centrality of Jesus Christ. It is in him alone that all revelation is made clear through faith.

FOR DIALOGUE

If you were asked to explain what a prophet is, what would you say? What do you think would be the difference between an Old Testament prophet and a modern expert in a certain field — such as a stockbroker or a scientist — who makes predictions about the future?

As we will see, prophets were men who devoted their energies to purifying the consciences of their people. Sometimes they spoke about the future coming of a Messiah. Why do we say these were generalized — though true — comments rather than concrete, detailed predictions? Why did we need Christ's revelation to know the real meaning of a Messiah?

Sometimes we say things that have more meaning than we realize at the time. What usually makes such meaning clear?

All seeing God, help us to gain the sense of the inner unity of Scripture. Show us how the New Testament lies hidden in the Old Testament — and how the Old Testament becomes clear in the New.

The historian is a prophet in reverse.

FRIEDERICH VON SCHLEGEL

CHAPTER 23

Isaiah Sees the Glory

Isaiah 6

Then the glory of the LORD shall be revealed, and all flesh shall see it together.

ISAIAH 40:5

It is often said that when people get power, they cease to read a good book, eat a bad meal, or hear the truth. In Scripture it is the role of prophets to make sure that the power people hear the truth, unpalatable though it may be. Nathan pointed an accusing finger at King David for his terrible injustice to Uriah: David sent Uriah to his death in battle and then married his wife. Elijah fumed with anger against the atrocities and idolatries of King Ahab and Queen Jezebel.

Isaiah is equally direct in accusing the ruling class of their basic sinfulness. His goal was to call them to repentance, conversion, and acceptance of the mercy of God. His insight into sin and conversion sharpened after his encounter with the glory of God, described in his vision that is preserved in the sixth chapter of the book of Isaiah. Having seen the absolute purity of God, he realized more fully the opposite state that is sinfulness.

ISAIAH'S VISION

In the year that King Uzziah died, the young aristocrat, Isaiah, went to the temple for some elaborate liturgical ceremony. Because of his privileged position in society, he was shown to one of the front seats. There he sat amid a heady atmosphere provided by clouds of sweet incense, rhythmic chant, the stately paces of liturgical movement, and the rich, colorful attire of the participants. The backdrop for the rite was the temple building. Inside it was the Holy of Holies wherein reposed the Ark of the Covenant. Resting on the ark were the angelic seraphim, upon whose wings would rest the cloud-glory of God's presence.

As Isaiah is caught up in this atmosphere, the Lord God lifts him up to the dimensions of vision. While Isaiah peers into the thick darkness of the room enclosing the Holy of Holies, the liturgy surrounding him gives way to a vision of a liturgical celebration in heaven.

Isaiah sees the Lord "sitting upon a throne, high and lifted up." His robe seems to fill the temple. This description means that the awesome presence of God penetrates the entire place. The servants at God's throne are seraphim — fire angels, associated with the glory of the Lord. Each angel has six wings and uses two wings to cover his face. This masking symbolizes the mystery of God, much the same as a masked face holds mystery for us, and sometimes terror. The angels appear to be saying: no one may look upon the face of God and live. As he looks upon the vision, Isaiah hears the chant about God's holiness and glory, as, in the New Testament, the shepherds one day hear angels on the hillside of Bethlehem sing about the glory of Jesus.

Isaiah Experiences the Holiness and Glory of God

The song about God's holiness is a way of emphasizing his opposition to sin. A German writer, Rudolph Otto, says that when we encounter the holy, we experience fear and fascination.

When Moses approached the holy ground of God's presence on Mount Horeb before the burning bush, he was fascinated by this marvel, yet fearfully he took off his shoes, bowing to the earth at a respectful distance from the bush. Peter, James, and John react in a similar fashion before the burning glory of Christ at his transfiguration.

Next, in the biblical account of Isaiah's vision, "the foundations of the threshold shook" (Isaiah 6:4). As thunder and lightning and the roar of the sea made primitive man understand the might of God, so here the trembling of the temple foundations brings Isaiah to know the Almighty. After this, the vision blacks out in smoke. Isaiah stands dazed, and alone. He gradually becomes aware of himself in contrast to what he has seen. In his weak and sinful condition, he has confronted the matchless holiness and glory of God.

Isaiah looks into his own heart and makes a serious examination of conscience. This scrutiny impels him to utter the anguished admission: "Woe is me! For I am lost; for I am a man of unclean lips." He goes on to assure us of the real reason why he can make this judgment of himself: "For my eyes have seen the King, the LORD of hosts!" (Isaiah 6:5) Unclean lips is an expression of human selfishness, a way of speaking about one's sinfulness.

A Burning Coal Cleanses the Lips of the Prophet

Now the cloud disappears, and the vision returns. One of the fire angels (a seraph) takes a hot coal from the altar of incense, and presses it against the unclean lips of the prophet, and recites what is reminiscent of a sacramental formula: "Behold, this has touched your lips; your guilt is taken away, and your sin forgiven" (Isaiah 6:7). The purifying coal of fire is a symbol of God saving people through his transforming power.

And now God speaks: "Whom shall I send, and who will go for us?" The Lord has a mission for the prophet. His words to Isaiah are framed in such a way that the prophet remains free to accept or reject the commission. The cleansed Isaiah, possessing a new heart forged by the divine courage, looks into the face of God and says: "Here am I! Send me!" (Isaiah 6:8).

Notice the rhythm of the movement in this vision. God advances first upon the prophet, breaking into his prayerful mood at a liturgical function. The actions of Isaiah are a response resulting from his awareness of the divine initiative. God speaks to him with a vision of his unapproachable glory and holiness. Isaiah responds with his confession that he is a sinful man. God speaks to the prophet again, this time with the purifying fire of the seraph, and a call to apostolic mission in this world. Isaiah makes the total response of obedience and love.

CHRIST CLEANSES US IN THE SACRAMENT OF PENANCE

This account of the call of Isaiah suggests God's approach to sinful people today. When God looks upon a sinner, he approaches the sinful person in some mysterious way, awakening in the sinner a sense of the divine purity and his contrasting sinfulness. Christ, the new pillar of fire, the new fire angel, descends upon the sinner with the glowing coal of the sacrament of penance, removing all guilt and sin. With this comes the immediate call to reaffirm the decision to really live as a Christian.

Isaiah, then, saw the glory of God. It was a shattering experience, making him radically reconsider the meaning of his own life, and undertake a new mission. He knew that this would not be easy. God's demand was strong: "Make the mind of this people dull, and stop their ears, and shut their eyes, so that they may not look with their eyes, and listen with their ears, and comprehend with their minds, and turn and be healed"(Isaiah 6:10, NRSV).

Faced with this difficult task, the prophet understandably and hopefully asks "How long, O LORD?" And God replied, "Until cities lie waste without inhabitant, and houses without men, and the land is utterly desolate" (Isaiah 6:11). This is not exactly the most comforting sort of future. Isaiah can anticipate a career that will meet with constant frustration and rejection because the people are spiritually blind and deaf. Hence the judgment will bring their lands to waste.

A FEW HEAR GOD'S WORDS AND REMAIN FAITHFUL

The encouraging part of God's message is that a remnant of people will remain. Isaiah can count on a small group who will indeed understand his message and remain faithful. They, too, will experience the fires of purification: "And though a tenth remain in it, it will be burned again.... Holy offspring is the trunk"(Isaiah 6:13).

Historically, the nation went up in flames at the time of the Babylonian invasion. The holy remnant was the group of Israelites that were taken into Babylonian exile where they underwent the purification of seventy years. They preserved the stirring memory of Isaiah, his vision of glory, his own painful purification, and his tireless efforts to summon the nation to penance and to encourage the faithful few. Read all of Isaiah, chapter 6, to get the flavor of the prophet's vision, purification, and mission.

REFLECTION

The sixth chapter of Isaiah describes his call to be a prophet. It involves his becoming aware of the magnificent holiness of God and his own sinfulness by contrast. He confesses openly his state of life and receives a forgiving purification from God. He hears that God wants a man for a mission and replies, "Here I am, Lord. Send me." He also hears that the mission will be hard work, but he is willing to take up the task.

This is an image of the conversion we need to undergo when God calls us to our mission in life. Whatever the state of life is that God calls us, we can go through a process of examining ourselves, seeking the purification needed to proceed, and pulling ourselves together to respond to God's call and mission.

The emphasis is on God's initiative in our lives. It is God who begins the process of our conversion and calling. Conversely, we do not call ourselves or make this up. St. Peter writes that a true prophet needs to be called. He cannot prophesy under his own authority. Self-styled prophets may be living under an illusion. Our calling is a gift from God who also endows us with the graces to live out our destiny. This is both a comfort and a challenge.

FOR DIALOGUE

What signs have appeared in your life, giving you direction concerning the path God is calling you to follow? This may involve a moral conversion from your sinfulness. What resources do you find in the Church to assist you with this conversion?

Why do we say that becoming a prophet to our society is something that is a call from God and not a self-induced idea? What basis for this is found in Scripture?

Who are prophetic figures in your world today? What is there about them that inspires you, disturbs you, causes you to wonder?

PRAYER

Loving Father, fill us with light to see the path you have designed for us. Give us the graces we need to respond to what you call us to do. In your kindness, walk with us as we seek to do your will.

The prophet himself stands under the judgment which he preaches. If he does not know that, he is a false prophet.

REINHOLD NIEBUHR

CHAPTER 24

Jeremiah: The Prophet of Moral Responsibility

Jeremiah 7

"Is it I whom they provoke? says the Lord. *Is it not themselves, to their own confusion?"*

JEREMIAH 7:19

History is full of stories of people who have failed to take personal responsibility for their actions. In recent years newspapers have been filled with stories and editorials dealing with the breakdown of personal responsibility in our times. There are those who have witnessed the rape of young girls and the murder of old men, and have not had the decency or moral strength to call for police help or to use their own abilities to defend the weak. This problem of accepting or avoiding personal responsibility is a very old one, and one that each generation must accept and face.

WHEN SECURITY WAS FOUND IN GROUP STRENGTH

In biblical times, people went through a twofold phase before the issue of personal responsibility was adequately faced. During the patriarchal and tribal confederacy periods, group or communal responsibility was stressed. Individuals generally found strength and identity in the collective power of the tribe. Their mentality normally was molded by the group, whether in such matters as finding a new water hole or in fighting off a hostile tribe, or in seeking revenge for the slaughter of a member of one's own tribe.

In such an atmosphere, it was only natural that the responsibility for a moral collapse would be considered communal. After all, punishment for sins was experienced in that way. For example, the army of Joshua experienced a puzzling defeat at the gates of Ai just after it had won a resounding victory at Jericho. The reason for the defeat was that one member of Joshua's army had sinned by stealing silver and gold from Jericho and had buried the treasure in the ground as a selfish hoard for himself. Nevertheless, the entire army (seen as the community) was held responsible for the crime and was therefore defeated (punished). The punishment of the individual criminal, Achan, was severe: he was stoned to death.

When the Sense of Sin Was Lost, No One Felt Responsible

The difficulty that arises with the group idea of responsibility is that sin can soon lose its personal aspect. If everybody sins, then it begins to seem as if nobody sins. Centuries of the group approach to morality tended to wither away the sense of sin. And this fact became all the more evident as the tribal form of society simultaneously disappeared. This is what had happened in Israel by the time of the prophet Jeremiah.

The fierce blood and social connections of Israel's tribal days had yielded to the fragmented life of the monarchy in which the aristocrats had formed their own social set, prophetic communities had become groups apart, and the poor had been dispersed into villages that soon forgot the fierce tribal loyalties of former days. With the disappearance of the strict tribal form, what remained of the idea of group morality made less sense to the Israelites.

Within the nation itself, it seemed that the sense of sin had been nearly lost.

The chosen people had retained a communal sense of responsibility while their community had substantially disappeared. But along the way, the idea of communal morality had been dropped. The idea of sin had been changed into some sort of impersonal "it" for which no one felt responsibility, either personal or communal. At this point, it is useful to study the temple sermon of Jeremiah in the book of Jeremiah, chapter 7.

In his blistering sermon on the false use of the temple, Jeremiah showed that just as the Israelites had a false notion of how God's blessings came to them, they had also a false notion of sin. He found them chattering the formula, "temple of the Lord," as though it were a magic chant that could charm away their sins and win blessings.

Sin Is a Personal Refusal to Love and Obey God

The temple was not supposed to be a mere thing. It was intended to be holy ground, the sacred space where man could enter into dialogue with God. And if the temple became an "it" because God was no longer seen as a "Thou" — a partner in a very personal relationship — then sin became no more than the violation of a command, and neither a communal nor a personal refusal to love and obey God.

Once God is depersonalized — seen as a "thing" — then sin, too, becomes a matter of offense against an "it." Instead of "thou" and "him," we now have an "it." And when this happens, we start to measure our lives against an abstract command, rather than against the love offered us by our Father who wants to save us.

Jeremiah stood by the crowded temple gate and raised his voice against the smug throngs gaily tossing off their sins by thoughtlessly muttering canned prayers. Jeremiah warned the people: "Put not your trust in the deceitful words: 'This is the temple of the LORD!'" (Jeremiah 7:4). He drew their attention to the real problem — the loss of genuine contact with God. He accused them of stealing, murdering, cheating, lying, and fornicating and then, hypocritically, rushing off to the temple with a twinge of conscience, to say they were delivered — and then continue these evil acts.

Jeremiah uttered words that later would be quoted by Jesus when he cleansed the temple: "Has this house, which is called by my name, become a den of robbers in your eyes?" (Jeremiah 7:11). Jeremiah reminded the people how God had destroyed the shrine at Shilo in the northern kingdom, where he had also established his name. God had wiped out that shrine because the people had made it a mere thing of magic. Jeremiah assured them that God is perfectly willing to repeat this performance.

Personal Responsibility before a Personal God

Jeremiah told them that they were a foolish people who rushed about baking bread and stamping the dough with the image of the pagan queen of the heavens. They, the holy people of God, blissfully ignored the primary address of God: "Obey my voice, and I will be your God, and you shall be my people; and walk in all the ways that I command you, that it may be well with you" (Jeremiah 7:23).

Fearlessly, Jeremiah pronounced doom for those who disregarded genuine contact with God and committed themselves to a purely external and materialistic religion. He warned them that such sinners would be food for the birds of the air, and none will frighten them away. The sound of mirth and the voice of gladness would disappear from the streets. The gay shouts of bridal processions would be heard no more, for the city would become a desolation. Bones of the dead would be taken from the grave and spread before the sun and moon that they loved and served, consulted and worshipped. These bones would be left as dung upon the face of the earth.

Jeremiah has placed before our eyes a scene from a religion of superstition rooted in the chill world of stones and charm formulas, a religion in which God is a thing and not a person. He has sketched for us the image of those who have lost their sense of a personal God. He has made a direct attack on the consciences of his listeners. By appealing to each one to turn to God as a "thou," Jeremiah has, at the same time, quickened the conscience of the individual and forced him to accept responsibility for his moral life.

SENSE OF SIN LOST TODAY

Many people today have also lost the sense of sin. Irreligious people simply say there is no sin. Religious people come to the same conclusion by hedging sin within some abstract category, absolving themselves from it by the uttering of some safe formula that charms away the guilt and produces the illusion of absolution. That is why Christians can stand by when others are being beaten and attacked, because for them sin has lost its personal meaning, and individual responsibility is meaningless.

Jeremiah's great gift to us is to call us to recover our sense of a personal relationship with a God who is loving and merciful and wants to fill us with forgiveness and hope. The counterpart to this is our willingness to take responsibility for our sins. Then we can identify quite well with the prayer of Jeremiah in chapter 17:14-17:

Heal me, O LORD, and I shall be healed;
save me, and I shall be saved;
for you are my praise...
Do not become a terror to me;
you are my refuge in the day of disaster.

REFLECTION

Sometimes it is important, when reading the Old Testament, to strip away the strange customs of ancient times, or to ignore for the moment the odd twists and turns of their wars and troubles, so that we might look as the basic truth being taught. When thinking of Jeremiah in this manner, we come to the bare bones of his message:

"Dear friends. Have you recently thought about God as someone who loves you, has a personal interest in your human fulfillment, desires to save you from your foolishness, self-deception, and self-destructive behavior? Do you really think your sin does not exist, that your evil ways have no effect on your spiritual health or on your community? Do you believe that you have no personal responsibility for your actions and their impact on society and the state of your soul?

"Is your religion little more than reciting vague formulas like 'the temple of the Lord, the temple of the Lord?' Souls have been lost and nations corrupted by the groundswell of the loss of the sense of sin and moral responsibility. God is not your enemy. God is your friend. God wants your happiness even more than you do. Begin now to say with your whole heart: 'Heal me, O Lord and I shall be healed.'"

FOR DIALOGUE

As you look at your own experience and those of others, what are some examples of failure to take responsibility for one's acts? How do such failings adversely affect your own life and the lives of others? Why do we say that acts have both a personal and social impact?

What are some examples of a loss of the sense of sin you have noticed in your experience? Why does Jeremiah insist on recovering a sense of a personal, loving, and merciful God in order to recover a sense of sin and moral responsibility?

In this process why is it important to be as attentive to themes of divine mercy, forgiveness, and hope — as well as sin? What happens when a society has lost its moral compass?

PRAYER

Forgiving and merciful God, you know our needs before we ask you. Yet we come to you, repentant for our sins, trusting in your healing power to help us to be cleansed and renewed. Convert us, O Lord, and we shall be changed. Thank you.

Jesus began to preach, saying, "Repent, for the kingdom of heaven is at hand."

MATTHEW 4:17

CHAPTER 25

Ezekiel: Reverence the Holiness of God

Ezekiel 34; 36-37

The Spirit lifted me up, and brought me into the inner court; and behold, the glory of the LORD filled the temple.

EZEKIEL 43:5

Space buffs might enjoy the science fiction atmosphere of the opening chapter of the book of Ezekiel. The prophet Ezekiel is seated along the banks of the River Chebar in ancient Babylon, having followed the Hebrew community into exile. The heavens open, the earthly scene fades, and the prophet sees whirling wheels, four-faced men, crystal skies, and a sapphire throne in a vision. This experience serves as the background of Ezekiel's call to be a prophet.

THE BOOK OF EZEKIEL

It is comparatively easy to see the outline of his book. After the story of his call to be a prophet, which occupies the first three chapters, there follows the series of sermons which Ezekiel delivered in Jerusalem. In these, he criticized the people for their evil ways and foretold their doom. This section is followed by angry warnings against the heathen nations and the Israelites who held beliefs similar to those of the Gentiles. The third section of the book is a diary of Ezekiel's sermons to the Jews now in exile. He changes from harsh condemnation to inspirational talks that attempt to strengthen their hopes.

The last part of the book (chapters 40 to 48) is the prophet's record of what the new temple should be like after the group returns from exile. Ezekiel not only details temple construction, but also outlines a sort of religious constitution for the community after the exile.

A Plan of Religious Living

The language used by Ezekiel to describe the new temple and form of religious discipline suggests that he is having a vision. But his purpose is to give the future congregations a plan of religious behavior that will ward off the kind of problems that have cast the present community into exile.

These closing chapters of the book of Ezekiel form the most original and influential part of the prophet's work. He gives a remarkably complete outline of the ritual and organizational structures that should be adopted by the new community. Here he was, a Jew living in exile with a people who, as an alien minority, had neither political power nor rights, nor any temple where they could sacrifice. This absence of ceremonial religion made it seem all the more important that they prepare for the restoration of divinely revealed worship.

Ezekiel had a detailed knowledge of Solomon's temple and its ritual practice. Much of this was used in his new plan. He leaves practically nothing out: the description of the temple courts, the sacristies for the clergy, the exact measurements of the structure, the ritual for the dedication of the altar, the plan for the temple kitchens. He ends with a vision of the glory of God taking up a permanent abode in the new temple after having abandoned the old temple of Solomon.

He Called for Worship Emphasizing God's Holiness

Before the exile, Ezekiel had emphasized the justice and mercy of God and the ethical demands made of a pious Jew. Now, as he looks ahead to the congregation of the future, he prescribes the walls that were intended to separate the holy from the common. The sanctuary should be in the inner court. Laity will worship in the outer court, and would not take part in the sacrificial ceremonies. In actual fact, however, the laity refused to give up their ancient right to offer their own sacrifices in the inner court.

Ezekiel eliminated the alien janitors. The Levites assumed these menial duties. The book of Deuteronomy equates the Levites with the priests. But from the time of Ezekiel, the Levites became only assistants to the priests. The prophet's attention to the most minute details of temple furnishing and ritual showed his consuming desire to keep the holy place from any profanation. He composed rules about such things as the offering of animals and vegetables, the materials and tailoring of the priestly vestments, the opening and closing of gates. Ezekiel's intense attention to such details was designed to protect the holiness, transcendence, and majesty of God in the awareness of the people.

Ezekiel was aware that human error and mistakes should be minimized. Hence, he prescribed purification rituals. His attention was focused totally on public worship, because his concern was to preserve a friendly relationship between God and the whole nation. He had little interest in private sacrifice. He concentrated on a worship that paid tribute to the divine and purified transgressions, unwitting or otherwise. Therefore, he introduced a solemnity to religious practice that suppressed the spontaneous gladness of earlier worship.

The Father of Judaism

So influential was Ezekiel's book on the religious life of Israel that he has been called by some the "father of Judaism." From him, the Jews inherited a personal sense of the need for repentance, an awesome sense of reverence for God, and an abiding hatred of idolatry. His liturgical reform was radical and lasting. It had the weakness of being overorganized, leaving little room for the spontaneous. But the reform did put fiber into the national religion.

His hopes eventually led to ritual legalism, but Ezekiel's legacy of the need to reverence the holy did not die. He was a stern and demanding prophet, but one whose basic wisdom instilled a sense of responsibility into a perpetually thoughtless people. Today, we might resist his insistence on external details, but we should celebrate and assimilate his "legacy of the holy" as we ourselves engage in our liturgical life.

REFLECTION

In our approach to God we waver between his majesty and his nearness. On the one hand God is a divine mystery, totally other, infinite and glorious. On the other hand, God is as near to us as a glove on our hand. Saints tell us that God is closer to us than we are to ourselves. Transcendence is the name we give to that aspect of God that refers to his absolute purity, majesty, and holiness. Immanence is the name we give that aspect of God that refers to his presence among us. If we only knew God as transcendent, we might think he does not care for us. If we only knew God as immanent, we might domesticate him and manipulate him for our own purposes.

Ezekiel strove to keep alive our experience of the transcendence or holiness of God, a reverence for God as mystery. This does not exclude our belief in God's love and mercy for us. Quite the opposite, since it posits a love that cannot fail and a mercy that is inexhaustible. It is in Jesus Christ that this seeming contradiction is resolved. In him the divine and the human are united in a wondrous manner. Christ as Son of God is transcendent, but as Son of Mary He is immanent — intimate, near, close to us as we would ever want. This mystery is offered to us at every Mass and in the reserved presence of Christ in the Blessed Sacrament.

Much as we hunger to have God near us, we also need a sense of his otherness and mystery. This is why we should be reverent in Church and adopt practices that foster respect, honor, and sensitivity to the presence of the holiness of God. Moral holiness is being without sin and guilt. Worship-holiness is a commitment to reverence for God that is a condition for moral rectitude.

It is not easy to hold onto the divine holiness of God. Details of piety have been a traditional way of helping us to do this. This was the plan Ezekiel provided for his people. We need to develop our own way of doing this today.

FOR DIALOGUE

Were you asked to explain the difference between the transcendence and immanence of God, how would you do it? If your listeners would ask you why the distinction is important, what would you say? Why did Ezekiel feel the need to stress God's holiness and transcendence for his people?

When you enter a Church these days or attend Mass, how strong would you say is the sense of God's holiness? What are some practices you would think might improve the practice of reverence at Mass?

In your personal prayer life how do you balance your approach to God as being both divine mystery and intimate divine friend? When you are having a crisis, how would both approaches to God be a comfort to you?

PRAYER

Almighty and glorious God, I kneel before you and adore your mystery and majesty. At the same time I thank you for your gracious and loving presence in my heart. Teach me the virtue of reverence that I may always honor your holiness.

As he [Jesus] died to make men holy, let us die to make men free.
JULIA WARD HOWE

CHAPTER 26

Daniel: A Teen Hero

Daniel 1-14

The king commanded his palace master Ashpenaz to bring some of the Israelites... young men without physical defect and handsome, versed in every branch of wisdom, endowed with knowledge and insight and competent to serve in the king's palace.

DANIEL 1:3-4

Teens have been accused of many things, but rarely have they been called prophets. The Bible, however, tells the story of a prophet who was a teenager. His prophecies and his life story are as unusual as the fact of his youth. His name was Daniel, which means "God has judged."

SIX STORIES AND FOUR VISIONS

The book of Daniel is made up of six colorful stories and four visions. It borrows images from natural disasters. The author of the book of Daniel lived under the Greek persecution of Antiochus the Terrible, from 167 to 164 BC. He was sensitive to the national despair brought on by this persecution, and so told six legend-like tales that survived the Babylonian experience years before. He used these stories as inspirational narratives to hearten the faithful of his time. Then he used the four visions of Daniel as ways of interpreting the meaning of the present crisis and establishing hope in the ultimate victory of the saints of God.

Daniel and His Friends Brought into the Service of the King

The first story about Daniel is placed against the background of the Babylonian captivity and the slave policies of the king. The monarch of Babylon had decided that the cream of the conquered youth should be brought into the service of the king.

Attention is drawn to the person of Daniel and his three friends. African-American spirituals have immortalized their three names: Shadrach, Meshach, and Abednego. Their first problem was one of diet. The rules called for them to become accustomed to Babylonian menus. But, unfortunately, this conflicted with the dietary rules of the Hebrews. To conform meant they would be unfaithful to their religion. "But Daniel resolved that he would not defile himself with the king's rich food, or with the wine which he drank" (Daniel 1:8).

Daniel Stands Up for His Beliefs

Daniel was not afraid to stand up for his beliefs, even against so imposing a figure as the king of Babylon. Daniel proposed a compromise. He insisted that he and his friends be put on a vegetarian diet, promising that they would be as healthy as the others after a ten-day period. The gentleman in charge agreed, and was pleasantly surprised to find that at the end of ten days, "they were better in appearance and fatter in flesh than all the youths who ate the king's rich food" (Daniel 1:15).

Then Daniel and his friends were presented to the king and found great favor with him. Daniel emerged as a wise man, even though he was still a youth. Each of the stories that follows this account illustrates in different ways Daniel's wisdom. He had become a wise man because, on the one hand, he did not fear the might of kings, and on the other, he stood by his conviction that obedience to his God was all-important.

Daniel Interpreted Dreams

By his obedience to the Lord, Daniel began to share in the creative power and wisdom of the Lord. One biblical way of illustrating this was by showing his ability to interpret dreams. The second story, then, is about a dream. The king saw a giant statue that had feet of clay. A small stone was enough to topple the image. When the king awoke, he did not remember what the dream was about, let alone understand its meaning. He asked his court advisers to help him out, but they were helpless.

Then Daniel came and interpreted the details of the dream and its meaning. The statue was made of various metals: these referred to the different empires that had ruled the world. The feet of clay meant that all of these empires were ultimately destined to fall. The small stone that rolled against the monstrous image and overcame it represented the small community who were faithful to God and were seeking justice. This little stone eventually rose until it became a mountain that touched the heavens. "But the stone that struck the [statue] became a great mountain" (Daniel 2:35).

This image of the small rock that became a mountain rising up to God and filling the earth may offer us some insight into the account in which Christ addresses himself to Peter the "rock," telling Peter that upon this small rock will be built the Church (Matthew 16:18). And this Church will be a mountain rising to heaven and surviving all empires that try to crush it — even hell itself.

The Den of Lions

The other stories about the wise and courageous young Daniel repeat the themes of his insight and religious dedication. His three friends were thrown into a fiery furnace, but were saved by the protective cloak of their faith. Daniel himself was hurled into a den of growling and hungry lions, but his faith subdued the angry beasts, creating a scene like the garden of paradise in which Daniel was a new Adam controlling the animal world.

Vision of the Four Beasts

Among the four visions in the book of Daniel, the one in chapter 7 deserves our attention. Daniel had a nightmare in which he heard the blast of the four winds of the world beating over the black waters of a vast lake. He saw a lion, a bear, and a leopard, and finally, a beast beyond description.

"After this I saw in the night visions, and behold, a fourth beast, terrible and dreadful and exceedingly strong; and it had great iron teeth; it devoured and broke in pieces, and stamped the residue with its feet. It was different from all the beasts that were before it; and it had ten horns" (Daniel 7:7).

The black lake represented the chaos that existed before creation. The four winds were symbolic of the creative breath of God that brought forth the first mankind. The four beasts represented the different empires of the old mankind who were given dominion over the earth. Picturing them as beasts with cruel intent taught that the first mankind did not really live up to being images of God and so did not deserve to inherit and rule the earth.

The dream next introduced a scene of light. An old man called "the Ancient of Days" ascended a throne of judgment: "The court sat in judgment, and the books were opened" (Daniel 7:10). The Ancient of Days declared that the dominion of the earth would now be taken away from the four beasts. Then he turned and saw the "son of man" coming toward him across the heavens. The expression "son of man" here seems to mean a messianic figure who will usher into our earth the kingdom of God. The saints — God's people — will receive this kingdom. "To him was given dominion and glory and kingship... the holy ones of the Most High shall receive the kingdom and possess the kingdom forever — forever and ever"(Daniel 7:14, 18).

The purpose of this vision was to encourage the Jews living under the persecution of Antiochus the Terrible. Beastlike tyrants like Antiochus would eventually be overcome by the power of God, as one day he would establish a new age that would be characterized by a faithful and obedient mankind.

Jesus Called Himself the Son of Man

In the gospels, we can note that Jesus was very fond of referring to himself as the "Son of Man," the title taken from the book of Daniel. In so doing, Jesus identified himself as the new Adam to whom has been given the lordship of the world, and who shares this loving dominion with the saints of the most high, namely, the Church. The Church is a dominion of a love and service that is truly creative.

The prophetic spirit of Daniel lives in many who have developed a sense of concern for people who are unjustly treated in our world.

REFLECTION

One of the special gifts of being young, besides strength and health, is idealism. Young people have the ability of reminding us that dreams can come true, that ideals are worth fighting for, that life is full of possibilities. The young have the energy and spark to look at life as an adventure. This fact applies not only to sports and romance, but also to religion. The biblical stories of faith surrounding the figure of the young prophet Daniel remind us that young people are capable of an enviable lively faith and a religious commitment.

If today's youth sometimes seem uninvolved with religion, it may be that adults have failed to offer them the invigorating challenges of faith. The young are the most eager to accept a challenge. Stretching their horizons is a way of life for them. The world is aware of this and thinks up dozens of challenges for today's youth. People of faith should be no less willing to propose to young people the gospel challenges that come from Christ.

In the Daniel story, we see a young man stand up for his beliefs against the threats of the most powerful ruler of his day. And he did this not just once but again and again. There is no reason why this should not happen today. Biblical youths were men and women of flesh and blood just like those today. Human nature has not changed, only the stage props have. Cowardice and courage still stalk the human heart. Youthful idealism has not disappeared with the advent of the technological world. But the condition for the possibility of such idealism being tapped for the cause of Christ needs to be revived.

God's call has not changed: "O man, arise! O woman, arise! Commit yourselves to Christ and the rebirth of his kingdom in this world. The stakes are as high as they ever were. You will know no greater joy or satisfaction than responding to Christ's call to participate with him in the salvation of the world."

No matter our age, we must uncover our idealism and exuberance and recommit ourselves to our Lord.

FOR DIALOGUE

What are some occasions in your life when you have been challenged to live up to your religious beliefs? When you did stand by what you believed, what were the resources that helped you do so?

Who are some people you know that inspire you to stay committed to your faith and practice? What do you think makes them tick, meaning what is the origin of their spiritual strength?

When it comes to promoting your idealism, what would you ask the Church to do to help you? What would you imagine helped the biblical Daniel to be so courageous in the face of a threatening ruler? Why does forming a group of faith-committed people reinforce one's own spiritual strength?

PRAYER

Lord Jesus, we thank you for the challenge to believe in you and practice what this faith implies. At the same time we need your spiritual powers to stay faithful. Give us, Lord, all the graces we need to accept this challenge.

Remember also your Creator in the days of your youth.
ECCLESIASTES 12:1

CHAPTER 27

Amos and Social Justice:
A Farmer Urges Social Reform

Amos 6

Woe to those that are at ease in Zion.

AMOS 6:1

The image that religious leaders often leave is that of refined and cultured men. It is, then, refreshing to come to the story of Amos, who was unashamedly a mountaineer, and had no intention of hiding his rustic ways as farmer and shepherd. He lived in 750 BC, in Tekoa, a mountain village in the wilderness of Judah.

Amos' call to prophecy came while he was watching his sheep. God summoned him to go from town to town in the northern kingdom of Israel and preach the cause of justice for the poor. Perhaps his most famous phrase is the expression he hurled at a self-indulgent women's club in Samaria where he called these ladies of high fashion, "cows of Bashan" (see Amos 4:1-3).

AMOS CRITICIZED LUXURIOUS LIVING

Like many of the prophets, Amos criticized luxurious living, especially when it blinded people to their social responsibility for the needs of the poor. He preached at the shrine cities such as Gilgal. His career was suddenly brought to a halt by Amaziah, the president of the royal sanctuary at Bethel. Amaziah accused Amos of heresy, a charge that was mixed with accusations of treason against King Jeroboam II. He succeeded in suddenly ending the prophetic activity of Amos after a few brief months. "O seer, go, flee away to the land of Judah, and eat bread there, and prophesy there; but never again prophesy at Bethel, for it is the king's sanctuary, and it is a temple of the kingdom" (Amos 7:12-13).

Amos retired gracefully, but with a biting rejoinder to the hypocritical Amaziah: "Your wife shall be a harlot in the city, and your sons and your daughters shall fall by the sword, and your land shall be parceled out by line;

you yourself shall die in an unclean land, and Israel shall surely go into exile away from its land" (Amos 7:17).

It is no simple matter to preach repentance to a prosperous people. Amos' prophecies coincided with the last burst of luxurious living Israel knew before her downfall. Israel had a boom economy because of several successful wars and, as a result, the merchant princes were living high. In the golden glow of this prosperity, the people could scarcely believe that the doom perceived by Amos could really happen. It is a tribute to Amos' genius that he really could sense the true threat presented by Assyria, even though at that time this threat was but a cloud on the horizon, no larger than a man's hand.

God Is Lord of All Nations

Amos was the first of the great reforming prophets. He was also the first to preach that God was the Lord of all nations, not just the Lord of Israel. In the general thinking of the time, each nation had its own God. Israel thought no differently. Yahweh was her God, greater indeed than all gods, but not the only god. But Amos spoke of Yahweh as Lord of every nation. He spoke of the Lord giving land to other nations besides Israel. It is true that God had put a special amount of attention on Israel, but only because he wanted a higher standard for her. "You only have I known of all the families of the earth; therefore I will punish you for all your iniquities" (Amos 3:2).

It is easy to see how Amos seemed like a real heretic: his message was so new; none of the other prophets had spoken this way. In fact, Amos did not want to be identified with the other prophets. "I am a herdsman, and a dresser of sycamore trees." But he also insisted that he truly represented the true message of the Lord: "The LORD took me from following the flock, and the LORD said to me, 'Go, prophesy to my people Israel'" (Amos 7:14-15).

He was not out to found a new religion, but to establish the old one in spirit and truth. He shifted the emphasis from external forms to the purification of the people's conscience. He insisted that Yahweh, the God of all nations, would not die with the fall of Israel. In fact, it is precisely this God who would annihilate Israel.

Israel Ignored the Poor and Practiced False Piety

As a genuine social reformer, Amos was horrified by the departure of Israel from even the simplest standards of decency that any civilized nation would uphold. He saw dishonesty: "Hear this, you who trample upon the needy, and bring the poor of the land to an end, saying 'When will the new moon be over that we may sell grain? And the Sabbath, that we may offer wheat for sale, that we may make the ephah [bushel] small and the shekel great, and deal deceitfully with false balances'" (Amos 8:4-5). He noticed the people's ruthlessness. In the face of such poverty, he was shocked by the luxury of the palaces and mansions of the rich. "Woe to those who lie upon beds of ivory... and eat lambs from the flock... who sing idle songs to the sound of the harp.... and anoint themselves with the finest oils, but are not grieved over the ruin of Joseph!" (Amos 6:4-6).

In condemning such self-indulgence, he used strong language.

"I abhor the pride of Jacob, and hate his strongholds; and I will deliver up the city and all that is in it" (Amos 6:8). The irony of it all was that the people of Israel not only forgot the plight of the poor, but cushioned their consciences by performing all the tried and true religious ceremonies that honored their God. In following the traditional acts of religious piety, they felt that that was all God needed to keep him from being angry or threatening them. They used the very liturgy itself as a wall to insulate themselves from any concern for the poor.

Even degrading aspects of their piety did not shame them. Amos noted that fathers and sons sinned with the same woman, even in the temple area, and got drunk there on wine purchased with money from unfair fines. It is understandable, then, that Amos had such hard words for a liturgy among such an immoral people. "I hate, I despise your feasts, and I take no delight in your solemn assemblies" (Amos 5:21).

Amos was not opposed to liturgy in itself, but to a worship performed by such an immoral people. God will not tolerate a liturgy divorced from a proper spirit. Splendid sacrifices, huge feast-day crowds, and loud music are not a substitute for clean lives. Some have accused Amos of being opposed to liturgy itself, but this is not true. His eye was on the heart, not the ceremony. Amos insisted on the need for social justice along with liturgy.

Real Meaning of Liturgy Is Seen in Social Justice, Right Living

The brief ministry of Amos gave the world one of the first documents of social protest. He had the courage to be a reformer, and the genius to see through the trappings of power and wealth to the rot that lay beneath. He showed that real liturgical relevance is not a matter of fresh ceremonies, but is rooted in right living and compassion for the poor and unjustly treated. Rough hewn as he was, Amos loved Israel. That love can be seen in this quiet lament: "Fallen, to rise no more, is the virgin Israel; forsaken on her land, with none to raise her up" (Amos 5:2). He scourged Israel because he loved her, and wept over her because she loved neither God nor man.

REFLECTION

One of the persistent problems of wealth is that it is too often linked to greed and to injustices that oppress the poor. The fatal flaw that can corrupt the rich is to forget that God planned that we should be conscientious stewards of the goods of the earth. The products of the earth are not just meant for the favored few. The goods of the earth are meant for the health and sustenance of each and every human person. This is God's will.

But wealth has a way of making people forget this fundamental moral principle. With money, people can insulate themselves from the problems of everyday life. In gated communities, guarded condominiums, luxurious resorts, and other protected environments, it becomes easy for the inhabitants to ignore the needs of the poor and even sustain social structures that keep the poor in misery.

The prophet Amos was God's mouthpiece speaking out against social injustice caused by the rich whose conscience had become dulled through self-indulgence. Amos made it clear that God was the one making this challenge through this farmer turned prophet. Divine revelation itself was taking up the cause of justice for the world.

Our own Church has developed a plan for social justice that asks us all to do what we can to heal the symptoms and causes of injustice and poverty. Two great women of our Church have been prophetic instruments of this vision. Mother Teresa of Calcutta taught us how to heal the symptoms of poverty as she went into the streets to pick up the bodies of the dying and bring them to her hospice and give them love, prayer, food, and care for their last days. She awakened our consciences to the needs of the poorest of the poor.

Dorothy Day did this also, but she drew our attention to the need to change laws and policies in our government and business practices so that workers could earn a living wage to support their families with a decent home and a future. She set out to heal the causes of injustice and poverty. In Latin America many Catholics have fought for a "preferential option for the poor" with the same goal in mind. The Church itself has joined this goal of an option for the poor. Archbishop Fulton Sheen argued that the poor should be the first citizens of the Church to get our attention and our support.

Amos would be pleased with these developments. But a lot of work remains to be done. Let us never "be at ease in Zion."

FOR DIALOGUE

What experiences have you had of injustice against yourself or those who have little or no power to protect themselves? How were you able to respond and correct the situation in your own case or those of others?

What do you find in the prophecy of Amos that resonates with your own desire to see justice in your world? How would you apply the principle that the goods of the earth are meant for the good of all?

How would you approach the call to alleviate the symptoms and causes of poverty and injustice? From what you may know of Mother Teresa of Calcutta, what would affect your own attitude to the poorest of the poor? How could you have a preferential option for the poor?

PRAYER

Jesus, when you told the story of Lazarus and the Rich Man, you called us to overcome our lack of attention to and compassion for the poor. Give us the graces to be aware of the symptoms and causes of poverty and injustice and help us to be active in healing them.

Care of the poor is incumbent upon society as a whole.

BENEDICT SPINOZA

CHAPTER 28

Hosea Celebrates God's Loyalty to His Covenant

Hosea 1-2

I will espouse you to me forever: I will espouse you in right and in justice, in love and in mercy.

HOSEA 2:21

It is common enough for an adulterous woman to be one of the central figures in a modern novel. But when this is true of a biblical book, we can understandably be surprised. Yet, this is precisely what happens in the book of Hosea, the prophet. Gomer, the prophet's wife, was unfaithful to him.

THE MAIN ISSUE IS ISRAEL'S FIDELITY TO GOD

It is true that there is some confusion about this. Chapters 1 and 3 have two different stories about what God really asked Hosea to do. The first chapter seems to indicate that he should marry a woman who would become an adulteress. The third chapter, on the other hand, seems to say that Hosea should marry a woman who is already guilty of adultery. While most critics will argue over whether chapter 1 or 3 is the true story, they all admit that the main issue is not really Hosea's domestic problems, but Israel's fidelity to God. At most, the faithless Gomer is an image of faithless Israel.

The Importance of a Person's Name

The opening chapter of the book of Hosea tells of Hosea's marriage to Gomer and the three children that she bore him. Great attention is paid to the names given the children, especially to their symbolism. At first sight this can seem unimportant to us, because we more than likely share Shakespeare's thought: "What's in a name? ... a rose by any other name would smell as sweet."

But for biblical people, a name was very important. It signified the power or office of a person. Names dealt with a person's destiny. For example, Abram became Abraham (Hebrew *Abraham*, "father of a multitude"), for he was to be the father of all nations. Simon became Peter (from the Greek

Petros, "rock"), for he would be the rock upon which Christ's Church would be built. And even in our own society, names can be more important than we might at first imagine. Salesmen know that their customers like to be known by name. Politicians have long known the same thing is valuable in vote-getting. The legendary Jim Farley, President Franklin Roosevelt's campaign manager, is said to have known fifty thousand people by name.

Hosea and Gomer gave their children symbolic names. They named their first son, Jezreel, which was the name of one of the royal residences. This residence had become a scene of horror where the king, Jehu, massacred the descendants of Omri, a former king. The name of Hosea's son was a reminder to King Jehu that God intended to punish him for this crime.

Israel, Like Gomer, Is Unfaithful

Then they had a daughter whom they named "Not Pitied." This was a way of telling Israel, the northern kingdom, that her days were numbered because of her infidelity. Their third child was another boy, whom they called, "Not My People." God's gift of election would now pass to the southern kingdom of Judah alone. Each child represented the increasing alienation of Israel from God, ending in total rejection.

The second chapter shifts from Hosea's domestic situation to a conversation between God and his faithless wife, Israel. Here we have a fascinating description of how God tries tirelessly to keep Israel united to him. At the beginning of the chapter, God assumes the attitude of a slighted lover. Then, by repeated attempts at correcting his beloved, he seeks to win her back. His first punishment is to treat her like a shameless woman, according to the customs of the time.

He will then rob the land of all fertility and prosperity. "Therefore, I will take back my grain . . . and my wine. . . . And I will lay waste her vines and her fig trees. . . . I will make them a forest and the wild animals shall devour them" (Hosea 2:9, 12, NRSV).

Return to the Innocence of the Days in the Desert

Happily, these corrective tests work, for, having removed the demoralizing luxury of Israel, God brings her into a desert where she can know him again. "I will allure her, bring her into the wilderness, and speak tenderly to her. . . . She shall respond as in the days of her youth" (Hosea 2:14-15, NRSV). The real clue in this passage is the word "desert." As the centuries passed, the memory of Israel's days in the desert during the time of the exodus was idealized. If distance lends enchantment to the view, then this is a fine example. The passage of time tended to glamorize the innocence and childlikeness of that early desert community.

It is perfectly human to gloss over the harsh features of the distant past and endow it with a dreamlike quality. After all, Israel's wanderings in the desert were a time when Israel knew no other God but Yahweh. That was when she really knew how to be his bride. Other prophets would be equally strong in picking up the desert theme as a lever for promoting reform among the Israelites. In other words, the prophets urged Israel to return to the ideals found in the origin of the race. It is something like telling present Notre Dame football players to remember former greats like Knute Rockne and George Gipp. This has an inspirational value as well as a current lesson for the hearers.

Thus, God, having removed the material prosperity of Israel, put her in a sort of desert where she could think about turning to him again in love. When she renewed her commitment to God, he would give her back the vineyards, send rain from the sky and harvests from the earth. Wild animals would not harm her, nor would enemy nations wage war against her. "I will espouse you to me for ever . . . in justice, in love, and in mercy" (Hosea 2:21).

God Remains Faithful to His People

The principal message of the whole book is brought out in this line: "I will espouse you in fidelity" (Hosea 2:22). The translation of the Jerusalem Bible is worth quoting here: "I will betroth you to myself with tenderness." Biblical commentaries are fond of using the Hebrew word *hesed* for faithfulness at this point. The basic meaning of the word is "bond," or "contract." If it is applied to human relationships, it takes on the meaning of loyalty. Hence, what is being said in this text, and indeed in the whole book of Hosea, is that God never ceases to be loyal to a people with whom he has pledged a contract.

No matter how faithless the people may be, no matter how often they may act like an adulteress, God remains loyal to his part of the covenant. And this is not just a passive loyalty, for he tries to woo them back to him. He makes efforts to discover ways to win their hearts back to him.

It is true that God cannot bless his people once they are faithless, but he always stands ready to grant his blessing, and he is anxious to grant it, once they are open to him again. So if Hosea is to be remembered for anything, it should not be for just the story of his fickle wife, Gomer. Rather, it should be because he celebrates the *hesed*, the incredible loyalty of God to a solemn agreement he has made with people.

We may run after other gods and seek false prophets who satisfy our itching ears for new winds of doctrine. God, who has a patience befitting his wisdom, pursues a thousand ways to win us back. We can do no better than quote the final wise advice of Hosea:

> *Let him who is wise understand these things;*
> *let him who is prudent know them.*
> *Straight are the paths of the LORD,*
> *In them the just walk,*
> *But sinners stumble in them.*

HOSEA 14:10

REFLECTION

For a culture where broken promises are as common as the vagaries of the weather, Hosea's emphasis on fidelity to one's promises is a welcome tonic. His message is all about staying faithful. Spouses who vow permanent fidelity on the day of their marriage should keep this promise. People who sign contracts are expected to live up to the terms. Should not business leaders be loyal to the customers who have invested in their enterprise? Ought not politicians keep their campaign promises? Would this not be a better world if we kept the promises to God made at our baptisms and confirmations? A society littered with the dead bones of broken promises becomes fragile, fragmented, and fatalistic.

The prophetic call to fidelity is linked to the meaning of covenant. The promises made in a covenant are meant to be as binding as the solemn vows made by monks to God or the spousal vows of eternal love made by bride and groom at a wedding. In a biblical covenant God and the partners to the covenant pledge undying loyalty to one another. Such promises are meant to have the sturdiness of passionate love and the durability of a rock. It demands perseverance, fidelity, and a seriousness of intent.

History and experience illustrate the difficulty of doing this. Human nature is weak, frail, and fickle. Unhappily, we often break our promises, act disloyally, and escape our responsibilities. But what makes our covenant with God different from all human encounters, is a divine partner who never breaks the promises, always offers love and forever seeks to mend any break in the relationship. God does not pout, give up easily, or write us off as a bad investment. As long as we live, we can count on God always looking at us with open arms, bearing a forgiving smile, welcoming us back to the covenant, and delighting to see us come home.

So do not be discouraged by failures in fidelity. Be prepared for a reunion with God. Keep your heart open to a revival of love and a restoration of a covenant relationship with God. The Lord is still saying, "I want to betroth you to me forever."

FOR DIALOGUE

How do you feel when someone breaks a promise to you? How do you react to a person who is disloyal to you? What lessons have you learned from disloyalty and broken promises? When people tell you they are fearful of making a lifelong marital vow, what do you say to them?

If you are questioned about the meaning of covenant in Scripture what is your reply? Why is the sense of security in a biblical covenant due to God's never failing loyalty so reassuring? What are some stories you can tell about friendships and marriages that witness fidelity?

In the life of Jesus we see an example of his loving his disciples to the end. He is faithful until death. What do you think can be done to restore this kind of fidelity in our culture?

PRAYER

Faithful Lord, we praise you for your loving fidelity to us and to our salvation. In your mercy teach us loyalty to you and give us the grace to live in fidelity to the covenant we have with you.

A faithful friend is an elixir of life.

SIRACH 6:16

THE NEW TESTAMENT

CHAPTER 29

The Revelation of Jesus Christ, Son of God and Son of Mary

Luke 2:1-21; John 1:1-18

Jesus... emptied himself, taking the form of a servant, being born in the likeness of men... At the name of Jesus every knee should bow... and every tongue confess that Jesus Christ is Lord.

PHILIPPIANS 2:7, 10-11

Now that you have read about the patriarchs, kings, and prophets of Israel, I hope you have found in them the breath of God and a sense of his beauty and goodness. I trust you have become aware of God's loving plan to save us as it unfolded in the history of salvation as it is recorded in the Old Testament. In a special way the prophets helped their people and us to sense the dynamic flow of history toward the birth of the Messiah, the Savior of the world.

Our principal source for the revelation of Jesus Christ is the gospels. The four gospels give us four portraits of Jesus. Each gospel offers us a unique vision of the person and message of Jesus. But all the gospels are united in proclaiming that Jesus Christ is the Son of God and the Savior of the world.

St. Paul gives us the first clue: "But when the time had fully come, God sent forth his Son, born of a woman, born under the law, to redeem those who were under the law, so that we might receive adoption" (Galatians 4:4). Through Jesus, we are adopted into the family of God. Jesus echoes this truth in his words to Nicodemus. "For God so loved the world, that he gave his only Son, so that whoever believes in him should not perish, but have eternal life. For God sent the Son into the world, not to condemn the world, but that the world might be saved through him" (John 3:16-17).

Each gospel portrait of Jesus gives us a unique vision of Jesus. In Matthew's gospel, Jesus centers his message and miracles on the arrival of the kingdom of God, a kingdom of salvation from sin and of justice, mercy, and love. Jesus links the kingdom to the church that will be its witness. The interior spiritual kingdom will be expressed in the public life of the church. Jesus establishes his church by choosing Peter to be its rock and shepherd. Further,

Jesus forms the twelve apostles to carry on the ministry of kingdom and church after he has died, risen from the dead, and ascended into heaven.

In Mark's gospel we behold a Jesus who concentrates on the formation of disciples. Central to this is Christ's challenge to deny the self, take up the cross, and follow him (cf. Mark 8:34-38). In a variety of ways Jesus shapes the beliefs, attitudes, and behaviors of those he calls to discipleship. Our relationship to Christ is more than that of a student and a teacher; it is the relationship of a disciple to a master. A student need not have any personal commitment to a teacher. A disciple not only believes what the Master says, but must enter into a bond as profound as love and to a behavior as challenging as the master's.

In Luke's gospel we encounter the human face of Jesus along with his divine presence. Jesus comes across as a people person, especially in his relationships with women who figure prominently in the narrative. Meals hold a prominent place in this gospel. Where else is one going to feel more human, more in touch with family and community than in the intimacy of a meal? Jesus appears frequently at table, using this personal environment as an excellent way to share himself and his vision. The human face of Jesus at these multiple repasts glows with affection for friends, frowns in anger at hypocrites, arches with mock despair at the follies of guests, smiles with welcome at their virtues, and sings heartily at festive meals. Aside from the Last Supper, no meal in the gospels is more beautiful that the one that takes place at Emmaus. In this gospel Jesus overflows with mercy and compassion. His humanity and divinity form a seamless garment.

In John's gospel the divine presence of Jesus is uppermost. Almost everything Jesus does reveals his glory — his divine appearance. The gospel starts with an account of the pre-existence of Jesus as the Word, the divine Son of God who becomes flesh from the womb of the virgin Mary. Constantly, Jesus uses the expression "I AM." God had revealed himself as I AM to Moses at the burning bush. Jesus repeatedly applied the expression to himself in this gospel: "I AM the living bread" (cf. John 6:51); "I AM the good shepherd" (cf. John 10:14); "I AM the resurrection and the life" (cf. John 11:25). Easter is the best perspective for appreciating the Jesus of John's gospel. The radiant glory of the risen Jesus shines upon the whole gospel. At the same time, the humanity of Jesus never fails to appear, for it is the sign through which his glory is revealed.

It is my hope that the following meditations on Jesus Christ will draw you to have a personal relationship with him. Bring your faith, hope, and love to these considerations. Only when you begin to experience the warmth of Christ's love for you will the significance of his revelation in the gospels begin to dawn on you. His story does not end with a death, but with a resurrection. Hence we who believe in Jesus do not simply look at him as one who lived in the past, but as one who is spiritually present to us today. Then you may begin to join the praise of Christ that resounds continually in heaven:

You are worthy to take the scroll and to open its seals, for you were slaugh-tered and by your blood you ransomed for God saints from every tribe and language and people and nation; you have made them to be a kingdom and priests serving our God, and they will reign on earth.

REVELATION 5:9-10

REFLECTION

The faith of the Church from New Testament times onward holds that Jesus Christ is both divine and human. Because he is divine, he has the power to reconcile us to God and overcome our separation from God due to our sins. Because he is human, he is able to achieve our salvation through the human nature that he assumed. The divine Word became flesh and lived among us.

In early Christian history there were some who found this too difficult to accept. Some denied that Jesus was human; he only appeared that way. He was God who just seemed to be human. Others denied he was fully God; he was godlike but not truly the Son of God equal to the Father. In each case the mystery of the union of the divine and the human in Jesus appeared to be impossible. It was not fitting that God should be confined in a human being. Recalling this dilemma, the poet W. H. Auden wrote:

How could the eternal do a temporal act?
The infinite become a finite act.

Eventually, the Church responded to these difficulties with ecu-menical councils that affirmed the ancient faith in the Incarnation of Christ. The council fathers found language that upheld this truth of faith so well that it is still prayed each Sunday in the Nicene Creed. We deepen our faith in the full truth about Jesus through our regular participation in the celebration of the Eucharist, our con-stant turning to Jesus in prayer, and our acquisition of the virtues of prudence, justice, temperance, and fortitude, as well as the virtues of patience and humility.

The best way to understand these truths about Jesus is to love him and live by his teachings. Christ calls us to friendship with him. Our union with Jesus brings about a transformation of our lives into his likeness. The more we do this, the more clearly we understand who he is.

FOR DIALOGUE

Why is it important to note that we need all four gospels to obtain a clearer understanding of Jesus and his mission? In other words, why not choose a gospel that appeals to us and let that be a sufficient source for our appreciation of the identity of Christ? Furthermore, what additional insight about Jesus could we obtain from the Acts of the Apostles and the New Testament letters?

It is claimed here that knowledge of Jesus is best achieved by loving him and imitating his life. What examples could you cite from your life where your knowledge of someone is greater because you have a relationship of love or friendship with that person? How true might it be to say, "To love me is to know me?"

Another path to realizing who Jesus is rests on the life of virtue. The classical virtues are prudence, justice, temperance, and fortitude, all of which are present in Christ's life and teachings. How would you measure your maturity in these virtues? Jesus also taught and witnessed patience and humility. How well do you practice these Christian virtues?

PRAYER

Lord Jesus, help us to know you by loving you. Awaken our need to practice the virtues you taught and witnessed. Grant us the grace to spend our time imitating your love, justice, mercy, and reconciling attitude and behavior. Make us living, active members of your presence among us.

Jesus, you came into the world heralding the new age foretold by the prophets. Give your holy people the gift of renewal in every generation.
INTERCESSION AT CHRISTMAS EVENING PRAYER

CHAPTER 30

St. Matthew's Account of the Birth of Jesus

Matthew 1-2

Now the birth of Jesus Christ took place in this way.

MATTHEW 1:18

S ongs, lights, gift-wrappings, smiles, ribbons, parties are part of the Christmas season in our culture. This is a season when the dream of Christian love becomes so real you can just about touch it. There is an ad that says, "A diamond is forever." The same is true of the meaning of Christmas. It introduces a spirit into our culture that, ultimately, will outlast the wars and human hate.

To discuss the meaning of Christmas we must turn to the scriptural record of the birth of Jesus. First we shall examine the birth account in St. Matthew's gospel, chapters 1 to 2, then the nativity account in the gospel of St. Luke.

JESUS' FAMILY TREE

Matthew's narrative of Christ's birth is made up of six stories: the family tree (genealogy) of Jesus; Joseph's dilemma; the wise men; the flight into Egypt; the slaughter of the holy innocents; the joyous return to Nazareth.

There was a time when people in our culture had little interest in their ancestral roots, but a change has occurred in which families are excited about researching their family trees. This is a recovery of an ancient tradition as exemplified in the beginning of Matthew's gospel. The strange names may be puzzling, but there are items of interest to attract us.

There are three sets of fourteen names in the family tree. The name "David" was "worth" fourteen; that is, the letters for "David," in the Hebrews' numerology system, added up to fourteen. Matthew used this image to show us that Jesus is the new David. He identified Jesus with the most loved public figure in Israel's memory. David had been promised that his throne would last forever. In political terms this did not happen, but in spiritual terms it did. Jesus was of the family of David, but his kingdom was a spiritual one of salvation, love, mercy, and justice. Matthew's family tree of Jesus is something like a cheerleading section shouting: "David! David! David!" The name was familiar. The reality was infinitely greater.

What Else Does the Family Tree Show Us about Christ?

These three sets of fourteen names also summarize the three main periods of Israel's history: the period of the patriarchs and judges, the period of the prophets and kings, and the period of the wisdom speakers and writers after the exile. Jesus will give meaning to the patriarchal period as the new Moses, to the kingly time as one greater than David; to the period after the exile as the real Son of Man and Wisdom Incarnate.

Lastly, the family tree shows that Jesus comes from a family of real people, and that he has a Jewish ancestry. The skeletons in the closet and the black sheep are there, including some of the least worthy kings of Judah. This is a case of history, "warts and all." And there is a sideline glance at Ruth, a Gentile girl among the Jewish women.

The notable sinners in the genealogy remind us that Jesus came to save all sinners.

Joseph's Dilemma

Joseph discovers that the woman he is about to marry is pregnant. Like any young husband-to-be, he is upset at this discovery. It takes a dream and a prophecy to calm him down. The angel of his dream assures Joseph that Mary has conceived by the power of the Holy Spirit. Matthew quotes the words of Isaiah about a virginal conception to confirm the dream, for Mary is actually the virgin who will conceive the promised Emmanuel-Child (Isaiah 7:14). This old prophecy had first been spoken to King Ahaz, who had been losing faith in God. He was assured of a son whom God would bless. The name "Emmanuel" means "God with us." Jesus would be the real Emmanuel, the Son of God made man.

The Story of the Wise Men, the Magi

The story of the wise men has, out of devotion, been embellished through the years. They are now pictured as being kings and numbered as three. Statues often portray them as Asian, African, and European. The imagery of kings arises from a meditation on Psalm 72.

> *May the kings of Tarshish and of the isles render him tribute;*
> *may the kings of Sheba and Seba bring gifts!*
> *May all kings fall down before him, all nations serve him!*
>
> PSALM 72:10-11

The adoration of the wise men brings full meaning to the forecast that the whole world would eventually pay homage to the Messiah (see Isaiah 60:6). The wise men have come to be numbered as three because of the three gifts gold: incense, and myrrh. The Fathers of the Church saw the gold as a sign of Christ's royalty, the incense as the mark of his divinity, and the myrrh as the indication of his passion and burial.

In this story, there is a star and a prophecy. The prophet Micah is recalled as the one who claimed the Messiah would be born in Bethlehem (see Micah 5:2). A mysterious star appears in the sky and, like a guiding angel, leads the wise men to the infant Jesus — the end of their quest.

The Flight into Egypt

Matthew recounts Herod's threat to kill Jesus. Once again, a dream and a prophecy are the way of solution and survival. The angel warns Joseph in a dream, and the holy family goes into exile. After Herod's death an angel comes to call the family back to Galilee. Matthew sees in this God's way of giving fuller meaning to the old prophecy of Hosea: "Out of Egypt I called my son" (Hosea 11:1). The first adopted "son" of God, Israel, had been called out of Egypt in the exodus. Now, God's real Son also is called to leave Egypt.

The Holy Innocents

The slaughter of a number of babies in the vicinity of Bethlehem by a jealous king is one of the darker pages of history. Herod was so threatened by the thought of a rival king that he lashed out against the defenseless infants of a quiet town. Matthew cites no dream or angel, but quotes a prophecy to accompany this story. "A voice was heard in Ramah, sobbing and loud lamentation, Rachel weeping for her children; she would not be consoled, since they were no more" (Matthew 2:18).

Jewish history recalls Israel's national mourning, symbolized in the voice of Rachel, at the time of the great deportation of the Jews by the Assyrians, during which a number of children and babies were killed. As Jeremiah put it, "Rachel is weeping for her children; she refuses to be comforted for her children, because they are no more" (Jeremiah 31:15).

The Joyous Return

The death of the old tyrant Herod was a signal for the end of the holy family's exile. Again we have a dream and a prophecy. The angel of Joseph's dream announces the good news that they can go home, but that they should settle in Nazareth. A popular prophecy of the ancient times supported the idea that the Messiah shall be called a Nazarene. There is no prophetic statement in Scripture exactly like this. Scripture does speak of "Nazirite Vows" taken by certain consecrated men (cf. Numbers 6:1-21).

But this does not refer to Nazareth. It is the title for men who followed a special type of spiritual discipline. It might be noted here that, in the early Church, the followers of Jesus were called Nazarenes in the Hebrew world. The Greek-Roman world called them Christians — the term that endured.

Birth of Jesus Linked to the Story of Moses

There are details in Matthew's account that link Jesus to the person of Moses. The infant Moses survived when many innocent Hebrew children were drowned, just as Jesus survived the killing of the innocents. Christ's temporary exile to Egypt is parallel to Moses' exile at Midian. Pharaoh's oppression caused Moses to leave Egypt, and Herod's death was the occasion of Christ leaving Egypt. These links with Moses, plus the prophecies and dream-angels, are woven into a pattern that links the birth of Jesus to the history of salvation. But Jesus is more than another David or Moses; he is the Son of God and Savior of the world.

The series of Old Testament promises and New Testament fulfillment also shows Jesus as the one who brings final meaning to the Old Testament theology. We have already noted in our treatment of the prophets that Jesus is the fullness of revelation. In him is the light that streams backward to give the full meaning of what God's plan of salvation was in the Old Testament and flows forward in the New Testament, Apostolic Tradition, and the history of our Church to help our faith to see the plan of salvation today. In our Christian interpretation of Scripture, Christ is the key to our approach.

Later on in Matthew, Jesus says he does not come to destroy the Torah, the law of the Old Testament, but to fulfill it. To modern eyes, this may seem like a complicated code, too troublesome to unravel. But to the eyes of faith of its first readers, this account was perfectly acceptable. The story still tells us today that Jesus is our Lord and king. He survived violence, jealousy, and exile to bring us a vision and a hope of freedom. His death and resurrection and sending of the Spirit is the ultimate key to the meaning of all history.

REFLECTION

Matthew's history of the birth of Jesus is popularly reflected in Christian art. The Old Masters loved to paint the adoration of the Magi, the Massacre of the Innocents, and the Flight into Egypt.

Our religious Christmas cards give us annual reminders of some of these scenes. The sense of a history of salvation in Matthew is important for our faith. In earlier cultures of Christian faith, history was never a purely secular matter. God's presence and plans in history were assumed. It was taken for granted that human history always had a divine dimension. We may say that Jesus split history into B.C. and A.D.

In our more secularized times, there is little or no reference to a divine action in history. Moreover, in a scientific culture where the pace is fast and furious, there is impatience with any kind of history whether sacred or secular. Efforts are made to make people pay attention to history with axioms like, "Those who forget history are condemned to repeat it." All of this is a pity especially for people of Christian faith, since the biblical account of creation, covenants, prophecies, salvation in Christ, the founding of the Church, the revelation of the Father, Son, and Spirit, the very gospels themselves is expressed in the form and context of a "history of salvation."

The particular gift of Matthew's infancy narrative is precisely the historical context. Now, we admit that he and other scriptural authors did not write history the way it is done today. But differing cultural styles must not be pitted against one another. Scientific ways of writing history should not cancel out earlier cultural methods, which were quite effective in transmitting history and its truths. Biblical history is written from the aspect of faith.

Consistent with the culture of those days, the authors used literary forms that employ figurative language, poetry, song, parable, facts, chronicles, and similar methods. The bottom line is that their faith helped them see God's providential presence and action in human history. Our faith is essentially connected to theirs through the action of the Spirit who opens our eyes and hearts to this divine, loving, and saving revelation.

FOR DIALOGUE

When you reflect on Christmas, what kind of thoughts and feelings arise? Which is your favorite feast in the liturgy — Christmas or Easter? Why?

When you read Matthew 1-2, you find him frequently quoting the Old Testament. Why did he do this? Our reflection notes he also records several dreams in which an angel appears to direct Joseph. What might be two reasons that God sent angels to Joseph?

Because of our faith we are able to see that Jesus fulfilled the promises of the prophets in the Old Testament. God kept his promises. What are examples of kept promises you can cite from your own experience?

PRAYER

Dear Jesus, Son of God and Son of Mary, thank you for coming to earth to save us from our sins and give us divine life. Help us always to rejoice in the mystery of your incarnation and to live out the consequences of our calling.

Sing, my tongue, the Savior's glory,
Of his flesh the mystery sing;
Of the Blood all price exceeding,
Shed by our immortal King.

ST. THOMAS AQUINAS

CHAPTER 31

St. Luke's Account of the Birth of Christ

Luke 1-2

"For to you is born this day in the city of David a Savior, who is Christ the Lord."

LUKE 2:11

Reading St. Luke's Christmas story, chapters 1 and 2, is like hearing the best-loved carols. It has the golden richness of an expensive Christmas card, the warmth of a Yule log, and the splendor of a midnight Mass. In all of biblical literature, Luke's Christmas story holds a unique place, both because of its poetic celebration of the birth of Jesus and its rich pattern of scriptural images.

THE INFLUENCE OF JEWISH THINKING AND MARY'S PRESENCE

To write his story, Luke consulted the traditional teaching and preaching of the apostolic community. His research into the development of the apostolic preaching showed him that the original sermons clustered around the public ministry of Jesus. By the time of his writing, interest in the circumstances of Christ's birth had surfaced.

We have no record of how Mary would have influenced Luke's account, but there are speculations. One view states that Mary told her story to the community of women who ministered to Jesus, most likely after Pentecost when the full picture of what Jesus had accomplished was revealed. They in turn would have passed her account on to the apostles. At some point an infancy narrative tradition would have developed.

In this view, one would see Luke's Christmas story as the poetic and exalted gospel which Mary, the virgin daughter of Zion, sang after she had contemplated this mystery in her heart over the years.

The Christmas narrative has the strong imprint of Jewish thinking together with the dominant presence of Mary. With this material, Luke presents us with his account of the origin of Jesus.

Luke's House of Parallels

One of the striking features of this narrative is Luke's use of numerous parallels. There are two annunciation scenes, one to Zechariah, the other to Mary. Zechariah sings the Benedictus (Luke 1:68-79) to welcome his son, John. Mary chants the beautiful Magnificat (Luke 1:46-55) to celebrate the approaching birth of Jesus. The birth story of John the Baptist is balanced by the birth story of Jesus. The visit of angels is matched by the visit of shepherds. Christ's presentation in the temple is echoed by the finding of Christ in the temple.

The Annunciation to Mary

The angel Gabriel appeared to Mary and addressed her as full of grace, a most highly favored one. The angel told her that she will conceive a son and call him Jesus. He will be called the Son of the Most High. He will mount the throne of David. His kingdom will last forever. Mary questioned the angel, asking how this could happen since she did not have relations with Joseph. Gabriel told her the conception would be caused by the Holy Spirit.

Now Gabriel waited for Mary's reply. God invited Mary to accept this gift. But even God must wait for an answer. In that silence Mary gathered up her whole soul for an answer. As her answer coursed to her lips, it arose from the depths of her heart. "Let it be done to me according to your word." Her "Let it be done" echoed God's creative words in Genesis, chapter 1. Her word was an act of faith and obedience. She conceived Jesus in her heart before conceiving him in her womb by the power of the Spirit. "And the Word became flesh and dwelt among us" (John 1:14).

The Visitation

Gabriel had told Mary that her cousin Elizabeth had conceived a child and was now in her sixth month of pregnancy. Mary journeyed to Ain Karim to be with Elizabeth. Her cousin greeted her with three "blesseds." "Blessed are you among women!" "Blessed is the fruit of your womb!" "Blessed are you for having believed Gabriel!" (cf. Luke 1:39-45). Elizabeth wondered how could it be that the mother of her *Lord* could be there.

These seven verses spoken by Elizabeth — filled with the Holy Spirit — are packed with invitations to prayer and contemplation. Mary did become the most blessed of all women because she is the mother of God, Jesus Christ — the fruit of her womb. The grace of God moved her to be the greatest woman of faith. Blessed is Mary for having believed. Finally, Elizabeth is inspired to say that Mary is the mother of her Lord, meaning her God. Mary brought Jesus who sanctified John in the womb of Elizabeth.

Mary's response to these wonders was her hymn, the Magnificat, a song of praise for God and a celebration of the gift of humility she had received from God.

Jesus Is Born in David's Royal City

Joseph and Mary journey to Bethlehem to register for the imperial census. While there, her time to deliver her baby had come. Since there was no room at the inn, they went to a cave that was used as a stable. There, Mary gave birth to Jesus. She wrapped him in swaddling clothes and laid him in a manger — a food bin for the animals. Jesus would one day call himself the Bread of Life. This food symbolism expands as we note that Bethlehem means "House of Bread."

In this humble setting the Son of God and Savior of the world was born. "Though he was in the form of God, he did not think equality with God something to be grasped. Rather he emptied himself, taking the form of a slave, coming in human likeness, and found human in appearance he humbled himself" (Philippians 2:6-7).

The Song of the Angels

In those days musicians would often come to a home where a new baby was born and greet the child with welcome songs. At a shepherd's field near the stable, angels appeared in the sky and supplied the welcome song, "Glory to God in the highest and on earth peace." They announced Christ's birth to the shepherds, telling them the world's savior was just born.

The Adoration of the Shepherds

After the angels disappeared, the shepherds searched for and found the cave where Jesus was born. They knelt in adoration of the child. They were filled with faith. They contemplated the mystery of Christ and rested in it. They beheld the God upon whom they depended for life turn to his mother's breast for the milk of survival. Shepherds were close to the mystery of nature and of God. Their appearance at the birth scene was relaxing and appropriate. The first people invited to the crib were persons whose faith and love would best appreciate what had happened. We pray with the shepherds, "O hold Jesus tenderly, dear mother, for he rules our hearts."

The Theme of the Temple

After the birth of Jesus, Luke's narrative moves from the crib to the temple. The first two chapters of Luke's gospel are like a piece of music that gradually grows louder until it reaches its peak in Christ's being brought to the temple. "And when the time came for their purification according to the law of Moses, they brought him up to Jerusalem to present him to the Lord" (Luke 2:22).

Hopes of the Prophets Realized

The infant Jesus came to the temple to seal the hopes and visions of the prophets. The aged prophet, Simeon, came forward and took the holy child in his arms. With tears of joy, he proclaimed that prophecy may now stop, since what was prophesied is now present. As he cradled Jesus in his arms, he swayed with joy. From Simeon Jesus heard the first human hymn that was composed out of love for him. Then the prophetess, Anna, came to the temple and publicly expresses her thanks. Her thanks reflected the gratitude of the people of God, acknowledging that their waiting and hopes have not been in vain.

The Finding in the Temple

When Jesus was twelve years old, the age at which he officially reached manhood, he went up to Jerusalem with his parents to celebrate Passover. At the end of the feast the women's caravan left first. The men's group left a little later. Jesus lingered at the temple discussing religion with the rabbis. Joseph and Mary, each thinking the son was with the other parent, met at the camp and discovered that Jesus was missing.

They returned to Jerusalem and found Jesus among the rabbis. Distraught, they asked him why he had done this to them. He replied, "Did you not know that I must be in my Father's house?" (Luke 2:49). They did not understand what he meant. He did return with them, remained obedient to them and grew in wisdom, age and favor before God and people.

Mary contemplated Christ's words and all the other experiences of the hidden life at Nazareth. In those quiet years, Mary was in daily contact with the human incarnation of the Son of God. Scripture draws a veil over those years of communion in which the mother shaped the Son — and the Son's mystery was revealed to her. Like any mother she was pleased to see him grow in wisdom and age. As the greatest believer who ever lived, she became the first and greatest disciple of her son.

REFLECTION

The figure of Mary pervades this meditation on the birth of Jesus. Her yes to God's call and the surrender of her undivided heart to the will of God stand before us as the attitude we need to bring to the understanding and witnessing of the incarnation. The warm glow of Christmas should not obscure the tough choices that Christ's birth implies for us. Mary was free from all sin — consecrated from the first instant of her conception — and filled with growing faith to the day Gabriel presented an incredible choice to her: "Mary, will you say yes to the call of God to be the mother of his Son?" God's grace and her obedient humility led her to say yes. She continued to do so for the rest of her life. God also calls us to say our own obedient yes in faith to him. It will take many forms and challenges. We always have divine grace and the indwelling of the Spirit to help us.

As Luke shows us, we must go beyond the crib to the temple. By all means, let us enjoy the wonder of a newborn baby, but we cannot be detained at the stable, no more than Jesus was. Jesus went on to the temple to anoint the holy place and seal the hopes of all people. This, also, is our Christian task. United with Mary we are to search into the riches of the mystery of Jesus Christ to bring his promise of fulfillment to all those who wait and hope. On the holy night we hear the carol: "O come, all ye faithful!" With Joseph, Mary, the angels, the shepherds, and the Magi we will join the liturgy of adoration, knowing that in the dawn we will bring this message of hope and salvation to our families, friends, and community.

FOR DIALOGUE

In Matthew's gospel we witness the adoration of the Magi. In Luke we see the adoration of the shepherds. What would you say has been the role of adoration of Christ in your faith life? Why is adoration so beneficial for your faith growth? What does adoration say to you about your relationship to Christ?

In Luke's presentation of the Christmas mystery, the Virgin Mary is the dominant presence. In what way have you found Mary helping you to get closer to Christ? As you meditate on Mary's faith, how does it help you deepen your own sense of faith? How does the silence of Mary affect your inner need to silently focus on Christ?

Christ's incarnation was an act of humility in which the Son of God took on the humble status of a human being. As you reflect on your soul, what do you see of pride, vanity, and arrogance? How would your union with the humble Jesus purify wrongful pride from your life and obtain for yourself the gift of humility?

PRAYER

Jesus Christ, in the wonder of your incarnation, your eternal Word has brought to the eyes of faith a new and radiant vision of your glory. In you we see our God made visible and so are caught up in the love of the God we cannot see. We join the angels in proclaiming your glory.

FIRST PREFACE FOR CHRISTMAS

Mary,
Answer with a word. Receive the Word.
Speak your human word. Conceive the divine Word.
Breathe a passing word. Embrace the eternal Word.

ST. BERNARD OF CLAIRVAUX,
MEDITATION ON THE ANNUNCIATION

CHAPTER 32

John the Baptist Preaches Conversion

Mark 3:1-17; John 1:19-34

John the baptizer appeared in the wilderness, preaching a baptism of repentance for the forgiveness of sins.

MARK 1:4

Preparing for the Second Vatican Council, Pope John XXIII sent out his call from the banks of the Tiber summoning the Church to spiritual renewal. Some years ago, Dr. Martin Luther King stood before the Lincoln Memorial by the banks of the Potomac and called on the American people to change their hearts about civil rights for blacks and other minority groups. And in the gospels we behold John the Baptist standing on Jordan's bank, shouting to Jerusalem and all Judea for a radical change of heart.

FOUR ELEMENTS IN THE JORDAN STORIES

There are four elements in the Jordan stories that need our attention here: (1) the Isaiah prophecy, chapters 40 to 66; (2) the judgment on the faith and morals of the people; (3) the reply of the people; (4) the baptism of Jesus. Let's look at each of these.

The Isaiah prophecy. Today, when an American politician needs something to support his speeches, he often turns to a familiar source — the Constitution. Just as a country's constitution is a favorite authority on political matters, so the book of Isaiah was the favorite prophetic source for the gospel writers. John the Baptist identified with the memory and teaching of Isaiah.

In Isaiah, chapters 40 to 66, the prophet consoled the Hebrew exiles in Babylon. Their seventy-year captivity was over, and they would return to see God's glory in the Holy Land. The joy of this historic return, however, would be but an image of the wonderful happiness that their descendants would know when the Savior would come to usher in the messianic age. Isaiah told of the herald of this good news — of the Messiah's coming — standing in the desert and calling for a preparation worthy of a king's arrival. In poetic language, the herald spoke of rolling away mountains and filling vast valleys to build a remarkable highway for the Lord.

Get Ready for the Lord

Now John the Baptist stood in the wilderness, which symbolized the desert of the exodus and the Israelites' glorious victory over Egypt. John became the herald of the good news and proclaimed the arrival of the messianic age. Get ready for the Lord! The highway that must be built for the coming Lord is one of repentance. The hills of pride and the valleys of despair must be swept away so that people may be open to the Lord's salvation.

The Greek word for repentance is *metanoia*. Its basic meaning is "conversion." John's urgent call was not just for external penances, though these are not excluded, but for an interior change of the attitudes of the heart. People's hearts must turn away from sin and turn towards faith and commitment to God. John practiced both. He lived on a diet that would put even a modern dieter to shame. Without embarrassment, he chose the harsh wilderness. But for John, the external penances were a sign of the purification of his heart. He sought the total gift of himself to God.

The Hour of Judgment

John's sermons were so rousing that he reminded people of ancient prophets like Elijah. The poor and the proud came out in droves to hear him. John was in no mood for sweet talk and soft words. Far from praising his listeners' pious interest in sermons, he attacked their spiritual blindness. "You brood of vipers! Who warned you to flee from the wrath to come? Bear fruits that befit repentance, and do not begin to say to yourselves, 'We have Abraham as our father'; for I tell you, God is able from these stones to raise up children to Abraham. Even now the axe is laid to the root of the trees; every tree therefore that does not bear good fruit is cut down and thrown into the fire" (Luke 3:7-9).

Shaking Up the Comfortable

John accused them of turning their religion into a lifeless formality. Their religion had hardened into mere bones on which the Spirit did not breathe life and, like a dead old tree, it must be cut down. Indeed, the ax was already measuring the root. With such strong language, John attempted to shake them from their contentment with themselves.

The People Reply, "What Shall We Do?"

John burned a path into the hearts of his honest listeners. He led them to question the meaning of their lives. On all sides, the cry arose: "What shall we do?" John aroused a sense of justice in the people. He bade the wealthy give food and clothing to the poor. He urged tax agents to renounce all crooked practices. He urged soldiers to refrain from armed robbery, and to learn how to be content with their army pay (see Luke 3:10-14). John pleaded for a moral change like that preached by the great prophets. This change of heart and behavior is the best preparation for the arrival of the Lord.

Jesus Comes to Be Baptized

Now Jesus makes his first public appearance as an adult. He comes to his cousin John to be baptized. John had been preaching that the Messiah would soon arrive, and now here he was. John tried to prevent him from being baptized, saying that he [John] should be baptized by Jesus. But Jesus urged him to proceed, "Let it be so now; for thus it is fitting for us to fulfil all righteousness" (Matthew 3:15).

> *John is the lamp in the presence of the sun, the voice in the presence of the Word, the friend in the presence of the Bridegroom, the one who leapt in his mother's womb in the presence of him who was adored in the womb.*
> ST. GREGORY OF NAZIANZUS, LH, VOL. I, P. 635

Jesus waded into the water but did not confess any sins, for there were none to tell. Humbly he adopted the posture of a sinner out of sympathy and compassion for sinners. In this way he let sinners know he loved them and would liberate them from humanity's worst problem, the problem of sin. He accepted this cleansing sign to show that this would be his own mission. The waters did not cleanse him. He cleansed the waters.

As Jordan's waters flowed over his body, the sky opened and revealed the mystery of God the Father. The Father spoke to Jesus words of love and delight. "Thou art my beloved Son; with thee I am well pleased" (Mark 1:11). Then the Holy Spirit, dovelike, rested over him. In the creation story, God's breathlike Spirit hovered over the chaotic waters and from them drew forth the dawn of a new creation. "Darkness covered the [earth], while a ... wind [God's creative breath-Spirit] swept over the face of the waters" (Genesis 1:2). Now over the waters of the Jordan, the Holy Spirit hovers to confirm the dawn of a new creation in Christ. This is a trinitarian scene with the Father's voice, the Spirit's creative presence, and the Son's humble redeeming act.

Jesus Brings Full Meaning to John's Teaching

At the Jordan, Jesus brings full meaning to the teaching of John. Jesus makes the dreams of the poor and humble come true. He establishes forever a vision that rescues the hopeless from despair. The best news of all is not just that he is dedicated to working for justice for all, but that he will make people just, save them from sin, and bring them the gift of divine life. Through his passion and resurrection, Jesus will enable men to be released from the heavy burden of guilt and sin that causes them so much anxiety. The saving work of Jesus will give people a sense of being just. This is not a self-righteous justice, born of false piety, but a humble and honest justice proceeding from God himself.

The liturgy of Advent and the feast of Christ's baptism recall and celebrate the Jordan baptism. All Christians again go down to Jordan to hear the plea for change, the reminder that the ax is laid to the root. In their hearts, the old questions about the meaning of their lives and the need to be saved from guilt and sin arise once more. And there is Jesus' blessed promise that we need weep no more.

REFLECTION

The account of Christ's baptism is an occasion for recalling our own baptism and what it means for our lives. Baptism initiates us into the life of the Holy Spirit, union with Christ, and membership in the Church. Baptism takes away original sin, any other sin, and all guilt from us. We are made spiritually new. Bathed in water and the Holy Spirit, we are baptized in the name of the Father and of the Son and of the Holy Spirit. We die to sin and rise to grace. Read St. Paul's explanation of this in Romans 5:1-5.

Though freed from sin, human weakness remains and the newly baptized must embark on a journey of faith growth, moral improvement, and spiritual development. Baptism takes away the sin, but not the damage sin created. The combination of God's grace and our spiritual development wears away the damage. Membership in the Church is not like graduating from school. Once you have the diploma, you have no more to do. Once you are part of the Church, you belong to a family in which your responsibilities have just begun.

The faith that brings us to baptism must not stop there. Growth in faith and grace must be a lifelong process. This should happen in one's personal relationship with Christ and also should involve an ever-growing and mature understanding of the teachings of Christ as mediated by the Church.

FOR DIALOGUE

Why do you think that God continues to send prophets and saints to awaken our moral and spiritual awareness? What would it be like if God did not send us such people to challenge our spiritual complacency? Why do the prophets and saints tend to afflict the comfortable and comfort the afflicted?

How do you think you would have reacted to the preaching and lifestyle of John the Baptist? Why did Jesus insist on being baptized by John? The mystery of the Holy Trinity is revealed at the baptism. What were some hints of the existence of the Trinity in the Old Testament?

How often do you think of your baptism? How should you extend the meaning of your baptism in your daily life and Christian witness? Why is it so important to do so?

PRAYER

We praise the Father, Son, and Holy Spirit in whose names we have been baptized. As we hear the call to conversion from John the Baptist may we renew our baptismal promises to renounce evil and be committed to the gospel with God's help and graces.

When Jesus comes to be baptized,
He leaves the hidden years behind,
The years of safety and of peace,
To bear the sins of all mankind.

ST. VENANTIUS OF WINCHESTER,
TR. STANBROOK ABBEY

CHAPTER 33

Jesus Is the Word Made Flesh

Matthew 1:16-25; Luke 1:26-38

He is the image of the invisible God.

COLOSSIANS 1:15

W ho is Jesus Christ? He is the Son of God and the son of Mary. He is truly God and truly man. The gospels were written, "that you may [come to] believe that Jesus is the Messiah, the Son of God, and that through this belief you may have life in his name" (John 20:31). Christian teaching speaks of the person and acts of Jesus in terms of "mysteries," because of the union of the divine and human in Christ.

In our study we will look at both aspects of Christ. In this lesson we will see the human aspect of Jesus and in the next lesson, his divine appearance. Such a separate study in no way divides Christ, but does help us appreciate in some small way the remarkable mystery of the Son of God who became human that we may be saved from sin and be given the gift of divine life.

"The Son of God ... worked with human hands; he thought with a human mind. He acted with a human will, and with a human heart he loved. Born of the Virgin Mary, he has truly been made one of us, like us in all things except sin" (*Gaudium et Spes*, 22).

No gospel is stronger in celebrating the lofty divinity of Jesus than St. John's. Yet he is equally insistent that Jesus was a real man. St. John's first chapter gives us a series of five testimonies about Jesus that underline some of Christ's human qualities. These five testimonies are given by: John the Baptist, Andrew, Philip, Nathanael, and Christ himself.

JESUS IS THE SUFFERING SERVANT

We hear first from the trumpet-like voice of the prophet, John the Baptist. He drew the attention of his congregation to Jesus and declared: "Behold, the Lamb of God" (John 1:36). The Aramaic word John used here was *talya*, a word that means both lamb and servant. When the audience seated along Jordan's bank heard this expression, they remembered the Old Testament poetry about the suffering servant of Yahweh.

These poems in the book of Isaiah speak of a mysterious man who will come one day to bring people freedom from their sins. He will be called, simply, the "servant." However, his work will summon him to suffer for the sins of people. He will be led like a lamb to the slaughter. Through this purifying suffering, people will be redeemed.

Hence, John presents Jesus as the real servant-lamb who has come to be the man for others and who is dedicated, even to death, for the cause of our salvation. By his loving obedience to the Father, Jesus fulfills the atoning mission of the Suffering Servant. Moreover, the fact that Jesus could truly feel pain, suffer, and die is evidence of his authentic humanity.

Jesus Is the Messiah

The second testimony comes from Andrew, the brother of Simon Peter. Andrew had stood on the Jordan's bank with the crowd that heard John the Baptist call Jesus "the Lamb of God." He found himself compelled to find out more about this man. Together with a friend, he approached Jesus and asked to stay with him for a while. Jesus said to them, "Come, and you will see." They stayed with him that day, for it was about the tenth hour. Andrew was so impressed that he rushed back to his brother Simon Peter and said, "We have found the Messiah" (John 1:41).

Andrew called Jesus the Messiah because he sensed in this man a religious teaching that really saves. He had listened to many men speak, and in his heart quietly asked, "Do you have a message that can really save me from sin and guilt? Can you speak to my loneliness? Are you a teacher who knows how to bring meaning to my life? Can you really tell me who I am?" In Jesus he found that the answer was a resounding yes! The Church today continues to proclaim this messianic promise of Jesus. The world questions the Church as Andrew questioned Jesus. And in word and sacrament, the Church brings to people the Christ who really saves them.

The Value of Faith-Filled Study of Scripture

We hear the third testimony from Philip who came from Bethsaida. He told his friend Nathanael: "We have found him of whom Moses in the law and also the prophets wrote, Jesus of Nazareth, the son of Joseph" (John 1:45). The word "law" here refers to the Torah, that is, the first five books of the Bible. Two of the main sources of faith for an Israelite were the Torah and the prophets.

Philip spoke here as a student. He had studied Scripture carefully and had lived by it with honesty. His studies, together with his deep faith, had given him an understanding of the work of God in the world. He was familiar with the mighty deeds of the God of the exodus and the teachings of the prophets. This was why his encounter with Jesus was a religious experience, for this man bore in his person a mighty breakthrough of the power of God and the vision of which all the prophets had spoken. Because of this, Philip is a patron of religious education. He is a reminder that religious studies are avenues to meeting the Lord Jesus. They are not meant to be a detached, academic work, but an opening to love and service in the name of Jesus.

Son of God and King of Israel

Our fourth testimony is delivered by Nathanael. He is best known for saying, "Can anything good come out of Nazareth?" Jesus said that Nathanael was a man in whom there was no guile. In other words Nathanael was an "innocent abroad," an honest man who felt no need to resort to tricks in his human relations. When he was brought to meet Jesus, he announced: "Rabbi, you are the Son of God; you are the King of Israel!" (John 1:49)

These two titles come from the Old Testament. The expression "Son of God" was not yet for Nathanael a reference to Christ's personal divinity, but a way of saying how close Jesus was to God. Of course, eventually Nathanael would come to know the deeper truth of this statement that Jesus was actually God's Son. "King of Israel" was a technical expression meaning the messianic spiritual leader of the people of God. Because Nathanael was an open man, the impact of Jesus was so great that Nathanael clearly saw the messianic role of Christ. The presence of Christ was powerful, causing people to become aware of themselves in a deeper way.

Jesus Is the Covenant Man

The final testimony comes from the lips of Jesus himself. He addressed it to Nathanael: "Truly, truly, I say to you, you will see heaven opened, and the angels of God ascending and descending upon the Son of man" (John 1:51). He recalls Jacob's dream about angels uniting him in a covenant with God. Jesus points to himself as the ultimate covenant man. Then Jesus applies to himself the title, Son of Man, taken from a vision of the prophet Daniel. "There came one like a son of man, and he came to the Ancient of Days [the LORD] . . . to him was given dominion and glory and kingdom . . . his dominion is an everlasting dominion" (Daniel 7:13-14). Here Jesus identifies himself as the true Son of Man who will usher in God's kingdom.

Hence, the testimonies that bear witness to Jesus and his meaning for us are: servant-lamb, Messiah, true meaning of religious study, son of God and king of Israel, covenant man, and judge. These testimonies help us see Jesus as a true man. At the same time we need always to see, in faith, the whole Christ in whom the Son of God maintains the harmony of humanity and divinity.

REFLECTION

In the early Church there were two heresies that undermined the identity of Jesus. The first one was called Gnosticism (or Docetism). This heresy denied the humanity of Christ. Its advocates could not accept the truth that God's Son had really assumed a human body and soul. They thought this was unworthy of God. The early Church Fathers countered that Jesus was really born of the blood and bone of the Virgin Mary. He had a true human nature.

The second great heresy was Arianism. The Arians denied that Jesus Christ was divine. They also felt it was improper for God to assume a human nature. Arius argued that God created a perfect creature — something like a super-angel, called a *logos*. [This is not the same as the divine *Logos*/Word in St. John's gospel.] The created *logos* was incarnated eventually in a human nature in Jesus Christ. So there would be nothing divine about Christ. He would be the embodiment of a created *logos*. He would never be God. This heresy was repudiated by St. Athanasius and the bishops of several Church councils, the first of which was Nicea in A.D. 325.

The Council Fathers reaffirmed the faith of the Apostolic Church that the Son of God assumed a human nature. He is not part man and part God, nor a confused mixture of humanity and divinity. There is only one person — the divine person of the Son of God — in Jesus Christ. This divine person unifies the divinity and humanity of Jesus into a harmonious unity.

Only our faith can grasp this revelation about Jesus. But our faith transmits light to our reason to help it appreciate the beauty of such an act of love for us from God. This truth about Jesus attracts us to him because its divine beauty is so compelling. Not only have billions of people been drawn to Christ over twenty centuries, but they have found that Jesus provides the love that satisfies our deepest longings and the light that enchants our constant and abiding attention.

Each time we are at prayer in Christ's presence, this truth becomes evident. Each eucharistic celebration brings us an increase of belonging to Christ. Each growth in our identification with the Church opens up the treasures of Scripture that is our privileged and meditative goal in this book.

FOR DIALOGUE

If you were to give a testimony about your relationship with Jesus, what would it be like? When you think of Christ, how do you experience Jesus as both human and divine? For your faith, why is it important to keep in mind the full revelation of Jesus as found in Scripture and the Church's teaching?

We have taken testimonies about Christ's humanity from the first chapter of John's gospel. It is necessary to recall that the first chapter begins with the pre-existence of the Word of God prior to the revelation of the Word becoming flesh in Jesus. Having said this, what are some reflections you have about the humanity of Jesus?

How have you grown in your relationship with Jesus throughout your life? How has prayer been an essential aspect of this relationship? How has adoration of the Blessed Sacrament helped you?

PRAYER

O Jesus joy of loving hearts,
The fount of life and my true light.
I seek the peace your love imparts,
And stand rejoicing in your sight.

ST. BERNARD OF CLAIRVAUX

Nobody knows the trouble I've seen,
Nobody knows but Jesus.

AN AFRICAN-AMERICAN SPIRITUAL

The Wedding Feast of Cana and the Cleansing of the Temple: Signs that Manifest Christ's Divinity

John 4:46-54; 6:1-21; 9-11

This, the first of his signs, Jesus did at Cana in Galilee, and manifested his glory; and his disciples believed in him.

JOHN 2:11

Great people evoke the uncanny feeling that they show something beyond themselves. Indeed when we read the lives of the great men and women of history who dedicated themselves to the betterment of the world, we see that all of them, in one way or another, illustrate a quality "beyond themselves." Jesus was a real man, the greatest man in history. But he was more than that. He was the Son of God. He manifested his divinity in an incomparable way. St. John says that in Jesus he saw the "glory."

THE GLORY

In the Old Testament the word "glory" was associated with images of the pillar of fire, the radiant cloud, the roaring wind at Sinai, the gentle whisper at Carmel, the burning bush at Horeb, and the breath of God that fluttered like a dove over the waters of chaos in Genesis. In other words, glory summed up the variety of Old Testament religious experiences of the living God.

To speak of the glory breaking through the person of Jesus is a way of saying that the divine presence was profoundly experienced by those who knew, believed in, and loved Jesus. Chapters 2-4 of John's gospel present an image of Jesus performing signs of the divine breakthrough. John records two events, the miracle of the wine at Cana and the cleansing of the temple, and follows these with two conversations that illuminate the meaning of the events. We shall discuss the events at Cana and the temple.

The Wedding Feast of Cana: Its Meaning

"On the third day there was a wedding at Cana in Galilee, and the mother of Jesus was there" (John 2:1). This tightly packed sentence has three major ideas that give us a clue to the meaning of the Cana story. First, the expression "third day" is a biblical way of speaking of a radically new experience. It has an Easter quality about it. Something entirely new was about to happen.

Second, the portrait of a wedding feast is the Bible's way of talking about the age of glorious happiness. In our terms, it is a way of speaking about heaven. A banquet was one of the most joyful things the biblical writers knew. Adding a wedding made it the summit of happiness imagery. These people had been taught that when the Messiah came to usher in the new age, it would be like an everlasting wedding dinner.

The third detail is the presence of Mary. She arrives as the woman who has summed up in herself the faith of Israel by uttering the great Amen to God. Jesus, as the new Adam, comes with Mary, the new Eve, to Cana, that there, as Man and Woman, they may announce the new age in the atmosphere of a messianic banquet. Mary initiates the event by telling Jesus the wine has run out. Jesus answers that his hour has not yet come, the "hour" referring to the start of his messianic mission as well as to his sacrificial death. He calls her woman instead of mother. He reveals Mary as a major participant in his act of salvation. Her last words in Scripture were heard at Cana: "Do whatever he tells you" (John 2:5). Mary begins her public spiritual mission as an intercessor for us. Jesus proceeds to perform the miracle of the wine, a sign of salvation, a sign of his divinity.

The giant water jars represent the purification rituals of the Old Testament. They symbolize the supremacy of the law in the Old Testament search for salvation. Jesus replaces this water with wine. The river of wine is a sign of the new blessings of salvation brought by Christ, namely through the power of the Spirit. The law washed only the outside of a man, as water removed the dust from his feet. The Spirit changes the hearts of people with divine love and life as wine loosens and rejoices the inner soul.

The prophet Amos hinted at this when he said: "Behold, the days are coming... when the plowman shall overtake the reaper and the treader of grapes him who sows the seed. The mountain shall drip sweet wine, and all the hills shall flow with it" (Amos 9:13). John concludes the Cana narrative with this interpretation: "This, the first of his signs, Jesus did at Cana in Galilee, and manifested his glory; and his disciples believed in him" (John 2:11). His revelation of his divinity calls the disciples to faith in him.

The Cleansing of the Temple

Right on the heels of the Cana story comes the narrative about the cleansing of the temple. Jesus appears as an angry, menacing prophet bent on purifying the temple. The story makes more sense when seen against the background of five Old Testament pictures.

First: Isaiah 1:10-18 — The prophet Isaiah delivers a sermon in the temple area to a well-fed and hypocritical audience. He tells them that God hates their liturgy, no matter how well done, because they are a selfish, unjust, and unconcerned people. God is only pleased with worship by people who seek justice and live honestly in their daily lives.

Second: Jeremiah 7:11 — The prophet Jeremiah stands at the doorway of the temple scolding the people for mere externalism in their worship, and for turning the holy place into a den of robbers. Like Adam, who stole the forbidden fruit, they rob the temple of the real meaning of worship.

Third: Zechariah 14:21 — Commenting on the messianic age, the prophet Zechariah foresees that the gross materialism of worship will be purged away. "And there shall no longer be any trader in the house of the Lord of hosts on that day."

Fourth: Psalm 69:10 — Here is a liturgical song about a just man who dedicated himself to the purification of the Church. He has already experienced the suffering that such work has brought upon him. "For zeal for your house has consumed me." It is a task that leads to suffering and even to death.

Fifth: Malachi 3:1-5 — "And the LORD whom you seek will suddenly come to his temple, . . . he will purify the sons of Levi [the priests] and refine them like gold and silver, till they present right offerings to the LORD."

These five passages form the spirit and content of the meaning of the temple cleansing. Jesus rails against the liturgy of the apparently just, accuses them of making the temple a den of thieves, drives out the traders, and opens himself to the threat of death. He symbolically destroys the temple, that is, the old way of worship, and replaces it with himself as both lamb and priest to offer a new and acceptable worship to the Father.

Two Events with an Important Message

The wedding feast at Cana and the cleansing of the temple are, then, two events with an important message for us. Jesus brings a new law and a new liturgy. Instead of legalism, he presents us with the freedom of the Spirit. Instead of a building full of selfish and hypocritical people, he offers us a worship that should grow out of a community blessed by the Spirit and filled with a record of works of love, justice, and mercy.

These are signs of his glory, of the manifestation of the divine, in the person of Jesus. These signs are works of divine majesty. They are public events that onlookers cannot avoid. The river of wine is a challenge to salvation by mere external performance of the law. The temple cleansing is a deliberate summons to stop all efforts to reduce worship to mere ritual performed by a self-righteous congregation.

The consecration of the wine at Mass recalls for us the marvel of Cana. The appearance of the new wine on the table of the Lord is our blessed assurance that Jesus lives on to give us his divine life that enables us to appreciate our human dignity as images of God, and to help others to sense this gift. Liturgical and social renewal, together with prophetic witness, are perennial forms of the temple cleansing, reminding us to bring justice, love, and peace to our communities.

In these ways Christ, who lives on in his Church, continues to teach today the message he taught at the wedding feast in Cana and at the cleansing of the temple.

REFLECTION

Mary's dialogue with Jesus at Cana again attracts our attention. Theirs is a communion so deep that the words on the gospel page need to be matched by the unsaid words, the signals based on understandings of the heart rooted in thirty years of familial communion.

On the surface Mary seems to be asking for little more than a practical favor, an act of simple charity for a distressed and embarrassed couple. But at another level Mary is asking Jesus to begin publicly his mission of salvation. At the Jordan River, the heavenly Father commissioned Jesus to his saving ministry. At Cana Christ's earthly mother released him from home life and urged him to start his active ministry.

This clarifies Christ's enigmatic response to her. Jesus completely understood what she meant. Had Jesus concluded that Mary was simply asking him for a pragmatic favor such as going out and buying more wine, he would not have responded with messianic language about his "hour."

If this were only a matter of solving a family problem, he would not have addressed Mary as woman. If he called her mother, he would refer to her physical parentage. By calling her woman, he elevated her to a maternal role in the process of salvation. He spoke to her motherhood in the Spirit, not just in the flesh. He calls her to be concerned with all human needs, especially for the salvation of every man and woman.

Hence Christ's words to Mary, which seem abrupt and even unfilial to us, actually confirm her spiritual motherhood in the Church. Christ's light shone on her faith and revealed to her the spiritual destiny that lay ahead. The future beckoned her to open her heart to all people. This was not a vague and fuzzy kind of call. It was specific and concrete. Mary tells the steward, "Do whatever Jesus tells you."

Mary is still asking us to do the same.

FOR DIALOGUE

When you think of Christ's miracles, what meaning automatically occurs to you? How does your association with miracles differ from the message we derive from the Cana wine miracle? How would you deal with apparent contradictions here?

What do you find so impressive about the dialogue between Mary and Jesus at Cana? Why might we cite this story as the beginning of Mary's intercessory calling in the Church? What is your own experience of turning to Mary for her prayers?

What are cases you could cite today that call for a "cleansing of the temple" in the present Church? Why should you expect this to occur from time to time? What are the spiritual safeguards that should accompany anyone involved in "cleansing the temple?"

PRAYER

Help us, dear Lord, to cleanse the temple of our souls before we try to straighten out anyone else. Mary, keep us in your love and prayers that we may be faithful to Jesus and the Church. Thank you.

Jesus accompanies his words with many "mighty works and wonders and signs," which manifest that the kingdom is present in him and attest that he was the promised Messiah.

CCC 547

CHAPTER 35

Nicodemus Learns How
Much God Loves Us

John 3:1-21; 19:39

*For God so loved the world that he gave his only Son, that whoever
believes in him should not perish but have eternal life.*

JOHN 3:16

JESUS WAS A THREAT TO SOME

Jesus presented a special problem to the religious leaders who were the
defenders of the established religion and the custodians of its truth and
practices. Jesus became a threat to them because his teachings challenged
many of their interpretations of the Torah and he was attracting an increasing number of followers.

The religious leaders found themselves unable to listen to him without
prejudice. They saw him as so far out that the best they could say of him was
that he was a religious crank; and the worst, that he was a blasphemer. His
message was a disturbance to the simple faith of the people and a danger to
their cautious relations with the Roman embassy at the Fortress Antonia. To
be seen with him publicly would be a security risk.

One of these men, however, was honest enough to recognize real worth
in the teachings of Jesus. His name was Nicodemus. He was a timid man,
afraid to risk his reputation by being seen with Jesus in public. So, he
arranged a meeting with Jesus in the middle of the night. The story is told
in the third chapter of St. John's gospel.

Does Nicodemus Truly Understand?

Nicodemus began the discussion by declaring that he thinks Jesus is a
true prophet of the living God. "Rabbi, we know that you are a teacher who
has come from God, for no one can do these signs that you are doing, unless
God is with him" (John 3:2). Nicodemus has read correctly the signs of the
glory that shone through Jesus at the Cana miracle and the cleansing of the
temple.

Jesus replied that Nicodemus must undergo a profound conversion if he is to receive the kingdom of God. This, so far, Nicodemus does not fully understand. Nicodemus must be changed by the Spirit of God so that he may begin to understand and enter into a new way of life. He will have to be born again of water and the Holy Spirit. Such is the meaning of Christ's words: "Amen, amen I say to you, no one can see the kingdom of God without being born from above.... No one can enter the kingdom of without being born of water and Spirit" (John 3:3, 5).

How May We Have Eternal Life?

This language is in keeping with the creation theme of the early chapters of John. The creation stories of the Old Testament are dominated by the two images of the dark lake and the breath-Spirit of God. Nicodemus has to be brought out of the dark lake of chaos and misunderstanding and led by the powerful breath of the Holy Spirit to a new life in God's kingdom.

The words Jesus addressed to Nicodemus also refer to the sacrament of baptism that is the public sign that accomplishes the transformation of which Jesus speaks. Nicodemus asked how this can come about. Jesus is not above a little humor at this point. He teased Nicodemus about being a teacher of religion who should know better. "Are you a teacher of Israel, and yet you do not understand this?" (John 3:10) Jesus then reminded Nicodemus of the old story of Moses and the bronze serpent, the tale of the Israelites forever complaining about the water shortage and the poor diet. The Lord punished the people by sending fiery serpents among them. They bit the people and many died.

The people repented and prayed for mercy. God instructed Moses to make a bronze serpent and put it on a pole. The pole symbolized majesty and God's power over the serpent, which was itself a symbol of sinful religious practices. All who looked upon the upraised figure were healed (see Numbers 21:4-9). Jesus then made the application of the story: "So must the Son of Man be lifted up, that whoever believes in him may have eternal life" (John 3:14). Jesus, as the new mankind, the Son of Man, must be raised up to the cross and to glory so that the reality Nicodemus searches for may come to pass.

The Work of the Trinity

Jesus then went on to speak to Nicodemus about his Father. The Father has given the world his Son that it might discover the way to salvation. The Father presents his Son to the world as a sign of judgment: "Whoever believes in him will not be condemned" (John 3:18). Further, the Father commands that the followers of Jesus must do their deeds in the light. This means that the Christian must always be faithful and obedient. "He who does what is true comes to the light, that it may be clearly seen that his deeds have been wrought in God" (John 3:21).

In effect, Jesus is telling Nicodemus that the work of the new creation is wrought by the Holy Trinity. The Spirit works mightily to draw men out of the chaos (see John 3:1-8). This is made possible through the death and resurrection of the Son (see John 3:9-15). And all this is set in motion by the immense love of the heavenly Father (see John 3:16-21).

"Love Lifted Me"

The most quoted line from Christ's dialogue with Nicodemus is in John 3:16 in which Jesus said that it was God's love that moved him to send his Son to redeem the world. The music of the spiritual "Love Lifted Me" echoes this wondrous loving act of God. Love and faith come together here.

When John's gospel talks about faith, it mainly refers to believing in Jesus, commitment to him as a person. This is faith as loving and being loved. It is love expressed through faith. Of course faith also refers to believing in a doctrine, a divine truth. But this view of faith should always be linked to faith as a loving union with Jesus.

A love for Jesus will always involve faith in his teachings, doctrines, and commands. A loving faith in him as a person must include faith in the standards and principles that govern our behavior. As a love song puts it, "Don't just talk, show me!" Faith in doctrines without faith in the person of Jesus could produce a dry, arid religion. But if we only deal with the person of Jesus, we risk a spirituality that is sentimental, vacuous, and weak.

Nicodemus appears to be one whose faith was too closely confined to its ritualism and legalistic customs without a vital relationship to God. Jesus gave him a bigger vision. Christ's talk about love and the Spirit was meant to convert Nicodemus to a love and transformation that would be his salvation. Love would lift Jesus up on the Cross and onto glory. That love will lift up Nicodemus and us through Christ's redemptive acts made available to us through the sacrament of baptism and the other sacraments.

REFLECTION

Jesus taught Nicodemus the need for a transformation by the power of the Spirit. He would need to be born again of water and the Spirit. Our baptism made that possible for us. But that is only the beginning of our spiritual lives. We need to permit the Holy Spirit to keep transforming us ever more deeply into Christ. This means we need to welcome the Spirit's influence on our lives. Scripture says that God is the potter and we are the clay. The image of clay implies malleability, the capacity for being shaped. We need to be more inward and meditative for this to happen.

Our souls have an inner space where we can nurture our personal relationship with God when we are at prayer. Some describe this as the still-point of our souls, that innermost space inside us where our transformation can begin. God wants our inner lives to be a harmony of thoughts, feelings, and spiritual encounters. Busy heads and turbulent emotions tend to cause a spiritual blackout.

Stillness, quiet, and meditation are the classical methods for sinking into our still-point. The fact that Nicodemus came to Jesus in the stillness of the night favored the possibility of his being gradually transformed by Jesus. This is where Nicodemus could meet the Spirit and permit himself to become the moldable clay. He could be prepared to be born again from above. Jesus invites us to the same adventure. We have been born again in baptism. What happened sacramentally must be lived in practice. Here we need to allow ourselves to be transformed by the Spirit who helps us with a gentle love. As water was changed into wine, so our sinfulness can be changed into sanctity with the grace of God.

FOR DIALOGUE

In his discussion with Jesus, Nicodemus was led into the first stages of conversion that would make him a loyal disciple of Christ. In your prayers when are you moved to have a "heart-to-heart" conversation with Christ? Why is such intimate sharing of yourself with Christ helpful?

Why do you need the help of the Holy Spirit to improve the depth of your spiritual life? Why does Christian self-improvement require something more than positive thinking?

Why do the gospels call us to have a faith that is a personal relationship with Christ? What is the connection between faith as a relationship to Jesus and faith as a belief in his teachings? Why are both forms of faith needed?

Lord Jesus, thank you for the sacrament of baptism by which we are delivered from all sin and guilt and initiated into the Church. Thank you for giving us your Holy Spirit to guide us and to help our spiritual and moral life to flourish.

The Spirit comes gently and makes himself known by his fragrance. He is not a burden for he is light.

St. Cyril of Jerusalem

CHAPTER 36

Jesus Converts the Samaritan Woman

John 4:1-42

Many Samaritans from that city believed in him because of the woman's testimony, "He told me all that I ever did."

JOHN 4:39

Nobody likes a phony. Unmasking the hypocrite gives us great satisfaction. To a certain extent, everyone has a cover story that eventually needs to be stripped away so that the true person may emerge. John the Evangelist, in the fourth chapter of his gospel, tells the story of how Jesus helped the Samaritan woman remove her mask and achieve the honesty that brought her salvation.

THE ANCIENT HOSTILITY BETWEEN JEW AND SAMARITAN

This story must be read against the background of an ancient hostility between the Jews and the Samaritans. After the death of King Solomon there was a civil war in Israel. The northern tribes broke away from the south and formed a separate kingdom. The capital of this new nation was Samaria. Consequently, the inhabitants of this northern nation became known as Samaritans.

The war also produced a religious division. The kings of the north forbade their subjects to worship at the temple in Jerusalem. Instead they provided a shrine for their people at the summit of Mount Gerizim. The passing years deepened the political and religious differences between the Jews and the Samaritans to the point where open hatred was commonplace.

Jesus Meets the Samaritan Woman

As this story opens, Jesus and his apostles are making a trip to Galilee. A quick way to get there was through Samaria. They paused by the well of Jacob. The well was situated between the holy mountain, Gerizim, and the mountain of the curse, named Ebai. The village of Sychar was just up the road. It was noontime, and Jesus was tired and hungry. He remained at the well to rest while his apostles went into the village to get some food.

Then "A woman of Samaria came to draw water. Jesus said to her, 'Give me a drink'" (John 4:7). This is the theme of the "cup of water." To give a cup of water to even the least of one of our brothers and sisters is to give it to Jesus and to find ourselves on the road to salvation (Matthew 10:42). We also have here a case of Jesus not being recognized, for the woman has no idea who he is, other than the fact that he is a Jew.

The Samaritan woman expressed her surprise that a male Jew would dare to ask a favor of her. He told her that he would give her living water. Compare this expression with the living bread Jesus would speak of in the sixth chapter of John. Living water is running water, in contrast to a stiff, stagnant pool. In a desert land like Palestine, running water was a valued commodity and a symbol of life.

In a sense, the woman is the parched earth, and Jesus has come to bring the refreshing waters of salvation to her arid spirit.

The woman remarked that it would hardly be possible for Jesus to give her water because he had no rope or bucket, and she asked him if he thought he was greater than Jacob, who gave this well to the people. Jesus overlooked her question and assured her that the water he would give her would be such that she would never thirst again.

Taking him literally, she thought, "What a convenience this would be." She would no longer need to haul water if what he said were true. "Go, call your husband," Jesus told her (John 4:16). With this command, Jesus struck at her cover story. He confronted her with her behavior. She insisted that she had no husband. But Jesus pursued the point, declaring that she had had five husbands, and the man she now lived with was not her husband.

Never in her life had she felt so embarrassed. The truth that Jesus confronted her with was so painful that she quickly searched for a way of changing the subject. Rather than discuss her personal life, she switched the trend of conversation to a discussion of religion.

She told Jesus that she could see he was a prophet, and she asked him where was the best place to worship. Was real religion to be found at the temple on Mount Zion in Jerusalem, or at the Samaritan shrine on Mount Gerizim? Jesus patiently took up her question and discussed it.

"Woman, believe me, the hour is coming when you will worship the Father neither on this mountain nor in Jerusalem. . . . But the hour is coming and now is, when the true worshipers will worship the Father in spirit and truth" (John 4:21, 23). In other words, today you can worship as one born anew by the Spirit. Today you can worship in truth, that is, with the blessed assurance that you worship as God wants you to.

He had finally reached her. She frankly admitted that she was in need of help. Wistfully, she talked of the contemporary hope for a savior who would bring forgiveness of sins and hope to women such as she. With that, Jesus revealed his identity and said, "I who speak to you am he" (John 4:26).

The Woman Receives Christ's Message with Joy

Alleluia! Great excitement took hold of the woman. Without another word she arose and ran into the town to tell everyone that she had met a man who had changed her heart, converted her from sin, and who had filled her with hope. She ran to spread the gospel of peace, and she became the first evangelist to the Samaritans.

The apostles returned just at the moment that the woman, with burning eyes, rushed past them. They wondered what had happened between her and Jesus. Jesus now seemed so absorbed that their presence was an intrusion. Bashfully they offered him food. He looked at them and asked them how they could talk of food when he had just saved a woman. How could they think of lunch when he had just brought spiritual renewal to a woman whose life had been meaningless and trapped in sin? He drew their attention to the grain fields. The tips of the wheat were white gold and ready for the harvest. He showed them that this is the symbol of the fullness of time when the whole world is ripe for his saving words and deeds. There no longer had to be a sense of being lost, for the inrush of his power had begun the saving task.

The scene closed with the arrival of the villagers of Sychar who came to hear the good news from the lips of Jesus himself. Their testimony was a confession of faith: "It is no longer because of your words that we believe, for we have heard for ourselves, and we know that this is indeed the Savior of the world" (John 4:42).

Centuries before, there was an intimation of what would happen at the well of Jacob in a hymn composed by the prophet Isaiah:

With joy you will draw water from the wells of salvation.
And you will say in that day:
"Give thanks to the Lord, call upon his name;
make known his deeds among the nations,
proclaim that his name is exalted...
Shout, and sing for joy, O inhabitant of Zion,
for great in your midst is the Holy One of Israel."

ISAIAH 12:3-4, 6

Christ's ministry to the woman at the well offers us a five-step method for evangelization.

First, begin at the human level. He does a simple human thing, asking for a drink of water. It was an icebreaker, an easy way to initiate a conversation. Despite her frosty reception, Jesus finds a way to establish a basic relationship. His approach may be summarized as: "Build the bonds of love before setting out the bonds of doctrine." Some evangelizers want to argue religion before they have even said hello. They forget Fulton Sheen's wise remark, "Don't argue. Win an argument. Lose a soul."

Second, introduce a sense of wonder and mystery. When Jesus tells her he could give her "living water," he was raising the issue beyond mere physical satisfaction. Wonder is the beginning of faith. Wonder is an attitude that unlocks the imagination and creates a feeling for searching the beyond. Once wonder is felt, then there is a receptivity to mystery.

Third, introduce the call to faith and the realm of mystery. Jesus tells her that he could give her the water that is eternal, that lasts forever. Jesus has drawn her to the gates of mystery. Slowly he inches her forward, quietly inviting her to the faith that will open the gates of mystery and eternal life. In confronting her with her immoral life, he connects faith with moral conversion. The discussion about which mountain is the correct one for worship shows that she has begun to see his offering.

Fourth, call for faith in Jesus. Now Jesus reveals he is the prophet whom she seeks. He is the one who offers salvation. He asks her for faith in him. He does this less with words than with an unfolding of his holy being. His self-revelation brings with it the invitation to faith. At no point has he forced her to this moment. The four steps have been a series of small revelations culminating in his final self-disclosure: "I AM ... he." In John's gospel these "I AM" statements are Christ's way of disclosing his divine identity, always with the intention of saving the one receiving this Good News.

Fifth, the converted one becomes an evangelizer. The Good News in her heart moves her to a joyful proclamation of Christ to her community in Sychar. She brings them to Jesus. They hear his message and are converted by him.

Embrace these five steps in your own sharing of your faith with others. Christ's gentle style attracts the listeners and draws them to wonder, mystery, faith, and conversion. It will be an excellent model for you as well.

FOR DIALOGUE

What experiences have you had in sharing your faith with others, especially those of other religions — or no faith persuasion? What have you learned from such experiences?

The Church teaches that we propose, not impose, our faith on others. "To be human, man's response to God by faith must be free, and . . . therefore nobody is to be forced to embrace the faith against his will. The act of faith is by its very nature a free act" (CCC 160). Why is it better to share faith in this way? When faith is forced on others, what goes wrong? What is the relationship between faith and freedom?

What impressed you most about the way Jesus invited the woman at the well to faith? What aspects of Christ's approach would help you in sharing your faith with others?

PRAYER

Father in heaven, thank you for the graces you gave me to believe in Jesus and in the truths that he taught. I praise you for the gift of belonging to the Church that sustains my closeness to Christ and faith in the truths that guide my life.

For this reason, because I have heard of your faith in the Lord Jesus and your love toward all the saints I do not cease to give thanks for you, remembering you in my prayers.

EPHESIANS 1:15-16

CHAPTER 37

Christ Is the Living Bread
Come Down from Heaven

John 6

"The bread which I shall give for the life of the world is my flesh... I say to you, unless you eat the flesh of the Son of man and drink his blood, you have no life in you."

JOHN 6:51, 53

The sixth chapter of John tells the story of Christ's bread miracle followed by the magnificent dialogue on the Bread of Life. It was springtime. The Passover was near. Jesus and his apostles sailed from Capernaum across the Sea of Galilee to the eastern shore for some solitude and prayer.

Thousands of people had come to Capernaum to hear Jesus preach the gospel and heal their sick. They saw Jesus leave and sail for the small fishing port of Bethsaida Julius. The lake was narrow at this northern end. The people could walk to the other town and meet Jesus. From his boat Jesus could see the people, marching in hope. He could hear them singing the psalms of desire for God. The great crowd met him when he landed.

Like a Good Shepherd, Jesus led them to a nearby hill where he spoke to them of hope, forgiveness, and salvation. He commented on the forthcoming Passover. As evening came near, Jesus knew they needed a meal. Phillip said that all the apostles had were five loaves and two fish. Jesus asked for this food. He took the loaves, blessed them, and had the apostles distribute them to the people. He did the same with the fish. His bread miracle fed everyone. The food was multiplied in the giving, much the same as love. There was enough food left to fill twelve baskets. The grateful and excited people shouted about making him a king. Jesus quietly disappeared and went off to pray.

The following day Jesus returned to Capernaum. This prosperous community owned the Seven Wells whose plentiful waters, conveyed by aqueduct, irrigated the nearby plain and drove the pottery and tanning mills. Today there are the ruins of the synagogue that existed in Christ's time. Throughout the centuries Christians have brought millstones for grinding grains and placed them around this site. They still up memories of wheat harvests, the smell of bread baking, and hearty meals of bread, lamb, salad, and wine. This was the setting for Christ's dialogue with the people and religious leaders about the Bread of Life.

Jesus had performed a miracle of bread, not only to still the pangs of physical hunger in the crowd of five thousand, but also to meet their spiritual hunger (John 6:1-15). Spiritual hunger can mean many things. The man who is starved for beauty knows such hunger. The woman who craves love understands spiritual hunger. The boy who yearns for justice and recognition has a clue to this hunger. The scholar who searches for meaning has a spiritual hunger. Anyone who realizes the need for salvation from sin, guilt, and evil has the deepest form of spiritual hunger.

JESUS BRINGS US HOME

Jesus thought of this hunger when he multiplied the loaves. In this miracle, he began his work to satisfy the spiritual hunger of men that he would fulfill in giving us the Eucharist. At the Mass, beauty, love, recognition, and meaning all have their place. The early Church loved to call the Mass the "breaking of the bread."

The Eucharist: A Sign of Community

One of the spiritual hungers most often spoken of today is the yearning for community. Jesus intended the Eucharist to be a sign and cause of community. "Holy Communion" is not just the union of Jesus and the individual, but also the union we have with one another. Ideally, it is not a meal of strangers, but of friends. If this is so, then the Eucharistic event should have community-forming details about it.

Forming a Community by the Sacrament of the Eucharist

It is Jesus who forms us into a community of self-giving love. We become ever more completely the Communion of the Church, temples of the Holy Spirit, living members of the Body of Christ. In fact, it is the Body of Christ in the Eucharist that forms the Body of Christ in the Church. The Eucharist makes the Church into a vibrant community of love. This is a process that intensifies through years of graces coming to us from the Eucharist coupled with our faith surrender to Christ. This is made concrete by loving and serving the Lord and one another.

The power of the Eucharist to form community is based on the truth that it is not only a holy meal, but it is also a sacrifice of love. This becomes clear in the gospel accounts of the institution of the Eucharist at the Last

Supper and the narratives of the passion and crucifixion of Jesus. There will be no community or love without sacrifice and pain.

In the Bread of Life dialogue, Jesus explained the central importance of what will be the Eucharist that he will create at the Last Supper on the night before he died. John's gospel does not have an account of the Lord's Supper since the other gospels and St. Paul have already done that. We recall this in every Mass:

> *On the night before he died, Jesus took bread, blessed it, broke it and gave it to his disciples, saying, "This is my Body which will be given up for you." Then Jesus took the cup of wine, blessed it and gave it to his disciples, saying, "Take this all of you and drink from it. This is the cup of my blood, the blood of the new and everlasting covenant. It will be shed for you and for all so that sins may be forgiven. Do this in memory of me."*
> SECOND EUCHARISTIC PRAYER

Jesus did this on Holy Thursday. On Good Friday Jesus offered to the Father the sacrifice of his Body and Blood on the Cross. It was the greatest act of love ever given on earth. What Jesus promised in the Bread of Life dialogue, what he instituted as Eucharist at the Last Supper, now receives its validity and fulfillment in the supreme act of love and obedience on the Cross. At every Eucharist we celebrate the mystery of Holy Thursday (the sacred meal), Good Friday (the sacrifice of the Cross), and Easter (our communion with the risen Lord).

Both Scripture and Tradition speak of the Eucharist as the "mystery of faith." At the conclusion of the Bread of Life dialogue, most people said that this was a hard and impossible teaching. They left Jesus because they could not accept the Eucharistic teaching. Jesus turned to the apostles and said, "Do you also want to leave?" Simon Peter answered him, "Lord, to whom shall we go? You have the words of eternal life, and we have believed and have come to know, that you are the Holy One of God" (John 6:67-69). Only our faith can see the truth of this central mystery of salvation. We praise God for these gifts of Eucharist and our faith.

REFLECTION

The Mass is both a holy sacrifice and a holy meal. The Eucharist is a *sacrifice* because it makes present the sacrificial act of Jesus at Calvary. The same Jesus who once offered himself in a bloody manner on the Cross to save us from our sins and give us divine life now offers himself on our altars in an unbloody manner. This sacrifice becomes the offering of the whole Church. At Mass, we unite ourselves with Jesus and identify with his Cross — an act that leads us to his resurrection where we rise with him.

The Mass is also a *holy meal*, a sacred banquet where we partake of the Body and Blood of Christ. We speak here also of the Real Presence of Jesus. Jesus is present to us in many ways: in the Scriptures, in the Eucharistic assembly, in the poor and the sick and those in prison, in the sacraments, in the priest — but above all in the Eucharist.

This presence is called real — by which is not intended to exclude other types of presence as if they could not be real too, but because it is presence in the fullest sense: that is to say, it is a substantial presence, by which Christ, God and man, makes himself wholly and entirely present.

PAUL VI, *MYSTERY OF FAITH*, 39

At Mass we adore the real presence of Jesus in the Eucharist by genuflecting or by bowing deeply. *And we adore the reserved presence of Christ in our tabernacles.* "Because Christ is present in the sacrament of the altar, he is to be honored with the worship of adoration. 'To visit the Blessed Sacrament is... proof of gratitude, an expression of love, and a duty of adoration toward Christ our Lord'" (Paul VI, *Mystery of Faith* 66 and CCC 1418).

The celebration and reception of the Eucharist should have an impact on our lives. As we finish Mass we always hear the priest tell us to love and serve the Lord. This is done practically by acts of love, justice, and mercy to one another, especially the poor.

You have tasted the Blood of the Lord,
yet you do not recognize your brother...
You dishonor this table when you do not
judge worthy of sharing your food someone
judged worthy to take part in this meal...
God freed you from all your sins and invited
you here, but you have not become more merciful.

ST. JOHN CHRYSOSTOM,
HOMILY ON 1 CORINTHIANS, 27:40

[This reflection is from *Celebrating the Mass*, by Father McBride, Our Sunday Visitor, pages 9-10.]

FOR DIALOGUE

If you had been present at the bread miracle, what do you think would have been your reaction? How did the bread miracle relate to the dialogue on the Bread of Life and eventually to the Eucharist?

When you hear that the Eucharist is a mystery of faith, how has that helped you appreciate what a great gift from Jesus it is? As you have grown up what has been your faith appreciation of the Mass? How does the Mass help you experience the parish community?

The Church Fathers taught that "The Body of Christ (Eucharist) makes the Body of Christ (Church)." Why do you think they taught that? Since the Eucharist is related to Christ's sacrifice of love on the Cross, what challenge does reception of the Eucharist present to you?

PRAYER

Bread of Life, Wine of Salvation, Jesus, I adore you, love you, and surrender myself to you. I believe. Help my unbelief. Stretch my inner spirit to receive an even greater fullness of your mystery and love. Fill me with the kind of love that opens me to appreciate the mystery that makes it possible for me to know you and benefit from your care for me. Put power in my faith so I will not be afraid to give myself to you. Teach me to see that being "taken, blessed, broken and given" actually heals me and those for whom I care.

Thomas answered him, "My Lord and my God."

JOHN 20:28

CHAPTER 38

Jesus Is the Living Water
and the Light of the World

John 7-8:12-20

"I am the light of the world; he who follows me will not walk in darkness, but will have the light of life."

JOHN 8:12

THE FEAST OF TABERNACLES

The sixth and seventh chapters of St. John's gospel recall Jesus describing himself as the light of the world and as the living water. These descriptions are set in the context of the Feast of Tabernacles, the most popular Jewish feast, though not the most important in their liturgical calendar. In many ways it may be compared to our Christmas celebrations with its lights and songs and general good feeling. Before it became a liturgical event, it was a farmers' celebration, a harvest festival.

Gradually it began to assume religious meanings. It was convenient for the harvesters to live in temporary huts in the fields during the gathering time. This was reminiscent of the years that Israel lived in tents in the desert, where God himself was enshrined in a tentlike tabernacle. The words "tent" and "tabernacle" are synonymous. To remember this, many of the celebrants constructed temporary tents made of branches from trees and bushes in which they dwelt for the week. Observant Jewish people today often make such a "tent" in their yards for the contemporary celebration of what they call "Sukkoth" or the Feast of Booths.

The passing years had glamorized the Israelites' desert experience to the point where they nostalgically thought of it as the ideal existence. When they were a pilgrim people, they were a pure people, an ideal community. The Hebrew name for their desert community was *qahal*. This name implied that they were not merely an organization or a motley group that happened to be together. Rather, they were a community summoned into existence by God and molded into his witness by his power and presence.

The Feast of Tabernacles began with a water ceremony and concluded with a fire ritual. Jesus used these dramatic scenes as an occasion for revealing himself as the living water and the light of the world. In each case he prefaced the revelation with the expression I AM, thus identifying himself with God who used these words as his name when he spoke to Moses at the burning bush. Our reflection here will begin with the water ritual and conclude with the fire ceremony.

The Water Ceremony

Tabernacles began with the procession to the pool of Siloam for the water ceremony. Anyone who knows farmers is aware of how concerned they are about rain. If there is no rain, there won't be any harvest. The water ceremony of the Feast of Tabernacles was meant to be a prayer for rain. Water was carried in procession from the pool of Siloam up to the temple where it was poured out over the altar. God was thanked for the water that brought about the harvests, and begged to send water again for future harvests. Texts from the book of Exodus were read that recalled how God had Moses miraculously bring forth water from the rocks of the desert.

Here was a seamless intermingling of human needs and religious faith. The Israelites needed rain to make their crops grow. Their faith easily associated the work of God as part of this growth process. They were keenly aware of the presence of God in all their human efforts.

Jesus Is the Living Water

It is in the context of this water ceremony that Jesus identified himself as the living water. "If any one thirst, let him come to me and drink. He who believes in me, as the Scripture has said, 'Out of his heart shall flow rivers of living water'" (John 7:37-38). He had already developed this teaching in his conversation with the Samaritan woman at the well of Jacob.

Those who long for God, who have a thirst for spiritual fulfillment, should come to Jesus. If they come to him in faith and drink of his wisdom and graces, he will satisfy them. Jesus was the living rain for the parched earth of hard hearts. This could also be understood as Jesus giving people the courage to make correct moral decisions. It really is not too farfetched to introduce the moral dimension here, because the Feast of Tabernacles had many overtones of the celebration of the giving of the Ten Commandments to Moses at Sinai.

The Feast of Tabernacles, therefore, did include a summons for greater fidelity to the law of God and the need for correct moral behavior. The desert days were lived out in the shadow of Sinai where the law was given. It's true that ultimately the Feast of Pentecost became the official celebration of the Ten Commandments, but Tabernacles never lost its memory of the great Sinai event, when God made a covenant with Israel and shaped them into his holy people.

Jesus still tells us who thirst for moral conviction and the courage to live by the will of God that we can find the power to do so by our faith-filled union with Christ. People whose hearts are dried out, who seem to have no nerve left to face the moral dilemmas of our time, are invited to put their faith in the immediate personal presence of Jesus and thus absorb the impact of the "rain" of his conviction and power.

The Fire Ceremony

The fire ceremony was the second ceremony of the Feast of Tabernacles. In a world without electricity, most people went to bed at sundown. They could not afford the oil or wax to keep torches and lamps going at night. But at this feast the night sky was ablaze with festal torches on Temple Mount. Four golden candlesticks, each so tall that ladders were needed to reach the tops, were capped with golden bowls of oil with lighted wicks floating in them.

This extravagance of night fire on the eight evenings of Tabernacles was one of the mystic delights of the feast. It probably had the same effect on those people that fireworks have for moderns. Selected men danced before the Lord while choirs sang God's praises, recalling how God walked before the ancient Israelites as a pillar of fire.

Onto this splendid stage walked Jesus on the last night of the feast. In a pause between the singing and dancing Jesus proclaimed, "I am the light of the world; he who follows me will not walk in darkness, but will have the light of life" (John 8:12). Using the powerful visual aid of the fire ceremony, Jesus endowed it with the ultimate meaning that God's plan intended for it.

The dance of the torches and the lighting of huge candles and lamps recalled the pillar of fire in the desert. The exodus story described God as a column of fire walking before the people who dwell in darkness. He led them through the darkness to the Promised Land. He liberated them from confusion and the wasteland into the territory of order and fertility.

Jesus used this context of the fire ritual to declare that he is the real light of the world. He is indeed the pillar of fire intent on bringing meaning to the lives of people. Because he is divine Wisdom made flesh, he has the gift of light that everyone needs to move with confidence through the mysteries of life. Jesus offers a light that both draws us to God and opens up the presence of God at each moment of our lives.

The Light of the World

It may be that for many people the complexity of modern life causes endless confusion. Self-understanding can become increasingly difficult in a world where a thousand conflicting ideals appear on every television screen and in every magazine advertisement. Well, where is the real ideal? Is the problem of finding meaning in life really solved by a good deodorant, a better mouthwash, a faster car, or a wilder dance?

It is sometimes hard to keep in mind the mystery that Jesus is a real man as well as truly God. Humanly speaking, Jesus faced temptations and tests of endurance just as we all do. He was faced with moral choices as described in his temptations in the desert and his life-and-death choice at the agony in the garden. Yet amid all these challenges, Jesus remained without sin. Jesus was in our world, but also perceived the divine presence — the will of his Father — in space and time. As many passages of the gospel testify, Jesus was possessed and led by the Holy Spirit. Father and Son and Spirit were always in union, ever connected by the light that linked eternity and time.

REFLECTION

At the Feast of Tabernacles Jesus faced some opposition from the religious leaders. Christ told them, "You are from this world.... If you do not believe that I AM, you will die in your sins" (cf. John 8:23-24). Jesus often speaks of the "world." Its usage has a complex meaning.

The world is not heaven. The world as we know it is a transitory place. Evil exists in it. Heaven is permanent and good. In this sense the world symbolizes what is opposed to God.

On the other hand God loves this world. Genesis describes how much love God put into creating the world. At the end of each day of creation, God looked at it and said, "That's good." Jesus taught that God loved the world so much that he sent his Son to save it from sin and guilt. Heaven and the world may be different, but God's affection for people has established a magnificent link between heaven and earth.

Still, something has gone wrong with the world. It does not recognize Jesus. Indeed it opposes him. The world has lost its original purpose. It represents evil and whatever breaks our relationship with God. But Jesus has come to resolve this impasse. Jesus has brought love and reconciliation to the world. God is in Jesus reconciling the world to himself. God has never lost his love for his creation or its people. Indeed because of Christ's reconciling redemption, there is a vision of a "new heaven and a new earth," beautifully revealed in the book of Revelation.

"Then I saw a new heaven and a new earth.... I heard a loud voice from the throne saying, 'Behold the dwelling of God is with men'" (Revelation 21:1, 3).

FOR DIALOGUE

How might you say that the American Thanksgiving Day is the modern version of a harvest festival? Why do you think that both Judaism and Christianity linked harvest festivals with religious feasts? Jesus invited the Samaritan woman and the celebrants at Tabernacles to faith in him as the living water. What does the image of living water suggest to you and your faith in Christ?

How is Jesus the light of your life? What is the symbolic value of fireworks on the fourth of July, of candlelight at a meal, of a bonfire at a sports rally? How might you use these symbols to apply to your faith in Christ?

What are the positive and negative uses of the word "world" in Scripture? How do you handle this complex use of the term "world"?

PRAYER

Jesus, thank you for calling me to faith in you as the living water and the living light. You satisfy the thirsts of my soul and clarify the various forms of darkness I experience. I believe in you and I love you with all my heart.

"If you continue in my word, you are truly my disciples."

JOHN 8:31

CHAPTER 39

Jesus Heals the Man Born Blind

John 9

"As long as I am in the world, I am the light of the world." As he said this, he spat on the ground and made clay of the spittle and anointed the man's eyes with the clay, saying to him, "Go, wash in the pool of Siloam." . . . So he went and washed and came back seeing.

JOHN 9:5-7

We all have compassion for the physically blind person and admiration for the courage and resourcefulness a blind one shows in taking hold of life. Other types of blindness may cause a negative reaction in us. Moral and spiritual blindness will prevent religious conversion, curb faith growth, and often cause harm to others. Both kinds of blindness occur in the ninth chapter of John's gospel.

THE SIMPLE BLIND MAN AND THE LEARNED SCHOLARS

When Jesus cured the man born blind, he set in motion a situation in which the leaders of faith reveal their spiritual blindness. The "ignorant" blind man verbally raps the knuckles of the clever religious teachers. Ultimately, the blind man becomes the very judge of those who accused him and thought of themselves as his judges. It is a case of he who "does not know" becoming the instructor and judge of those "who do know."

The scene is a crowded street in Jerusalem during the Feast of Tabernacles. Jesus had just claimed that he is the light of the world, and he demonstrated it by bringing sight to a well-known blind beggar. The apostles see the beggar and make a typical pious statement about the relation between the sin of this man and his blindness. Or was it his parents who were the sinners?

Too Much Talk and Not Enough Action

Jesus had no patience with religious quibbling that masks unbelief. He is tired of the endless, learned conversations about the poor which kept people so busy talking that they never got around to doing something about the problem. Jesus sees a man, not a moral problem. This is no time for lofty moralizing. Hope and salvation must be brought to a man who sits humbly on the bare edge of existence. The man, after all, is blind. He needs vision, both to see flowers in spring and to have hope in salvation.

Jesus sends the blind man to the holy pool of Siloam. There he will gain physical sight and raise his eyes to Mount Zion, where the glory of God rests in the temple. Locked within this blind man is a faith that groped through the darkness for salvation. His faith responded to God's call.

After the blind man's cure comes questioning. The neighbors are astonished and question him closely about how his cure happened. He is then brought to the Pharisees who are dismayed when the blind man, in his simple wisdom, unhesitatingly declares: "he [Jesus] is a prophet" (John 9:17).

Then his parents are brought in for questioning by the Pharisees. These religious leaders threaten the poor couple that if they are not telling the truth, they will be excommunicated from the temple. If this happens, the parents will be disgraced, shamed before their neighbors and friends, and deprived of whatever little consolation they received from singing the hymns and hearing the sermons. In their old age, they will be robbed of the experience of being in the very presence of the "glory." Consequently, the parents refuse any responsibility for their adult son. They point out that he is a man now and must speak for himself.

The Blind Man Answers the Pharisee

By this time, the Pharisees appear as desperate men who must corner their victim at all costs. They pursue the absurd line of argument that Jesus must be a sinner for showing such human concern. The cured man is not one bit ruffled and counters, quite logically, that Jesus, far from being a sinner, is like the prophets of old. He shifts the conversation so that now he is the one asking the questions.

He taunts the Pharisees by remarking that their interest in Jesus is just a bit too intense. If they are so absorbed in such a man, are they planning to become his followers? Is this really just a kind of research project? Is this a method that learned people go through to find out the truth? Are they just trying to prepare themselves to be his disciples? Do learned people always follow such a difficult path?

Their Studies Have Closed Their Minds

This attack has the desired effect of making the Pharisees admit what is really on their minds. They protest their loyalty to Moses and their disdain for Jesus. They are the protectors of the formal religion and are not easily fooled by any so-called new prophet. They reserve for themselves the right to prophesy, and to anoint a man whom they would consider heir to the mantle of the prophets. They feel, after all, that their long years of religious study have made them professionally competent to recognize the work of God in the world.

They can't believe that such an insight could come from a man who has no formal education. But the cured man is not impressed. In effect he tells them that, in their case, their studies have closed their minds. All their years of combing the Scriptures, analyzing the words, and talking about the laws have not given them insight, but blurred their vision. They, who should have been the light of the people are, instead, blind guides. Their training which was meant to be a fire that illumined their minds and warmed their hearts, hardened their hearts instead.

The Learned Man Must Guard against Pride

This story is not meant to be an attack on the intellectual life or religious studies. It is, however, meant to draw our attention to the dangers of religious studies that mask unbelief and obstruct others' belief. The simplicity of the cured blind man drives the learned Pharisees into a rage: "You were born in utter sin, and you would teach us?" (John 9:34) And they threw him out.

Now it is Jesus who comes seeking this simple man. Jesus crowns the hope of the man who was blind by introducing him to the final purpose of life — belief in the Son of Man. Jesus asks the man to trust that the hope of all people is found in him. He invites the blind man to believe in him in order to enter God's kingdom and receive the gift of salvation. And the man who could have passed no extended Scripture exams kneels before Jesus, and says, simply: "Lord, I believe" (John 9:38). And he worshipped Jesus.

This story is a warning to every Christian whose pride blocks an appreciation of the mystery of God. It is a reminder that arrogance is the fatal fault of those who trust too much in their religious learning and who forget that God does the revealing to those who come in faith. It is a tale that tempers the proud and calls for a celebration of the most authentic Christian, a truly humble person.

REFLECTION

The liturgy of the Church assigns this text in Year A for the Fourth Sunday of Lent. It is meant to draw people's attention to the candidates for the Rite of Christian Initiation of Adults (RCIA) — those who are preparing for baptism as well as those getting ready for full communion with the Church. In the early Church, catacomb art used this story seven times as a picture of Christian baptism.

This beautiful narrative is filled with observations about spiritual growth based on an openness to Jesus. Those who are closed to Jesus will experience spiritual decline. Faith in Jesus results in a commitment to him that culminates in baptism. Only a Jesus-centered faith ensures the spiritual development envisioned by the gospel.

Some people want a Christianity without Christ — a religion that has no faith teachings or moral requirements. Jesus is offstage longer here than in any other gospel text. Those who want to keep him away fall into radical disbelief. This happens today when some people want to distract us from thinking of Jesus, praying to him, being near him in the sacraments, especially the Eucharist. A loss of faith is the outcome.

The scrappy, street-smart blind man is the perfect antidote to any effort to block contact with Jesus. This nameless man is the patron saint of Christian realists. His stubborn loyalty to Jesus opened him to the gift of faith. He will be a good companion for us on our faith journey.

FOR DIALOGUE

What are some details in this narrative of the cure of the man born blind that relate it to baptism? Why do you think John's gospel has so many references to faith and baptism? What would be the value of the blind man's cure in John's ministry to converts in the early Church?

The students of religion do not come off well in this account. What might be three reasons you could cite that account for their inability to believe the blind man's story and their hostility to Christ? Why is religious learning not a guarantee of faith? On the other hand how does religious learning help faith to grow?

Why does this story fit so well in the process of preparing people to join the Church in the RCIA? What have you learned from the blind man's behavior?

Jesus, open the eyes of my heart to see with faith what you are trying to reveal to me. Let me learn of you both from my faith, and prayer as well as study.

Amazing grace, how sweet the sound that saved a wretch like me.
I once was lost but now am found, was blind but now I see.

REVEREND JOHN NEWTON

CHAPTER 40

Jesus Is Our Good Shepherd

John 10

"I am the good shepherd. The good shepherd lays down his life for the sheep.... I am the good shepherd, and I know my own and my own know me."

JOHN 10:11, 14

Psalm 23, the shepherd psalm, is the best loved of all the psalms. Jesus must have loved it too since he liked to use the image of the shepherd both about his own ministry as well as God the Father's approach to us. Let us begin with a reflection on Psalm 23 and then proceed to the tenth chapter of John's gospel where Jesus explained what a good shepherd should be like.

TRUSTING SHEEP

The opening verse, "The LORD is my shepherd, I shall not want" (v. 1), refers to the trusting attitude of the sheep. They know the shepherd will care for them. Jesus is our shepherd who loves us. We need to respond with a trust based on the conviction that Jesus wants to care for us.

The psalm continues, "he makes me lie down in green pastures" (v. 2). In biblical times the grazing habits of sheep were structured. They were awakened at 3:30 a.m., when they began grazing and continued until 10:00 a.m. when they paused to rest. The shepherd directed them first to the rough herbage and then to the smoother grass, and finally to the rich, fine, sweet grass of the green pasture. Then he made them lie down contentedly in the verdant pasture.

Jesus feeds us first with the rough herbage of challenging Christian ideals. He does not offer us a soft religion, but one that opens us to the difficulties of loving others, serving their needs, struggling for justice, visiting the sick, and overcoming evil. But he knows we also need the smoother grass of affirmation. He touches our hearts with his love and consolation, assuring us that he loves us. Lastly, he makes us lie down in green pastures, knowing we need the quiet of prayer and the rest of contemplation where our souls are refreshed with God's divine energy.

Sheep will not drink from running streams. Hence the verse, "He leads me beside still waters" (v. 2). The shepherd must often construct little pools of still water so that the sheep can drink it. In our case we live on the fast track of modern life. Our frantic lifestyles will never satisfy the deeper thirsts of our souls. Jesus brings us to the inner stillness that permits us to drink of the fountains of grace he offers us. At Tabernacles he called himself the living water, the source of the salvation we seek.

The Narrow Path

Everyone knows the next verse, so familiar, so consoling. "Even though I walk through the valley of the shadow of death, I fear no evil; for thou art with me" (v. 4). There is a mountain pass in Palestine that once bore this name. It stretches for four miles from Jerusalem to the Red Sea. The walls of the valley are 1,500 feet high and the width seldom exceeds 15 feet.

The path through it is narrow. Twice a year the shepherds took their flocks through it in search of greener pastures. The sheep faced several dangers. There was a ravine midway through the pass. The sheep must be coaxed to leap over it. [The absence of a small bridge is not explained.] Sometimes the shepherd carried the mother sheep across it so the lambs would be encouraged to jump it to be with her. If they fell, the shepherd used the crook (the curved end) of his staff to rescue them.

Another danger came from the wild dogs and wolves that prowled the valley. The lead sheep gave the signal should they appear. The shepherd rushed forward, using the pointed end of his staff to drive away or kill the enemy. The psalm remembers this with the words, "thy rod and thy staff, they comfort me" (v. 4).

Jesus knew that the shadow of death hovers over all people. He accepted his own death as the price for being human. He endured a violent, sacrificial death to save us from sin, conquer death, and give us a share of divine life. He left us the sacrament of reconciliation to pull us up from our sins so that we can renew our discipleship with Christ. His "rod and staff" protects us.

At night the sheep, one by one, entered the sheepfold. There was only one opening. The walls were made of piled up stones and topped with thorn bushes to keep out predatory animals. The shepherd inspected each one for cuts and fever. The shepherd anointed with oil any sheep wounded that day by sharp rocks or thorns. Then, to cool the fever of any animal, the shepherd plunged the head of the sheep into a basin of cool water to lower its temperature. The psalm pictures this for us: "You anoint my head with oil. My cup overflows" (v. 5).

Jesus Is the Gate

Jesus said he was the gate of the sheepfold. There was no door for the enclosure. The shepherd lay down at the one opening. He became the living door to the fold. He guarded them with his body. To enter Christ's community we need to go through him into the fold. He inspects each of us for the cuts of sin and the fever of passions. He plunges our heads into the cool waters of baptism to allay the fevers of the passions that draw us to sin. He anoints our cuts from sin with the oil of confirmation that we may have the divine courage to withstand evil.

Jesus Is Our Shepherd

Jesus knows each of us by name, certainly by our baptismal name. Through prayerful communion with him, we begin to "hear" his voice, affectionate, affirming, ready to feed us with the life of the Spirit. This is most evident in the lives of the saints who converse so intimately with him. Jesus also speaks of hirelings who are the false shepherds who lead the community astray. The hireling takes care of the sheep so long as there is no trouble. If the wolves come, the hireling runs away and leaves the community at the mercy of the "wolves," predators who destroy the flock.

The good shepherd works for love. The hireling works for money. Love is the substance of courage. The shepherds of the Church come in many forms: parents, teachers, nuns, priests, bishops, and popes. Leaders who are only interested in money will abandon their responsibilities to families, schools, parishes, and communities. Leaders who are "wolves" will prey on the weak, even children, as became evident in the priest-abuse scandals. Good shepherds are brave. They defend people even at the cost of their lives. Jesus states the principle by which a good shepherd must live. "I will lay down my life for the sheep" (cf. John 10:15).

REFLECTION

We cannot overcome our sins by human effort. A brilliant mind is not enough. Fierce willpower and rugged determination is insufficient. Conversely, simpleminded solutions won't work. Clever manipulation of our situations are of no help. Sin is a condition from which we need to be rescued. Evil is a situation from which we are saved by a redeemer. Jesus uses many ways to teach this fundamental religious lesson. He says, "I am the living bread. I am the living water. I am the good shepherd."

Knowing that we need a number of ways to understand what Jesus asks of us, he develops a number of compelling pictures that still engage our imagination and connect us to the sacraments of salvation. Bread. Water. Wine. Lambs. In every case Jesus is our savior reaching out to us, offering us salvation from sin, inviting us to take divine life from his outstretched hands.

When we fail to see this truth, we turn to our own devices. Typically we trust in money, sex, power, drugs, and even lies, violence, and domination. Many choose evil methods to overcome evil. It does not work. Satan cannot be made to overcome Satan. A house divided against itself cannot stand.

When there is solid leadership in the family, parish, school, community, and workplace, then the condition for the possibility of salvation is available. This is why we need good shepherds among our parents, teachers, religious, and political leaders. These shepherds do not save us, but they do lead us to Christ who has the power to save us. We pray to Christ, "Shepherd of souls, come heal and save us."

FOR DIALOGUE

Jesus uses the shepherd image to help us understand what he offers us in his redeeming sacrifice and ministry: The good shepherd is willing to die for the sheep's safety. He knows our name. He is the gate by which we enter the community. What impressions of these various aspects of the good shepherd have you received? Which aspect touches you most?

Does some form of being a shepherd come hand-in-hand with becoming an adult and having a leadership role? How does Christ's witness as a good shepherd shape your vision and practice?

How could you avoid being a false shepherd who exploits those committed to your care? Just as important, what will you do to avoid being a "wolf," one who acts as a predator upon helpless people?

Lord Jesus, loving shepherd of my soul, feed me with your Bread of Life. Anoint me with your healing oil in confirmation. Lift me from sin in your sacrament of reconciliation. Teach me to pray so that I may recognize my need of your salvation and be ever open to receive it.

"And I have other sheep, that are not of this fold; I must bring them also, and they will heed my voice. So there shall be one flock, one shepherd."

JOHN 10:16

CHAPTER 41

Jesus Raises Lazarus from the Dead

John 11:1-44

Martha said to Jesus, "Lord, if you had been here, my brother would not have died" . . . Jesus said to her, "Your brother will rise again."

JOHN 11:21, 23

A DEATH IN THE FAMILY. A DEATH OF A FRIEND

Everyone of us will experience this. Our materialistic culture is of two minds about death. On the one hand it wants to deny death and hide it. Yet, every day the newspaper carries an obituary column, stories about murders, fatal accidents, assassinations, suicides, wars, executions, and lethal tragedies of all kinds.

Scripture teaches it is better to think about death than deny it. Death should never be an "X-rated" topic. One person may look at death and see in it a challenge to make meaning out of life. Another will ponder death and be motivated to explore life's possibilities. Others will see in death the bridge to eternal life. This is what Jesus did for us. When he cured the man born blind, he demonstrated he was the light of the world. When he raised Lazarus from the dead, he made concrete his claim that he is the life of the world. With this in mind, we proceed to meditate on the eleventh chapter of John's gospel where Jesus raises Lazarus from the dead.

Three Parts to the Narrative

The story is divided into three parts: the prelude; the dialogue; the miracle. The prelude introduces the problem, namely, the critical illness of Lazarus. The dialogue illustrates the meaning of the miracle that is to occur. The miracle is another sign of Christ's divinity being manifested and his call to faith in himself.

In the prelude Jesus and the apostles have gone into seclusion at a hideaway, on the east side of the Jordan, not far from where John the Baptist held his calls to conversion and baptism. Messengers bring Jesus news of the quickly failing health of his close friend, Lazarus. As happens so often in

John's gospel, Jesus is presented with a dilemma — and he appears strangely indifferent to it. At Cana, he doesn't seem to share his mother's concern about the empty wine jugs. On the mountain, he doesn't seem alarmed by the food shortage. Now, hearing that Lazarus is dying, he says that the illness will not end in death but manifest the glory of God, "that the Son of God may be glorified by means of it" (John 11:4). He loved Martha and Mary and their brother Lazarus, yet he remained in the place where he was for two days. We might be taking the next plane to be at the bedside of a loved one. Oddly, Jesus stays put. As we find out, he permits Lazarus to die and stay in the grave four days so that the death is certain and then the resurrection will be authentic.

Jesus Wants People to See a Crisis from God's Point of View

You must not think that this means that Jesus is indifferent to human problems or, on the other hand, that he is like a gambler who delights in knowing that he has the winning ace in his hand. The "delay stories" are meant to show that Jesus wanted to help, but to do so from the divine perspective. He asks us to look at a crisis situation from God's point of view. There are issues deeper than temporary embarrassment at a wedding or a shortfall of food at a prayer meeting. Jesus persistently reveals God's presence and his own glory-divinity in each of these crises.

He invited the apostles and later the family and friends of Lazarus to join him by looking at the event with faith. He wants them to share with him the agony and struggle necessary to prepare for the divine breakthrough. He is attempting to drive the magical elements out of faith, to nudge them to understand that faith is not a childish hope for a supernatural trick, but the mature obedience of men and women open to the great power of God.

Jesus wanted to situate their faith in the environment of struggling hope and trust. When Jesus feels they have begun to sense the drama of the faith need, he gives the instruction: "Lazarus has died. And I am glad for you that I was not there, that you may believe. But let us go to him" (John 11:14-15).

Jesus Speaks of Resurrection from the Dead

In his dialogue with the grief-stricken sisters of Lazarus, Martha and Mary, Jesus strives to awaken their faith in the resurrection of the body. Not all Jews believed this. The Pharisees taught the resurrection, but the Sadducees denied it. This teaching was underdeveloped at the time. It was Christ's intention to prepare his listeners for the full revelation of this truth.

Martha and Mary were more interested in the life of Lazarus here rather than his resurrection at some distant date. They both tell Jesus that their brother would not have died had he been there. They fully expected him to perform a healing miracle for his best friend. After having healed so many strangers, surely he would cure someone so close to him.

He assured them that their brother would rise again. They are not very impressed with his answer because they think he is referring to the religious belief that all faithful Jews will rise on the last day. This article of faith is of little comfort to them, who want a living brother now rather than in the obscure future. To them, Christ's reply avoided the real issue.

This sets the stage for the beauty of Christ's response. He wanted to enrich their faith in the final resurrection. His daring promise is that, for people of faith, there is the assurance of eternal life beginning now. Their brother will rise today. "I am the resurrection and the life; whoever, believes in me, even if he dies, will live, and everyone who lives and believes in me, will never die"(John 11:25-26).

Far from avoiding the problem, Jesus addresses himself to it immediately. He is teaching the two women — and all of us — that he is bringing us ultimate freedom from death. He is making the most extravagant claim that Christianity will proclaim through the ages. He is not excluding the possibility of physical death. He is saying rather that this dark hour is not so dark after all.

He is calling all people to trust that in him everyone can survive death and enter into everlasting life. We can receive the beginning of eternal life now. At death life is changed, not taken away. Freedom from death means liberation from the fear that death is the end of everything. Freedom from death implies that we now can attend to the responsibilities of living because we have the glorious promise of living on in Christ Jesus.

The key words in this hope of freedom from death are "responsible living." Wrong attitudes toward death result in either a reckless wasting of life, or a neurotic, convulsive hold on life. Jesus wants to free us from such extreme reactions. The resurrection relieves us of the worry about the afterlife so that we can pay attention to the needs of this life. Naturally, the burden of death, the stages of grief, the sense of loss of a loved one, and some of its mystery endure, but Christ's promise makes such a burden light.

Suffering and Sadness Remain

In the miracle scene, seldom has the humanity of God shone forth so convincingly as it does when Jesus weeps before the tomb of Lazarus. In his talk with the sisters, Jesus makes clear that, even when people have faith, they must still face the suffering and sadness of human life. The vision of faith that Christ brings to us cannot erase the burdens of human life. Expertly, that is shown to us in this story.

The event ends with Jesus confidently calling forth Lazarus from the grave. Here is an ultimate breakthrough of God's power in history and the confirmation of the promise of life after death.

As you can see, the issues in the Lazarus story are not a superficial report of "life on the other side," but rather a forceful declaration that there is life in the beyond. This incident is a page in the story of freedom that Jesus brings us. In this case, the freedom from death is explained. Here is a religious statement of deep meaning for all those who wish to live this life to the fullest in faith and as responsible and mature Christians.

REFLECTION

The poet Dylan Thomas looked at death and said we should not go gently into that good night. We should "rage, rage against the dying of the light." Those words express our survival instincts and our tight hold on life. Yet this poet also speaks of Christianity's compelling message about life after death and the resurrection.

And death shall have no dominion
Dead men naked, they shall be one
With the man in the wind and the west moon . . .
Though they sink through the sea, they shall rise again.

St. Paul said this of Jesus, "Death no longer has dominion over him" (Romans 6:9). An even better text is Paul's entire fifteenth chapter of his First Letter to the Corinthians, where he lyrically celebrates the revelation of Christ's resurrection and his own.

Facing the reality of death will be easier when we take seriously its impact on helping us to live the present life to the full. Looking at death becomes even more valuable when we see it as the door to eternal life. Some of today's self-help books promise happiness through certain techniques that deter us from looking squarely at pain, tragedy, and death. Instead of going through the sorrow, we are encouraged to run around it. This approach views life as a headache, quickly cured by an aspirin. But much of life is a heartache whose healing requires faith, trust, and surrender to the mystery of God's plan for us.

The Christian view of death teaches us there is another life beyond. This is the lesson of Christ's raising of Lazarus from the dead. It forecasts Christ's own resurrection at Easter that made possible our own share in eternal life both here and hereafter and our future resurrection on the last day.

FOR DIALOGUE

What has been your experience of the various ways people speak of death? How do people differ about having wakes with the coffin open or closed? What do you think about this variety in dealing with death?

How are you affected by Christ's reaction to the death of Lazarus when he comes to the grave of his friend — "He trembled with deep emotion"? When some people speak of death as a mystery, what response would you give?

In what way does Christ's raising of Lazarus help you to deepen your Christian faith in the teaching that at death, "Life is changed, not taken away"?

PRAYER

Thank you, Jesus, for the gift of eternal life, received already here and then in the future life. Thanks, too, for the promise of the resurrection of the body on the last day. Help us to live in faith and responsibility here that when we die, we may live in joy with you.

"Did I not tell you that if you would believe you would see the glory of God?"

JOHN 11:40

CHAPTER 42

Jesus Is Tempted

Matthew 4:1-11; Luke 4:1-13

For we have not a high priest who is unable to sympathize with our weaknesses, but one who in every respect has been tempted as we are, yet without sin.

HEBREWS 4:15

Removing evil from the world is no easy matter. In the Garden of Eden there might have been two ways to prevent Adam and Eve from sinning. First, get rid of the serpent so that no temptation could occur. Second, deny Adam and Eve the gift of freedom so that it would be impossible for them to choose to sin. But this reduces man and woman to a subspecies, closer to the animals than to God. They would be superior "pets" who have no freedom, no struggles to choose God and the good act, no temptations, no capacity to express sacrificial love.

MADE IN THE IMAGE AND LIKENESS OF GOD

In God's plan we are made images of God, with the ability to think, to make decisions, and to enjoy the gift of freedom. As images of God we still have that dynamic drive toward God. This is a force within us urging us to love God and one another and to know and live by the truth. But we also bear the effects of original sin, a counterforce that inclines us to evil and to succumb to temptations to sin.

Jesus emptied himself of the status of glory as Son of God and humbled himself to be like us in all things except sin. As part of his life as a man, he experienced temptations to sin, but never gave in. Just after his baptism at the Jordan at the beginning of his public ministry, Jesus spent forty days of fasting in the desert. At the end of that spiritual discipline he faced three temptations from Satan.

Extensive fasting produces three stages. At first the person just notices the lack of food and the desire for food disappears. As the body fails to receive any outward feeding, it begins to feed on itself.

At a later stage the body starts feeding on essential organs. This causes a brutal hunger that consumes the person's instinct for self-preservation. At the same time, the one fasting feels light, free, even a sense of floating beyond usual boundaries. Physical weakness is countered by spiritual power. But the person is also subject to a dangerous loss of self-control. The usual cautions are hard to maintain.

The Temptations of Jesus

The following quotes from the temptation are from Matthew 4.

In a state similar to this, Jesus faces three temptations. The tempter approached him and said, "If you are the Son of God, command that these stones become loaves of bread" (v. 4). The small round toast-colored stones had the appearance of loaves of bread. The Tempter asks Jesus to use his power to satisfy himself. He asks Jesus to misuse his extraordinary powers for his own benefit. Jesus refused to exploit his gifts in such a manner. He replied, "Man shall not live by bread alone, but by every word that proceeds from the mouth of God" (v. 4). We must have earthly bread to stay alive. But we must also have the hunger for the bread that is the Word that comes from God's mouth. Bread for the soul is as essential as bread for the body.

Next Satan took Jesus to the top of the highest tower of the temple. From this vantage point there was a 450-foot drop to the bottom of the Kedron valley. This summit was the place where a temple priest stood each morning and sounded the *shofar* (the ram's horn) when the first glint of dawn hit the Hebron hills. It was the call to come and present sacrifices to God. Satan said, "If you are the Son of God, throw yourself down; for it is written, 'He will give his angels charge of you,' and 'On their hands they will bear you up, lest you strike your foot against a stone'" (v. 6).

Satan seemed to be saying, "It is clear you are a born religious leader. But you need to do something to attract people's attention. Look at the crowds down there in the temple court. Jump from this tower! Descend from the heavens! Did not the prophet Daniel say that you would come in the clouds of heaven. Do not fear. Angels will cushion your fall."

Jesus replied, "Again it is written, 'You shall not tempt the Lord, your God'" (v. 7). Basically Jesus was saying to Satan, "It is evil to try to force God's hand. You are wrong to think that I should use my powers to amaze people, to awe them with a theatrical entrance as you suggest. You may not tempt God or people with astonishing gimmicks. There will be signs and wonders, but these are part of a gospel strategy that begins small and humbly, planting tiny mustard seeds that grow quietly and slowly. You want me to build idols in the temple. I will call people to meet the living God."

Then Satan took Jesus to the summit of a very high mountain and showed him all the kingdoms of the world. They could see the splendor of Jerusalem, the gold of the temple, and the spacious courts of Herod's imperial palace. Satan tempted Jesus again. "All these I will give you, if you will fall down and worship me" (v. 9). Satan could add, "Beyond the seas are great kingdoms and cities — Alexandria, Athens, Carthage, and Rome. You want a better life for your followers. You need power to do this. I can teach you how to take over the very throne of Caesar."

Jesus needed no such power. He could have said, "Power corrupts those who seek it. And absolute power corrupts absolutely. You offer a power where the strong bewilder the weak. If there must be power, let it be the power of love that comes from God. I will not bruise the tender reed."

Satan would never buy this approach. "You are wrong. You will fail if you do not listen to me. Put yourself in my hands. Adore me and I will give you the world." Jesus could have replied, "Never! You lie! I hate what you ask." Jesus quoted Scripture again, "You shall worship the Lord, your God, and him alone shall you serve" (v. 11). We might hear Jesus say also, "Be gone, Satan! Get out! Oh God. Abba. Father.... Help me." And angels came and comforted him.

In the furnace of the desert solitude Jesus was strengthened for his mission. In experiencing temptations in the midst of a weakened condition brought on by extensive fasting, Jesus knew in a very intense manner what many of us go through. By resisting temptations, Jesus not only gave us a good example, but also won for us the graces we will need to overcome temptations. We speak of the mysteries of Christ's thoughts, words, and deeds. Because they are performed by the Son of God, though in a human nature, they have redemptive power. We can draw from him not just the inspiration of an admirable model, but also the powerful graces that overcome evil.

REFLECTION

In our meditation on the temptations of Jesus we can find the sources of spiritual energy that he used to drive away the tempter. Among these are silence, fasting, and prayer. In each element there was the effective presence of the Holy Spirit.

Silence. External silence makes us aware of the "twenty-four-hour movie" that keeps running inside our heads. Outward silence is a method for gaining interior quiet. Inner quiet is meant to help us pay attention to God's efforts to reach us. A spiritual giver needs a spiritual receiver. Heart can only speak to heart. Silence helps us to be receivers and have an open heart. The calming voice of the Holy Spirit invites us to the inward energy we need in the battle against temptation.

Fasting. (Before undertaking a fast be sure you consult your doctor and your mentor or guide lest you do harm to your health.) Spiritual guides have always recommended fasting as a path to holiness. Gandhi used the fast to intensify what he called his "soul force." Dieting slims the body and focuses the mind. Fasting for a religious purpose increases our attention to the Holy Spirit. Religious fasting is to the soul what aerobic exercise is to the body. Fitness experts speak of the "training effect" one receives from regular exercise. As we grow stronger we do daily tasks with less effort. The same is true in spirituality. The inner strength that comes helps one resist temptations.

Prayer. During his forty days in the desert, Jesus prayed. At the other key moments of his life, such as the baptism, transfiguration, the choice of his disciples, Gethsemane, Jesus handed himself over to the Father in prayer. The apostles were so impressed with his prayer they asked him to teach them how to pray. Jesus taught them the Our Father. It was the prayer of a beggar, with seven petitions. The first three petitions ask God to sanctify his name, establish his kingdom, and accomplish his will in the world. The last four deal with human needs — daily nourishment, forgiveness, and all the graces possible to withstand temptations and evil. This is the greatest prayer and one that should govern all of our prayers.

Jesus gives us a spiritual plan for a spiritual battle. In the desert He worked in cooperation with the Holy Spirit. So should we. Our victory over sin means that we will be liberated from self-destructive behavior. At the same time, we are freed to love God, others, and self. We learn how to perform small acts with great love.

FOR DIALOGUE

What have you found helpful in resisting temptations to sin? Why do we say that forming good habits, which involve the practice of virtues, help us avoid sin? What are some external forms of temptation that you would say come from the culture?

How would silence, fasting, and prayer help you ward off temptations? Why is it absolutely necessary to have God's graces to help you resist temptations?

Why do you think so many people find it hard to resist temptations to sin? Who are people you know personally — or from reading about in books and newspapers — that impress you with their commitment to virtues and resisting sin?

PRAYER

Jesus, send us your Holy Spirit to form our consciences in such a way that we recognize sin and evil when faced with temptations. Give us every grace we need to overcome any temptation to evil.

"Father . . . lead us not into temptation, But deliver us from evil."
MATTHEW 6:9, 13

CHAPTER 43

Christ's Gospel of Love — The Sermon on the Mount

Matthew 5-7

"Think not that I have come to abolish the law and the prophets;
I have come not to abolish them but to fulfill them."

MATTHEW 5:17

THE SERMON ON THE MOUNT

Christ's Sermon on the Mount (Matthew 5-7) is the greatest sermon on morality ever preached. The context is love and happiness. Jesus taught that the greatest moral commandments are the love of God and neighbor. A scholar of the law asked Jesus, "Teacher, which is the great commandment in the law?" Jesus said to him, "You shall love the Lord, your God, with all your heart, with all your soul, and with all your mind. This is the great and first commandment. And a second is like it, You shall love your neighbor as yourself" (Matthew 22:36-39).

These love commandments already existed in the Old Testament. The call to love God is in Deuteronomy 6:5. The love of neighbor is in Leviticus 19:18. Jesus connected them and made them the standard for all other moral thinking and behavior. These laws of love permeate every line of the Sermon on the Mount.

The other theme dominating the sermon is happiness. Jesus taught that the desire for happiness is an excellent motivation for being moral. There is in fact no better way to be happy than to be moral. As Son of God he is the author of human nature and knows best what will make us joyful. It is a pity that Christ's moral teachings are often presented without the two themes of love and joy. Because of this lack, the moral life seems like a burden and a gloomy prospect for a life plan. St. Augustine brings his usual wisdom to the connection between happiness and being moral:

We all want to live happily; in the whole human race there is no one who does not assent to this proposition, even before it is fully articulated. How

is it then that I seek you, Lord? Since in seeking you, my God, I seek a
happy life, let me seek you that my soul may live, for my body draws life
from my soul and my soul draws life from you.

ST. AUGUSTINE

Happiness Requires God

Other great Church teachers echoed Augustine. St. Thomas Aquinas wrote that, "God alone satisfies." In his greatest work, the *Summa Theologica*, he dwelt on the role of happiness as the goal of the moral life, before he wrote about the rules and responsibilities of morality.

The Beatitudes

Jesus began the Sermon on the Mount with the eight beatitudes. The word beatitude means happiness. Traditional translations use the expression, "Blessed are you . . ." It would be just as true to say, "Happy are you . . ." How shall we be happy? By being poor in spirit, mourning, being meek, hungering for justice, being merciful, being clean of heart, peacemaking, and suffering persecution for God's kingdom, we receive the key to happiness.

For each of these pathways there is a divine reward that includes inheriting God's kingdom, receiving God's consolation and mercy, seeing God, becoming children of God, finding real justice. Of course, such happiness occurs imperfectly here, and completely hereafter. "The beatitudes teach us the final end to which God calls us: the Kingdom, the vision of God, participation in the divine nature, eternal life, filiation, rest in God" (CCC 1726). Our sinful inclinations prevent us from being totally happy on earth. In heaven we will have perfect joy.

After the beatitudes, all the rest of the Sermon on the Mount is a series of practical applications by which Jesus shows us how to live the eight pathways to happiness and love of God, others, and self. Every so often Jesus explicitly adds his own authoritative interpretation of one or other of the Ten Commandments, bringing out the need to correct the attitudes as well as attention to external acts — and even correcting an interpretation as in the case of hating enemies.

"You have heard it was said to the men of old, 'You shall not kill. . . .' But
I say to you that every one who is angry with his brother will be liable to
judgment. . . . You have heard that it was said, 'You shall not commit adultery.' But I say to you that everyone who looks at a woman lustfully has
already committed adultery with her in his heart. . . . You have heard that

it was said, 'You shall love your neighbor and hate your enemy.' But I say to you, Love your enemies and pray for those who persecute you."
MATTHEW 5:21-22, 27-28, 43-44

Other ways of stating the goals of the moral life are perfection, mercy, and holiness. In Matthew's gospel Jesus asks us, "Be perfect, as your heavenly Father is perfect" (Matthew 5:48). But in Luke's version of this sermon, Jesus speaks of the goal in terms of mercy. "Be merciful, even as your Father is merciful" (Luke 6:36). God the Father puts it this way, "Be holy, for I am holy" (Leviticus 11:45). We deduce from these texts that the Father is perfect, holy, and merciful. Those are the traits of his identity.

In the 137 verses of the Sermon on the Mount, Jesus outlines a number of practical ways to achieve such ideals. Beyond these are all the teachings of the whole Bible, the teachings and examples of all the saints and holy witnesses of Christ from the early Church to the present. In addition we have the resources of the sacraments, especially the sacraments of reconciliation and the Eucharist. We benefit from the prayers of the Communion of Saints, those in heaven, purgatory, and on earth. We do not exist in a moral and spiritual vacuum. There is a mighty power of prayerful support, especially with the Blessed Mother and the saints as well as of Jesus himself, standing before the Father, always interceding on our behalf.

REFLECTION

In the moral life there are always two movements: God in search of us. Man and woman in quest of God. The poet Francis Thompson described God's attempts to reach us in terms of God being the "Hound of Heaven." Thompson said he felt God coming after him, yearning to give him love. But the poet was not ready.

> *I fled him, down the nights and down the days;*
> *I fled him, down the arches of the years.*
> *I fled him, down the labyrinthine ways*
> *of my own mind. I hid from him.*

A Spiritual Adventure

At the same time, God has stamped in our souls a longing for himself. We are born with an inner drive to God, a longing for the divine that cannot be satisfied by anyone or anything short of God. We are created to be seekers for the absolute love, which is God.

Francis Thompson not only experienced God as the hound pursuing him, he also felt his own hunger and thirst for God. One day he stopped running away from God. He turned and rushed toward him begging for love.

Naked, I wait Thy love's uplifted stroke!
My harness, piece by piece, Thou has hewn from me,
I am defenseless utterly.

And God, the other seeker, in this spiritual drama says:

Rise, clasp my hand, and come!

The Holy Spirit presided over this spiritual adventure. The Spirit's action within us is sometimes hidden and we feel that God is far away. The consoling presence is not here. Spiritual writers remind us that our duty is to "seek the God of consolations, not the consolations of God." Even Jesus on the Cross confessed to feeling abandoned and forsaken by his Father. These times of being in a spiritual desert are challenges for us to remain firm in our faith. As the old saying puts it, "When the going gets tough, the tough get going."

FOR DIALOGUE

When you think about morality, what issues come to your mind? If you have a negative reaction, what might be the cause of that? If your response is positive, what are the experiences that made that possible?

Jesus proposed happiness as the motivation for being moral. How often has that idea occurred to you? Why does it make sense that being moral is the best way to be happy? Of course Jesus is thinking of the kind of joy that lasts forever, such as that associated with heaven, but already occurring here. How do you link earthly and heavenly joy?

Why do so many people find the moral life so difficult? Which passages of the Sermon on the Mount appeal to you? Why? What are some moral challenges you face these days?

Jesus, help me to be perfect, holy, and merciful just like your heavenly Father. Lead me to be patient and open to the graces that will make this possible in my life. O Lord, be merciful to me a sinner.

Jesus said to the woman taken in adultery, "Neither do I condemn you. Go and do not sin again."

JOHN 8: 11

CHAPTER 44

Jesus Performs Miracles — Signs and Wonders

Matthew 8-9; Mark 1-5; Luke 4-5, 7-8; John 2:1-12, 4:46-53; 6:1-21; 9:1-40; 11:1-44

Jesus said to him, "Rise, take up your pallet, and walk." And at once the man was healed, and he took up his pallet and walked.

JOHN 5:8-9

SIGNS OF GOD'S PRESENCE

People talk of miracles every day. We constantly hear of the "miracles of science." Five million people every year journey to Lourdes either hoping for a miraculous cure or for an increase of their faith. Men walk on the moon; pharmacies sell miracle drugs; and research centers promise even greater signs and wonders.

Today the World Talks of Man's Miracles

Has it occurred to you that in our so-called scientific age, many persons cast doubt on the miracles of religion, then use the idea of miracles for man-made wonders? To paraphrase the "Ancient Mariner": "Miracles, miracles everywhere — and not a drop of faith." The word "miracle" formerly meant a special sign of God's presence and action in history. Today, it is used almost exclusively to praise human cleverness.

All this is not to say that we should not gratefully praise the tough-minded achievements of science. But we should regret the scorn sometimes heaped on religious claims to miracles. And we should be appalled by those who deny that Jesus performed the signs and wonders attributed to him in the gospels. Finally, let's be aware that many fail to see any religious meaning in the wondrous productions of our laboratories.

Let us applaud the winners of the Nobel Prize, but let's shy away from making gods out of our white-coated researchers. It would be a mistake to put our wonder-workers on altars. Ultimately, it is God to whom the glory should be given.

The Ten Miracles in Matthew's Gospel

This may become clearer to us if we first take a closer look at the miracle stories in the gospels. In St. Matthew's gospel, chapters 8-9, we find an account of ten miracles of Jesus, followed by an explanation of the role of these wonders in the apostolate.

It will be easier to appreciate Matthew's point if we remember the general presentation he had in mind. He wanted to portray Jesus for his Jewish readers as the greatest person imaginable. Up to this time, no man had greater claim to Jewish esteem than Moses. Hence, Matthew surrounds Jesus with qualities and details that were typical of Moses, thought to be the writer of the first five books of the Bible. The common Jewish name for these books was Torah or "the law." Moses was called the lawgiver. In imitation of this, Matthew divided his gospel into five parts. In each section, he drew a parallel between Jesus and Moses. He used this technique both to show the greatness of Jesus, and his superiority to Moses.

The Ten Miracles of Jesus and the Ten Plagues

In our previous chapter, we studied the Sermon on the Mount. Jesus is like a new Moses, a new lawgiver on a new Sinai. In his ten miracles as reported by Matthew, Jesus seems to echo the mighty works of God wrought through Moses by the ten plagues of Egypt.

The plagues of Egypt were ten signs of God's displeasure with the Pharaoh, who stood as the symbol of the evils of injustice and cruelty. The Egyptian leader had dehumanized and enslaved the Jews. He robbed them of their rights, their religious heritage, and human dignity. The ten plagues signaled the advance of God against such a kingdom of evil.

We can find the same meaning, only in a richer fashion, in Matthew's account. Jesus cleanses the lepers, thus restoring their human dignity. They need no longer be outcasts of society. Jesus cools the fever of Peter's mother-in-law, raises people from the dead, relieves the embarrassment of the dumb, erases the humiliations of the paralyzed, and eases the torments of the mentally afflicted.

As God once made the Red Sea safe for passage, so now Jesus calms a storm at sea. As Moses, by the power of God drove out the devils of Egypt, so now Jesus drives out the demons that would elude and enslave the helpless.

The new "pharaoh" is the sum total of human ills that frustrate the growth and dignity of people. The new pharaoh is the presence of evil in the world. The new pharaoh is the old demon, Satan, who sows evil in the hearts of people who yield to his temptations. Such evil causes people to refuse to see anything beyond the human. The evil spirit flatters us into denying that there is anything beyond ourselves, and urges us to forget the presence of the divine in the midst of the world.

God Is at Work in the World

Over and over again, it becomes clear that miracles are signs of God's saving and providential presence. They are wonders that prove God's intention to raise us to the peak of human dignity. They are examples of the graciousness of God who rescues us from the sin, guilt, and chaos that comes from forgetting him altogether.

Miracles are that extra dimension of life that should cause us to stop and take notice. They should stimulate a shock of recognition: we are not alone in the world; God is in our midst. Jesus told his followers that the miracles are a way of saying that the kingdom is at hand. By the kingdom, he meant God's rule of salvation, love, justice, and mercy in the world. Jesus gave us the Church to be the witness and communicator of God's kingdom.

Through the Church, through Christ's community of believers, God is powerfully at work in the world to accomplish his will for all people. God's plan includes salvation from all sin, guilt, and evil so that there will be peace for the world, the victory of God's love in human hearts, the establishment of divine justice, and the promise of eternal hope for everyone.

The miracles tell us that the kingdom is always at hand. What we, as the community of believers, must do, is work to make this kingdom a reality for everyone. We must act as if all depended on ourselves and pray as if all depended on God. We live with our human energies supported by the powerful graces of God. God has not gone back on promises. It is the Church that must make these promises available in a practical way. Don't forget that the Church is the community of believers.

The Miracle of Love

The kingdom is at hand, but no one will know it if we do not show it. The miracle we must perform is the mighty work of love. To you and me, as to all Christians, is entrusted the miracle of making love a standard of action in the world. Still, we must always remember that we do not act alone. The love we wish to bring to the world originates in God. "God's love has been poured out into our hearts through the Holy Spirit which has been given to us" (Romans 5:5).

Technology is the world's miracle of our time. This is a triumph of reason, which is itself a gift from God. But love remains the enduring religious miracle of all time. Miracles are victories of faith. Scientists can make the bomb, but only love can control it. Technicians can make the automobile, but only human concern can keep it safe. Botanists can make new possibilities for millions of tons of wheat, but it takes love to make sure the world does not go hungry. We must pledge ourselves to the miracle of love and believe that it will work.

REFLECTION

While we have noted that God's love manifested through our Christian concern and love for others is like a continuing miracle in the world, we must not forget there are still miracles in the stricter use of the term. Pope John Paul II canonized 464 saints during his papacy. The canonization process includes verifying a miracle attributed to the intercession of the candidate for sainthood. Such miracles have occurred and have been validated.

Moreover, the famed shrines such as Lourdes continue to report miracles of healing, not in great numbers, but from time to time. It takes a lot of time to authenticate them.

In the gospels Jesus performed miracles of healing (sight for the blind, hearing for the deaf, mobility for the lame, exorcizing demons); miracles of nature (multiplication of the loaves, calming the storm at sea, cursing the fig tree); miracles of resurrection of the body (raising Lazarus, the son of the widow of Naim, the daughter of Jairus). In particular, though, his miracles of healing in which he drives out illness and evil spirits, Jesus demonstrates both his compassion for bodily ailments and his intention to overcome the power of Satan in this world. These are signs of his redemptive power that will save us from the control of sin and death.

In John's gospel, Christ's miracles are signs of his divinity. John uses the term "glory," adopted from the Old Testament terms *Shekinah* and *Kabod* that referred to the visible, radiant cloud and pillar of fire by which God manifested his presence to Israel. In multiplying the wine at Cana and the bread in the wilderness; by curing the blind man and raising Lazarus from the dead, Jesus released his inner glory that showed his divinity and called the beholders to faith in him. Christ's miracles did not force people to believe. His miracles invited people's faith in him.

FOR DIALOGUE

What would you do if you were privileged to witness a miracle? Why do you think faith is so important when dealing with miracles? Why are Christ's gospel miracles excellent ways to perceive God's saving presence and providential care in the world today?

Why do millions of people make pilgrimages to Lourdes, Fatima, Guadalupe, and other shrines? Why does the Church look for miracles as part of the canonization process in making saints? Why did so many miracles happen in the ministry of Jesus as well as in the New Testament Church? Why are miracles less frequent today?

In a broader sense we speak of the "miracle" of love and Christian witness. Why is this a legitimate observation?

PRAYER

Jesus, we pray that you will continue to heal our souls through the sacraments and heal our attitudes through our life of prayer. We also pray for your graces of healing for the sick and those suffering from other causes. Be merciful, O Lord.

But Peter said, "I have no silver and gold, but I give you what I have; in the name of Jesus Christ of Nazareth, walk."

ACTS 3:6

CHAPTER 45

Jesus Describes God's Kingdom and Church in Parables

Mathew 13; 18; 20:1-16; Luke 8:4-18; 10:29-37;
12:16-21; 14:15-35; 15:1-32

"The kingdom of heaven may be likened to a man who sowed good seed in his field...." All this Jesus said to the crowds in parables.

MATTHEW 13:24, 34

Sometimes it is better to describe than to define. A definition has a way of putting an end to a discussion because of the limits that it sets. I have seen some blank looks on the faces of people when they hear others defining a Catholic. Description is a little easier to take because it doesn't close the question. A description is gracious enough to imply that there is something more. A Catholic is much more than a definition can indicate.

A CHALLENGE TO BE ACCEPTED OR REJECTED

When Jesus wanted to portray the kingdom of heaven he was bringing, he chose to describe it, rather than define it. This is why he used parables. Parables describe; they don't define. Parables have the power of poetry. Poetry, as a descriptive device, always hints that the reality is greater than any one thing you can say about it.

The reality of the kingdom is much greater than any one picture we can give of it. Parables emphasize the mystery of the kingdom as a work and revelation of God. Today we generally speak of the kingdom of "God." In Christ's time it was customary not to speak the name of God out of reverence for the Lord. So Jesus substituted the word heaven in its place.

Scan the thirteenth chapter of St. Matthew's gospel and you will find Christ's parables of the kingdom. Here, Jesus presents you with a set of images that attempt to give you a feel for the meaning of the Church. While the Church is not identical with the kingdom, it is called to be a witness to it and should represent what Jesus wanted us to know about the kingdom and how that should appear in the Church.

The kingdom is God's rule for us — the divine dimension of his presence among us. St. Paul beautifully describes the kingdom for us. "For the kingdom of God is not food and drink but righteousness and peace and joy in the Holy Spirit; he who thus serves Christ is acceptable to God and approved by men. Let us then pursue what makes for peace and for mutual upbuilding" (Romans 14:17-19). Since the realities of Church and kingdom are so closely related, for the sake of convenience, we will use the terms interchangeably.

Each of these parables fills out the broad view of the meaning of the Church. The longest and most famous of these stories is the parable of the sower. When the Christian missionary proclaims the kingdom of God, he is like a farmer scattering seed. The farmer knows that some of the seeds will find good ground and grow. Other seeds will meet obstacles and fail to take root.

Good Christian missionaries announce the kingdom to all available people. They know that their missionary work faces both the pleasing prospects of success and the depressing results of failure. Some people will accept the kingdom with joy. Others will consider it an intellectual curiosity and dismiss it. A third group will reject it altogether and, perhaps, even work to frustrate its progress. The missionaries present the Church as a challenge that must either be accepted or rejected. They are so serious about this challenge that they will not let anyone be indifferent to the gospel, just as the farmer is not indifferent to his hopes for a harvest.

Christ Warned about Evil in the Church

Jesus tells a second parable about the wheat and the weeds. An enemy sows destructive weeds in the field that threaten the vitality of the crop. In this story, Jesus draws our attention to the existence of evil in the life of the Church. Everybody in the kingdom is not a saint. Sadly, there may be a Judas in your congregation. In your enthusiasm for the integrity of the Church, you may want to root out the sinners and the traitors.

Because of this, Jesus urges a realistic and healthy caution. "No; lest in gathering the weeds you root up the wheat along with them. Let both grow together until the harvest; and at harvest time I will tell the reapers, 'Gather the weeds first and bind them in bundles to be burned, but gather the wheat into my barn'" (Matthew 13: 29-30).

You must not think that Jesus wants you to be indifferent to the evil people in the Church. Rather, he wants you to have the hard-eyed realism to know that such things happen in a sinful world. You may, indeed, work to convert the sinners and soften their harmful influence on the community. But a fanatic campaign to stamp them out may threaten the existence of the good people as well as the bad. Plainly put, sinners will live within the community of faith. This is an unpleasant picture, but a true one. It is part of the description of the Church and Jesus tells us so. Since all of us need conversion from sin and the graces of Christ's redemption, this should give us a humble attitude in this matter.

The Humble Can Put the Strong to Shame

Jesus continues his description with the images of the mustard seed and the leaven. The smallest of all seeds grows into the biggest tree. The tiny piece of leaven enlarges the dough into a fine loaf of bread. Jesus teaches that the beginnings of the Church are always small. The kingdom is not promoted by sending a huge expeditionary force to land on the beaches of the pagans. Big publicity campaigns, flashy advertising, and strong-arm tactics are not the true way to present the gospel. The weak, that is the truly humble, are to put the strong to shame. If it is the other way around, then we raise a doubt about the honesty of the faith. The growth and progress of the Church is primarily the work of the Holy Spirit. The more we depend on the Spirit, the greater will be the results.

The Church is a community of faith and grace. The act of faith must be made in freedom. Massive conversion techniques would be like a bulldozer. Rather than inviting people to believe from the vantage point of freedom, you might find yourself forcing them to believe. To either trick or force people into the Church fails to be like the mustard seed or the leaven.

Membership in the Church Makes Serious Demands

The last series of parables in Matthew is about the hidden treasure, the merchant in search of fine pearls, and the sorting of the good and bad fish. The treasure and pearl stories focus on the candidate for the Church. The parable of the fish concerns the role of salvation and judgment in the life of the kingdom.

The candidates for Christianity will be people of absolute commitment. Once they have discovered the message of Christian love, nothing will hold them back. They will sell all they have to possess this treasure. This means they will be willing to surrender all the values of their former lives that are inconsistent with Christ's call to love. They will see that this vision of the possibilities of Christian life will make them new people.

The separation of the good and bad fish highlights the theme of salvation and judgment in the parables of the kingdom. The church of Christ is ultimately an either-or affair. The kind of love to which Christ calls us is either practiced or it isn't. Those who embrace this love will be saved. Those who refuse will be judged. "Judged" is a biblical way of saying we will be held accountable for our behavior before the judgment of God. We can see the seriousness of Christ's message.

Membership in Christ's church is not to be taken lightly. It is not to be reduced to the position of a pleasant and casual social club. It is far more important than being a leader in a civic group or running a business.

The demand of Jesus is for trust in the power of love. Those who parade under the name of Jesus, yet fail to accept salvation from sin and guilt and witness the mercy of Christ will be liable to lose salvation. Still, we all try to work together. We do our best to be a community, helping one another, giving good example, sharing our gifts, and shouldering one another's burdens. Praying to the Spirit helps us live the ideals of the kingdom.

REFLECTION

The fifteenth chapter of Luke gives us three parables Jesus taught that describe him as eager to save the lost ones. Jesus gave us the parables of the Lost Sheep, the Lost Coin, and the Lost Son (Prodigal Son). In each case it is God who looks and searches for the lost to bring them back home to his love. In our country we have millions of inactive Catholics. Almost all families have members who have drifted away from being practicing Catholics. They do not benefit from the blessings of parish community and the renewing graces of the sacraments.

The Church responds to this by an active evangelization. In his parable of the Lost Sheep, Jesus gives us three elements to guide us in reaching out to inactive Catholics. First, trust that the "ninety-nine" are not going to feel neglected when we devote energy to bring others home. In fact evangelizing parishes grow bigger.

Second, become convinced of the need to share your faith with those who have drifted away or formally rejected the Church. You must believe that evangelizing is part of your baptismal commitment. This is not an attempt to force conversions. Your style must be loving, invitational, and affectionate. You need to believe that Jesus is intrinsically appealing and inherently attractive.

Thirdly, this should be done with joy and lightness of heart. We do not need the stern pose of the debater nor the lusty militancy of the hunter. The Holy Spirit is the strong and gentle persuader who does the real work. Let us be like the shepherd who generously seeks the lost sheep. Let us imitate the woman who scours her house to find the lost coin. If we lose a wallet filled with credit cards and a driver's license, we turn our rooms upside down to find it. Use this energy to share faith with inactive Catholics. Lastly, let us imitate the loving father who goes to the top of the hill every day scanning the roads for his lost son. Love never abandons the beloved.

FOR DIALOGUE

What are three stories (perhaps from sports, pop music, or films) you like to tell that put across a point you want to share? Why do you find yourself using stories? In reflecting on your most recent conversation, how often do you tell a story?

How does your own practice correspond to Christ's using stories-parables to get his point across? Why do people love stories? Which three of Christ's parables do you like the best? Why?

Why is it important to link the kingdom of God with the Church? In other words, what is the connection between your Christian behavior and God's kingdom?

PRAYER

Jesus, you taught us to pray, "Thy kingdom come, thy will be done." In these words you invite us to pray that kingdom behavior will be living and active in our lives in the Church. Give us the grace to say these words sincerely and put them into practice.

"Son, you are always with me, and all that is mine is yours. It was fitting to make merry and be glad, for this your brother was dead, and is alive; he was lost, and is found."

LUKE 15:31-32

CHAPTER 46

Jesus Forms His Apostles for Ministry

Matthew 10; Mark 6:7-13; Luke 9:1-6, 23-27

These twelve Jesus sent out, charging them, "Go nowhere among the Gentiles, and enter no town of the Samaritans, but go rather to the lost sheep of the house of Israel. And preach as you go, saying, 'The kingdom of heaven is at hand.'"

MATTHEW 10:5-7

After the Vietnam War, documents were found that described in detail the training of Vietcong soldiers. The documents dealt with the ideals that should inspire the soldiers, the different strategies for guerrilla warfare and mass-army warfare, and the collection of taxes to finance the military. There was a similar case in China for training the Red Guard. Armed with the sayings of Mao, they marched forward as apostles of radical communism, faithfully carrying the small book of the master's sayings with them.

PERSONAL EXAMPLE

Jesus was equally absorbed in forming his men for an infinitely better cause — the ministry of salvation. The central lesson in this formation was the example of Jesus himself. The apostles had the privilege of contacting the greatest personality who ever lived. This touch with divine greatness at so intimate a level was the central feature of their training.

Heal the Sick

But Jesus also gave them healing gifts. St. Matthew's gospel, chapter 10, documents how Jesus did this. Jesus gave the apostles the power to cast out devils and to heal the sick. He taught them how to relieve people from the demons that tormented their souls. This healing ministry did not exclude family care and medical help.

Almost every Christian family has a story about a "miracle" of healing that was attributed to profound prayer and the faith of the loved ones at the bedside. This does not, in any way, lessen the need and respect for the professional doctor and psychologist. It is just that faith adds a dimension to the mystery of human healing that Jesus does not want us to forget.

Help for the Lost and Lonely

Jesus then directed the apostles to go to the lost sheep of Israel first. They should announce that the kingdom of heaven is at hand. In modern terms, this would mean going to the lonely and the lost in our society. It does not mean dealing only with Catholics and forgetting non-Catholics. It is a call to bring the joy of the gospel to any rejected person anywhere.

Who are some of the lonely and the lost, today? The teen who is confused about the meaning of life and the darkness of the future. The rich man who finds that his vast bank account still leaves him empty inside. The African-American who has no hope of ever advancing in society. The despairing poor of Appalachia. The bewildered families of war-torn countries. The social outcasts on skid row. The aimless, middle-aged woman in suburbia who has turned to alcohol. The old people who are forced to live on the edge of society. The apostle should go to them with the good news that the kingdom is at hand.

Apostles will not only tell them of the kingdom. They will also bring the kingdom to them by their compassionate acts. Apostles will work to bring justice to the poor, provide care for the elderly, inspire aimless people, support the cause of peace, and witness loving compassion. In other words, they will bring a living gospel that will provide help and encouragement for all who are in need. Effective apostles will combine a grace-inspired presentation of Jesus and the gospel along with its practical application.

Travel Light

A third point that Jesus insists on is: travel light.

"Take no gold, nor silver, nor copper in your belts; no bag for your journey, nor two tunics, nor sandals, nor a staff." (Matthew 10:9-10). Travel light! Apostles must have the mobility of someone who can be free to reach all kinds of people. They cannot be weighed down with the concern for large property holdings, extensive investments, and vast possessions. Such things tie them down. They become caretakers, not evangelizers. And, as in the parable of the wedding feast, they might refuse to go to the banquet because they must take care of their property.

The greatest examples in history of the "travel light" theme are Jesus, St. Paul, and St. Francis of Assisi. Of course, all the apostles and saints are good illustrations of this. It is just that these three are obvious examples. St. Francis is the most romantic picture of this theme. He literally gave up his estates so that he could travel light. In giving up all, he gained all. He sang along the highways of Europe as a troubadour for Christ.

Expect Opposition

Next, Jesus firmly warns his apostles that they will face opposition and severe criticism. They may even have to die for the cause. After all, the disciple is not above the master. Christ's followers can expect to be stoned like Stephen, imprisoned like Paul, and crucified like Peter. Christian apostles today may hear the screams of those who oppose their stand on justice for minorities or defense of the life of the unborn. They can experience the stinging rebukes of those who oppose them and sweep up the glass from the windows broken in their homes by hostile neighbors. Many apostles have died for their faith, such as the countless who were persecuted for their commitment to Christ.

There Is a Risk Involved in Standing Up for a Cause

Once you stand up for a cause, you take the risk of knowing opposition. Once you decide to carry out Christ's challenge that there be justice and charity for all, you are open to attack from those who refuse to allow such justice and charity to occur. Even so remarkable a woman as Mother Teresa, who traveled the world helping the poorest of the poor, faced opposition to her beliefs in Christ's moral teachings, especially her defense of the life of the unborn.

Jesus realized his apostles would be storm centers. "Do not think that I have come to bring peace on earth; I have not come to bring peace, but the sword" (Matthew 10:34). It is not that Jesus really wishes such division, but he knows full well that justice and charity are only achieved with a struggle. The dark forces of evil must be fought, not sweetly tolerated. The Church experienced severe persecution in the twentieth century during which thousands died for their faith in Jesus. Such persecution continues today, and many more will face death for their belief in Christ.

Carry these sayings of Jesus (from Matthew, chapter 10) with you as faithfully as the apostles did in Roman times when they gave their lives for the cause and whose blood became the seed of the growth and progress of the Church.

REFLECTION

The term *disciple* is closely related to the word discipline. It has always been known that becoming a disciple of Christ requires discipline. There is a small saying that captures the essence of discipline:

Sow an act and reap a habit.
Sow a habit and reap a character.
Sow a character and reap a destiny.

Those who seek discipline soon learn the need to be an orderly person both in external behavior and internal self-mastery. This includes rational control of one's schedule as well as one's inner passions and drives. Repeated acts toward this goal over a long period of time usually bring growth. This does not mean becoming a rigid robot. Nor can it tolerate inner and outer chaos. In these complex times, flexibility without compromise is essential.

Being goal-centered makes a difference. The goal here is to become a disciple of Jesus. We hope to be disciples who lose the self (let go of selfishness), take up the Cross (willingly accept the challenges of the life of faith), and follow Jesus (he leads us to personal fulfillment and true joy). This means keeping our eyes on the prize that is the kingdom of God, experienced partially here on earth and perfectly in heaven.

FOR DIALOGUE

Another name for discipleship is hero-worship. Who are some of your heroes or heroines? What attracts you to them? How do they affect your behavior? When you are passionately attracted to someone, how difficult is it to imitate such a person? How can Jesus enter your life and become a star for you to follow?

Since discipline is part of being a disciple, what parts of your life already demand discipline so that you can appreciate its value in a relationship? Where have you been successful in acquiring good habits as a result of discipline? Why is being goal-centered a method for motivating yourself toward discipline and discipleship?

Why was Christ's example a powerful means for training his disciples? If teachers fail to practice what they say, what will be the response of the students? What is the impact of a leader who is inspiring, encouraging, patient, and understanding?

Lord Jesus, you call us to be your disciples, to lose our selfishness, to carry the Cross, and to follow you. Give us the grace we need to remain faithful to you, with our eyes fixed on the prize of the kingdom of heaven. Walk with us so that we may never wander from this path.

Be kind to one another, tenderhearted, forgiving one another, as God in Christ forgave you.

EPHESIANS 4:32

CHAPTER 47

Jesus Establishes His Church

Matthew 16:13-20; John 21:15-19

"I tell you, you are Peter, and on this rock I will build my church, and the powers of death shall not prevail against it. . . ." Jesus said to Simon Peter, "Simon, son of John, do you love me more than these?" He said to him, "Yes Lord, you know that I love you." He said to him, "Feed my lambs."

MATTHEW 16:18; JOHN 21:15

THE CHURCH AS AN ORGANIZATION (MATTHEW 16:1-20)

On the slopes of Mount Hermon was built the city of Caesarea Philippi. Below the city was a cave shrine, holy to Greeks and Romans, where they worshipped the god Pan. The god was associated with fertility, and mating rites were part of the cult. The mouth of the cave was called the Gates of Pan.

Pan was also associated with chaos. This is the origin of Pandora's Box. Take off the lid and unleash pandemonium, anarchy, turmoil upon the earth. The Gates of Pan were like the lid of Pandora's Box that kept within it the bedlam and disarray that destroyed law and order in society. It also assured that the wildness of passions could be restrained.

Jesus selected the setting of the city on the rock and the cave of Pan as the backdrop for his choice of Peter as the head of the Church he was founding. Jesus began by asking the question, "Who do [people] say that the Son of Man is?"(Matthew 16:13). Jesus frequently applied this title to himself. It is an Old Testament image. Ezekiel used *son of man* seventy times and applied it to sinful human nature. Jesus used Ezekiel's meaning to refer to his own humanity — but without the weakness of sin.

Daniel 7:13-14 also used the son of man image, a figure who comes on the clouds of heaven toward the throne of the Ancient of Days (the LORD). To him is given a saving dominion over the earth. It is a messianic image. Jesus identified with this meaning of the term as well. He knows he is human and that he is the Messiah with a mission to save the world.

"You Are the Messiah"

Though assured of his identity, he raises the question about what others think. The apostles reflect the popular opinions of the time: Jesus is the reincarnation of John the Baptist, Elijah, Jeremiah, or some other prophet. Jesus surely knew what people were saying about him. The apostles' answer sets the stage for the second question. "But who do you say that I am?" (v. 15) Silence. That silence was not just the fear of giving a wrong answer. Jesus was their friend and leader, a man of unbelievable wonder and depth. Who had ever known a man such as this? Was it possible to find words that do justice to a description of Jesus? Finally Peter spoke: "You are the Christ, the Son of the living God" (v. 16).

The richness of Peter's reply is dazzling. In the light of God's fire he spoke like an oracle. What neither the religious learning of the Pharisees, nor the peasant cunning of the people, nor the intimacy of being apostles could discern, Peter is the first to see. His words are born of a religious inspiration. The Holy Spirit took hold of the heart of the blunt fisherman and offered his mind this luminous insight. Peter is the first apostle to realize in a rudimentary manner the mysterious identity of Jesus — human, messianic, divine. Jesus is a man. He is the Messiah. He is Son of God.

Jesus replied with a burst of joy:

"Blessed are you, Simon [Son of Jona]! For flesh and blood has not revealed this to you, but my Father who is in heaven. And I tell you, you are Peter, and on this rock I will build my church, and the powers of death shall not prevail against it. I will give you the keys of the kingdom of heaven, and whatever you bind on earth shall be bound in heaven, and whatever you loose on earth shall be loosed in heaven."

MATTHEW 18-19

Jesus used a play-on-words, since "Peter" means "rock." This was like saying, "Rock, upon you, the rock, I will build my church." Jesus anointed the leader who will carry on his work after he is gone. By speaking of Church, Jesus declared his intention to found a permanent community, an organization that would witness and communicate his saving presence and powers. By the Gates of Pan, Jesus said nothing will eliminate the Church, not even the gates of hell [older translation]. Jesus reminded Peter and the others that flesh and blood had not given Peter this insight. Rather it was a revelation that came directly from God. Jesus further invested Peter with the "keys of the kingdom," the power to forgive sins. All the apostles would receive this power on Easter night (John 20:22-23). They would pass on this gift to bishops and priests.

THE CHURCH AS A COMMUNITY OF LOVE (JOHN 21:15-19)

In one of his resurrection appearances, Jesus gave Peter another role to play in the Church. At Caesarea Philippi, he made Peter the rock, the organizational leader of the church. By the lake of Galilee, the risen Jesus made Peter the shepherd and pastor of the Church as a community of love. Jesus asked Peter if he loved him more than the others. Peter said that he did. Jesus commissioned him to feed his lambs. Jesus repeated the question again. Peter once more affirmed his love and was told to feed the sheep. A third time Jesus asked Peter if he loved him more than anyone else. Distressed that Jesus seemed not to believe him, he complained that Jesus knew everything. He certainly knew that Peter loved him. He could read hearts. Jesus again commissioned him to feed the sheep.

Peter's public declarations of love put behind him once and for all his triple denial during the passion. Seldom have we heard a more touching call to leadership. Here is a vision of leadership based on love and affection between Jesus and Peter — and between Peter and his potential associates. This "love model" of leadership balanced the "institutional model" seen at Caesarea Philippi. The total ministry of Peter would embrace his call to be Rock and Lover.

Peter would never be a St. John taking spiritual flights like an eagle. Peter could never match the eloquence and literary genius of St. Paul. He had a humbler form of genius, the capacity to become the first chief shepherd of the Church. He remained lovingly faithful to Jesus until his martyrdom in Rome some thirty years later. Michelangelo memorialized these dual qualities of Peter (and the Church) in the base of the great dome and a transept of St. Peter's Basilica in Rome. Inscribed there is the "Rock" text of Matthew and the "Love" text of John. Jesus knew his man and was not disappointed by the choice.

As to what this Church would be like, read again the previous lesson about the kingdom and the Church. Christ's parables are wonderful descriptions of what the mystery of the Church is like. St. Paul has given a wonderful image of the Church as the Body of Christ in which Jesus is the head and we are the members. At the Last Supper Jesus spoke of the Church as a relationship of vine and branches. Jesus is the vine; we are the branches taking our life from the vine. The Eucharist is the event where head and members, vine and branches come together. The Church is the living Body of Christ and temple of the Holy Spirit and the communion of believers, the assembly of the redeemed.

REFLECTION

Nine days before Pentecost Mary, the apostles, and disciples gathered in prayer for the coming of the Spirit. Art always pictures Mary, the mother of Jesus, as seated in the center of this holy gathering. The setting is one of prayer and contemplation. Mary is the principal contemplative, the woman wrapped in the silence of prayer. The contemplative dimension, with Mary at the center, prevailed.

At Pentecost, the Holy Spirit descended on those gathered in the Upper Room. The Spirit manifested and revealed the Church publicly. Now Peter became the visible leader, the Shepherd and Pastor and Rock. Pope John Paul II, reflecting on these scenes, taught that the Marian dimension of Church precedes the Petrine one. The environment of prayer is the womb from which the Body of Christ is born. Because of this, prayer, contemplation, and the adoration of God have the primacy in the Church.

Finally, we repeat that the Church as communion is our loving fellowship and union with Jesus and other baptized Christians in the Body of Christ. Its source and summit is in the celebration of the Eucharist by which we are joined in divine love to the communion of the Father, Son, and Holy Spirit. In this communion the members are called to love God, others, and self and so be a communal witness of the love by which Christ saved the world. This communion also finds an expression in the parish, the diocese, and the universal Church. Its faith is nourished by the teaching of Tradition, Sacred Scripture, and the Spirit-guided Magisterium — the teaching office of the pope and bishops.

FOR DIALOGUE

How would you defend the need for the Church to have an organizational component? In other words, why did Jesus make Peter the rock, the Rock of the Church?

Why must the Church also be a communion of love? In what way does the celebration of the Eucharist express the truth of the Church as a communion of love?

What is the significance of noting the centrality of Mary as the contemplative leader of the gathering of apostles and disciples nine days before Pentecost? What did Pope John Paul II mean when he said that the Marian vision of the Church precedes the Petrine one?

PRAYER

Jesus, we praise you for the gift of the Church and the role of Peter as Rock and Loving Pastor. We also praise you for Mary's prayerful leadership at the dawn of the Church just before Pentecost.

You may know how one ought to behave in the household of God, which is the church of the living God, the pillar and bulwark of the truth.
                                                                    1 TIMOTHY 3:15

CHAPTER 48

Jesus Defends Two Women

Luke 7:36-50; John 8:1-11

Therefore I tell you, her sins, which are many, have been forgiven, for she loved much.... "Woman, where are they? Has no one condemned you?" She said, "No one, Lord...." Neither do I condemn you; go and do not sin again.

LUKE 7:47; JOHN 8:10-11

In his conversation with Nicodemus, Jesus explained that he had come not to condemn people, but to save them from their sins. "For God sent his Son into the world, not to condemn the world, but that the world might be saved through him" (John 3:17). Two unforgettable stories in the gospels illustrate Christ's teaching. One took place in the house of Simon the Pharisee; the other happened near an execution wall.

JESUS DEFENDS A WOMAN AT A DINNER PARTY (LUKE 7:36-50)

A Pharisee named Simon invited Jesus to dinner. He omitted the usual courtesies due a guest. Jesus expected a formal greeting kiss, water to rinse the dust from his feet, and a few drops of perfume sprinkled on his head. Even the poorest family would treat a guest this way. Simon ignored these customs.

A sinful woman learned that Jesus was Simon's guest. The context implies that she was a known prostitute. Unannounced she crashed the party, shocking the guests by her unwanted presence. She offended their sensibilities approaching Jesus, kneeling before him, shedding tears on his feet, rubbing them with water from her eyes, and kissing them with her lips. She dried them with her hair. She brought an expensive alabaster phial of perfume, all of which she emptied upon his feet, filling the room with its fragrance.

Simon and his companions were disturbed. Why did Jesus allow her to do this? Why did he not pull away in disgust or demand the servants have her removed? How could he let this scandalous woman touch him?

Jesus was not upset with her. He smiled at her and made her feel welcome. Jesus was displeased with the reaction of the others. He told them a story about a moneylender. One person owed him a large amount, another, a small debt. The lender forgave both debts. Which one would love him more? Simon replied that the one with the big debt would feel the most love and gratitude.

Jesus agreed and proceeded to contrast their discourteous treatment of him with the kindly treatment from the woman. Then he compared the way they thought of the woman with his. They dwelt hypocritically on her sins; he looked at her humble love. They saw moral ugliness; he saw her potential for conversion.

The dinner guests heard Jesus tell them that the woman's great sins were forgiven because her love was so great. She believed she could be forgiven. Jesus looked at her with great love. "Your faith has saved you; go in peace" (Luke 7:50). We never get to know her name. In a sense she stands for every woman and every man who believe they can be changed from a sinner into one whom Jesus will forgive.

Love surrounds the whole conversion event. Love brought her to Jesus. Jesus brings her greater love, for she is forgiven and redeemed directly by the Son of God. Jesus tried to open the hearts of Simon and the offended guests. They stonewalled him. He succeeded with the woman. The proud have a hard time accepting salvation because they do not think they need it. Only the humble appreciate what a gift they can receive from Jesus.

JESUS DEFENDS A WOMAN AT AN EXECUTION WALL (JOHN 8:3-11)

A self-righteous group of men brought a woman "caught in the act of adultery" to Jesus. They asked him to judge her case. It was a trap. If he recommended stoning, he would break Roman law that reserved to itself the right to capital punishment. He would also lose his reputation as a friend of sinners and a man of compassion. If he rejected stoning her, he would break the law of Moses which called for capital punishment for an adulteress.

Jesus reacted with the two-step process. First he responded with silence. He knelt down and began tracing on the ground with his finger. Christian imagination has long speculated about what he was doing. Did he write out the sins of her accusers? Was he just doodling? Was he simply letting silence rebuke them? The last interpretation seems the most likely. Jesus used silence to calm their passions and get them to reflect. Now their heavy and obscene breathing sounded awkward. The silence was like the sound of one hand clapping. He gave them no hand to clap against.

Only when that little army of hypocrites found they had no war to fight did Jesus advance to the next step. Jesus straightened up and said, "Let him who is without sin among you be the first to throw a stone at her" (John 8:7).

While they absorbed his challenge, he resumed writing on the ground. The beauty of this scene is that Jesus did not engage these "little murderers" on their own terms, but on his. He deftly changed the focus from the woman to their own sinfulness.

One by one, they dropped their stones and crept silently away. He was left alone with the woman. St. Augustine visualized this part of the scene with these words that include a Latin pun: "There remained a great *Miseria* (misery) and a great *Misericordia* (mercy)." A miserable woman. A merciful savior. Jesus stood up and looked around. Possibly with a smile he could have said, "Oh! Where did they all disappear to? Look at all the unused stones. Didn't anyone condemn you?" "No one, sir." "Nor do I condemn you. You may go now. Do not sin any more." (See John 8:10-11.)

Jesus treated her with pastoral honesty. He let her know he realized she had sinned. She became aware that he had forgiven her sin. He defended her from other sinners who had planned to ignore their own immorality and condemn and stone her to death. Jesus gave her a second chance and challenged her to sin no more. He did not give her easy forgiveness — cheap grace. He appealed to her capacity for conversion and moral change. He made her feel it was possible. A sinner can be redeemed.

REFLECTION

Visualize the ceiling of the Sistine Chapel. God rides on a cloud toward Adam. Weak and dreamlike, Adam stretches his arm toward God and extends one finger to be touched by the hand of God. In the fresco, a small space remains between God's hand and Adam's finger. There is no touch. But every one of the millions who have seen the fresco knows that God's creative life is about to surge into Adam.

Here is another scene, one from the twentieth century. We go to the game preserves in West Africa where researcher Diane Fossey has been observing gorillas, their habits and mannerisms. She wants to see if one of them will come near her gently. She lures them as though she were in a park tempting a squirrel with a nut. A 400-pound ape, a real King Kong, approaches her. He picks up her pencil. She touches him softly. And then he reaches out his paw, capable of bending iron, and he taps her so gently that she can scarcely feel it. It is a tender and halting start of a friendship and is a parable of how we could come to one another in a healing manner.

In each of these pictures we have hints of the exquisite silence and respect that Jesus demonstrated toward the two women He defended and healed in the gospel narratives we have just read. Jesus is like a revered artist stretching out his hand to give life and forgiveness to the woman mistreated by Simon and his guests. No one of us can reverence human dignity more elegantly that Jesus did. He was also like that anthropologist who used infinite patience to make contact with the wild one. Jesus is a master of patience. His majestic composure is matchless in his capacity to wait and invite the sinner to come to conversion. Such was his silence and solitude with the "little murderers" at the execution wall, ready to stone the woman.

FOR DIALOGUE

What are some stories you could tell about hypocritical behavior in which people express disdain for a so-called undesirable person? As you think about this, what would you say are the causes of the hypocrisy?

Why does it take courage, patience, and insight to help a person who is being mistreated? What did you find to admire in the way Jesus defended the two women in the gospel narratives?

How can people open their hearts and be converted from their sinfulness? How would you picture Jesus today bringing forgiveness to people?

PRAYER

Merciful Jesus, inspire us to seek your forgiveness in the sacrament of reconciliation. Help us see our sinfulness and be ready to confess and repent our sins.

"But the tax collector, standing far off, would not even lift up his eyes to heaven, but beat his breast, saying, 'God, be merciful to me a sinner!'"

LUKE 18:13

CHAPTER 49

Jesus Reveals His Glory at the Transfiguration

Matthew 17:1-13; Mark 9:2-8; Luke 9:28-36

And after six days Jesus took with him Peter and James and John, and led them up a high mountain apart by themselves; and he was trans-figured before them, and his garments became glistening, intensely white, as no fuller on earth could bleach them.

MARK 9:2-3

THE TRANSFIGURATION

The gospel says that six days after Jesus appointed Peter to be the rock on which he would build his Church, he took Peter, James, and John up a mountain where the transfiguration took place. Tradition says this happened on Mount Tabor in northern Palestine. It overlooks the plains of Esdraelon where Deborah led the Israelites to victory against a bronze-age enemy. The village of Naim is located in this area. Near that town Jesus raised the widow of Naim's son from the dead.

A pilgrimage church crowns the mountain. Enshrined in its dome is a white and gold mosaic of Christ transfigured in glory. Opposite the mosaic is a window in the dome through which the morning sun shines, causing the figure of Jesus to glow like the sun and his clothes to seem white as snow. Chapels have been erected in honor of Moses and Elijah so that the wish of Peter that "tents" be built for them has been fulfilled. The Eastern Church celebrates this mystery of Christ as the feast of Taborian — the Tabor event.

The gospels frame the transfiguration with Christ's predictions of his passion and death. The image of the Cross stands before and after the sign of glory on the mountain. At Tabor Christ's divinity is manifested. Coming immediately after Christ's prediction of his passion and death, the transfiguration put into perspective what had upset their assumptions about what a Messiah would be like. Surpassing glory lay beyond the humiliation of the passion.

The vision on the mountain also foresaw the kind of transformation that the saved would be given. Redeemed people would share in Christ's glory. The just will shine like the sun in the kingdom of God. St. Paul echoed this when he wrote, "I consider that the sufferings of this present time are not worth comparing with the glory that is to be revealed to us" (Romans 8:18).

After they had reached the mountaintop, Jesus became absorbed in prayer. While he was praying, he was transfigured before them. His face shone like the sun, and his clothes were dazzling white. This was not a light that shone upon him; it was a glory that came from within him. It was not a spotlight. It was his intrinsic, divine glory. This was not theater; this was a revelation.

Moses and Elijah then appeared with Jesus. Moses represented the Torah of God, the law that was a light for the spiritual and moral growth of Israel. Elijah stood for all the prophets who called Israel back to the practice of the covenant with God when they had strayed from obedience to God. The two greatest religious leaders of Israel and the three major apostles of the New Testament witnessed this remarkable revelation of Jesus.

Five Witnesses — Two Testaments

These five witnesses were the trumpets of the two testaments, resounding in harmony their music about the eternal Word of God. Ancient prophecy and gospel proclamation sing with one voice the praise of Jesus. The stained glass windows of France's Chartres cathedral mirror this biblical unity when they depict the apostles sitting on the shoulders of the prophets. Christ in glory is their colorful focus.

During this revelation, the three apostles were filled with awe and prostrated themselves in adoration. Peter, overwhelmed by the joy of this experience, said, "Rabbi, it is good for us to be here; let us make three dwellings, one for you, one for Moses and one for Elijah. He did not know what to say, for they were so terrified" (Mark 9:5-6). This revelation was too much for them. It would take time for them to realize what it all meant.

Many years later, Peter could speak of it with greater faith and understanding. He was explaining to his readers that the gospel was not a myth such as pagans teach, but the very truth of God.

For we did not follow cleverly devised myths when we made known to you the power and coming of our Lord Jesus Christ, but we were eyewitnesses of his majesty. For when he received honor and glory from God the Father and the voice was borne to him by the Majestic Glory, "This is my beloved Son, with whom I am well pleased," we heard this voice borne from heaven, for we were with him on the holy mountain. And we have the prophetic word made more sure. You will do well to pay attention to this as to a lamp shining in a dark place, until the day dawns and the morning star rises in your hearts.

2 PETER 1:16-19

A cloud rested over the mountain. From it came the voice of the Father, "This is my beloved Son. Listen to him" (Mark 9:7). The scene recalls Christ's baptism. At the Jordan the Father spoke about his beloved Son. The Spirit hovered like a dove over Christ. Father, Son, and Spirit begin Christ's ministry of salvation. At Tabor the Trinity is again manifested as the divine persons contemplate the outcome of salvation in the foretaste of Christ's resurrection.

Easter and Good Friday

Then the vision disappeared. The apostles saw only Jesus, and the glory was gone. Some commentators have noted the similarities between this event and the Agony in the Garden. In both events the visible appearance of Jesus changed. On Tabor the dominant color is the white light of glory. At Gethsemane it is the red blood of agony.

Peter, James, and John witnessed both appearances. On Tabor the apostles seem to sleep in awe. At Gethsemane they slumber with fatigue. Prophets speak to Jesus at Tabor. Angels comfort him in the garden. On the mount the covenant is spoken of in its fulfillment in glory. In the garden the covenant is spoken of in terms of the shedding of blood.

The two events are images of Easter and Good Friday in reverse. At Tabor Jesus wanted the favored three to get a glimpse of the glory so that they could endure the loss of Christ at the Cross with faith and trust. After the revelation at Tabor, Jesus again predicted his passion. This grieved them. They did not understand him. They were afraid to question him about it. Only when they met the risen Christ at Easter and received the Spirit at Pentecost did this all become clear.

REFLECTION

One of the persistent problems of our faith is that we spend too much time with words and thoughts "about" Jesus and not enough time on a prayer experience "of" Jesus. Many people study Jesus but never meet him. They enjoy the word games and one-upmanship of scholars and substitute this for an affectionate relationship with Christ. The "blah-blah" of theological words replaces the encounter with the divine.

Religious studies are clearly important, but they work best when they flow from and flow toward a life of prayer. Religious discourse should be among people who devote themselves to the adoration of God in meditative prayer and the worship of God in the liturgy. Position papers divorced from prayer are tiresome. We have the right to hear the resonance of God's presence in the religious speech of others.

This is one of the lessons of the mystery of the transfiguration of Jesus at Tabor. Peter, James, and John have heard Christ's sermons. They have experienced him as a person, sensed the power of his personality, felt his affection, and witnessed his miracles. What they needed was a defining experience of Jesus by which they could get beyond a superficial appreciation of his wonder and greatness. Jesus knew this and decided to reach them in the most silent part of their souls.

He showed them his glory. They did more than physically look at Jesus. Their vision of him was actually more interior. The text says they were overcome with awe, prostrated in adoration, and "slept." This sleep was the rest of adoration, the prelude of their receiving of the revelation of the mystery of Christ. "Peter and his companions had been overcome by sleep, but becoming fully awake they saw his glory" (Luke 9:32). This helped them receive Christ's teaching into their hearts. This is the message of this event for us. All our studies and thoughts must become connected to our hearts. It is love that brings the best understanding of what Jesus tells us.

FOR DIALOGUE

Why must there be a more intimate link between your religious studies about Jesus and your prayerful union with him? What would happen if you failed to do this?

Which aspect of the mystery of the transfiguration touches you most? Why do you think this is your response? Why did Jesus favor Peter, James, and John with this vision?

When Peter said, "Lord, it is good for us to be here," what did he mean? In what sense could you use his words when you are before the Blessed Sacrament?

PRAYER

Jesus, when you showed your glory at Tabor, you strengthen our faith in the hope of our resurrection. We pray that we may inherit eternal life with you.

Christ Jesus, you are the splendor of the Father and the perfect image of his being; you sustain all creation with your powerful word and cleanse us of all our sins. On this day you were exalted in glory upon the high mountain.

ANTIPHON FOR THE
CANTICLE OF MARY ON THE FEAST
OF THE TRANSFIGURATION

CHAPTER 50

Jesus Comments on the Perils of Wealth and Concern for the Poor

Mark 10:17-31; 12:41-44;
Luke 12:16-21; 16:19-31

"'Fool! This night your soul is required of you; and the things you have prepared, whose will they be?' So is he who lays up treasure for himself, and is not rich toward God."

Luke 12:20-21

Arguments about money bring out the worst in people. Someone asked Jesus to make his brother share the family inheritance with him. Jesus refused to get in the middle of the family quarrel about the details of a will. At the same time he used the incident to warn them about the peril of wealth when it leads to greed. "Take care! Be on your guard against all kinds of greed, for one's life does not consist in the abundance of possessions" (Luke 12:15, NRSV).

THE RICH FOOL

While Jesus extolled detachment from money, he favored a decent way of life for all. He came to bring Good News to the poor, a message of salvation from sin, but also a kingdom of justice and peace for all. Jesus liked to highlight the truth that financial security without spiritual maturity made little sense. That was the lesson of his story about a rich farmer who built a new barn, settled his financial affairs, and sat down to enjoy his hard won prosperity. Alas, the man died at that very moment.

His economic goals had little to do with concern for the poor, a thirst for justice for the oppressed, a responsibility to be generous to those in need. Moreover, he had no interest in God or the state of his soul. To Jesus he is a rich fool. "Fool! This night your soul is required of you; and the things you have prepared, whose will they be? So is he who lays up treasure for himself, and is not rich toward God" (Luke 12:20-21).

The Poor Widow's Contribution

One day Jesus was sitting near the temple treasury that had thirteen trumpet-shaped collection boxes. Each one had a special purpose, one for oil used for the lamps, one for ceremonial needs, one for the temple upkeep, and so on. Rich people were donating large sums of money. He saw a poor widow put in two mites, a word that literally means a thin coin, worth one tenth of one penny. It was all she had.

Jesus drew his disciples' attention to her humble offering. He told them the rich were giving from their abundance. But this lady gave from her poverty. The rich had plenty of money. The poor widow gave all she had. Jesus used the incident to teach them about sacrificial giving. This is giving until it hurts. It means giving without counting the cost. It is a generosity that gives without expecting a return. This is a donation that illustrates our faith-filled surrender to God.

What a beautiful gift Jesus presents to us by using as an example of generosity a tiny coin that was the last money the woman had in her purse. "Truly, I say to you, this poor widow has put in more than all those who are contributing to the treasury. For they all contributed out of their abundance; but she out of her poverty has put in everything she had, her whole living" (Mark 12:43-44).

The Rich Man and Lazarus

Jesus then told his wonderful story about the rich man and Lazarus. A self-indulgent rich man feasted every day. A poor man named Lazarus sat at the door of the mansion and ate the garbage from the rich man's table. Dogs licked the poor man's sores. When Lazarus died, he went to heaven (the bosom of Abraham). The rich man died and went to hell. The tormented rich man begged Father Abraham to let Lazarus cool his tongue with one drop of water. But the gulf between them could not be bridged.

The rich man asked that Lazarus be permitted to visit his five brothers and warn them about the consequences of having no concern for the poor. Abraham said that they already have the teachings of Moses and the prophets about a loving and practical compassion for the poor. The rich man argued that his brothers would listen better to those teachings if a man risen from the dead tells them. Abraham replied that if they were not open to God's will now, they will not be convinced by a man who comes back from the dead. People against their will are of the same opinion still.

The rich man wanted mercy after he died. But he showed no mercy when he was alive. "Blessed are the merciful for they shall obtain mercy" (Matthew 5:7). The rich man did not have a social conscience. He had no interest in the political and economic causes of hunger and homelessness. Worse yet, he did not even notice the misery of a poor man on his doorstep. Self-absorbed, he paid no attention to the needs of others. His belly was warm with food, and his heart cheered with wine. Rich enough to indulge his appetites, he failed to nourish his conscience. Because, in his greed, he never gave mercy, he cannot receive mercy.

So dull was the rich man's conscience that he was blind to the poor man's need. In the laziness of his sin, he sank into the cushions of his dining room and let alcohol numb his brain and fat foods weigh down his body. The result was a dead soul that one day would cry out for mercy when it was too late.

If we want to test our capacity for love, we should examine how well we bring mercy to those in need. Jesus taught that whatever we do to others, we do to him. Mercy is both an expression of love and a precondition for bringing justice to our community. The act of giving mercy is already a reception of mercy. A doctor who treats his patients with compassion is already increasing his capacity for compassion. A parent who treats a child tenderly has just received a gift of tenderness. The benefactor who educates a poor student receives an even more generous spirit from the deed.

REFLECTION

The best way to help the poor is to begin with the sacred dignity and image of God found in every human person. To this vision should be added the kind of conscience formation which will uphold the beliefs, attitudes, and practices that make avoiding greed and concern for the poor possible. "Having" more is never enough. We should always begin with the principle of "being" more.

Economic development without a social conscience creates moral and spiritual poverty. It actually leads to the greed and avarice condemned by the tenth commandment. An excess of affluence is just as bad as an excess of poverty. When faith and God's plan for human dignity are central to our thinking and behavior, then the processes of economic, technological, and political development take their proper place.

E. F. Schumacher has this to say about the problems generated by greed and envy:

I suggest that the foundations of peace cannot be laid by universal prosperity, in the modern sense, because such prosperity, if attainable at all, is attainable only by cultivating such drives as greed and envy, which destroy intelligence, happiness, serenity, the peaceableness of man. It could well be that rich people treasure peace more highly than poor people, but only if they feel utterly secure — and this is a contradiction in terms. Their wealth depends on making inordinately large demands on limited world resources and thus puts them on an unavoidable collision course — not primarily with the poor (who are weak and defenseless) but with other rich people.

No one is really working for peace unless he is working primarily for the restoration of wisdom.

E. F. SCHUMACHER, *SMALL IS BEAUTIFUL*

FOR DIALOGUE

In Christ's parable about the rich fool, what was the fatal mistake made by the man? What form would that person's behavior take today? How widespread would such an attitude be in our culture? Why does this happen?

The widow who gave her last coin to God is an example of sacrificial giving. How would you persuade people to adopt some form of sacrificial giving? Why is it a good idea?

Pope John Paul II used the story of the Rich Man and Lazarus to apply to the rich nations of the world and the very poor ones, indicating that prosperous countries should avoid the crassness of the man in the story. What are ways in which this has happened? What more needs to be done?

PRAYER

Jesus, you have taught us that being "poor in spirit" is the first step toward happiness. We ask for this gift as well as a lively spirit of compassion for the poor.

But those who desire to be rich fall into temptation, into a snare, into many senseless and hurtful desires that plunge men into ruin and destruction. For the love of money is the root of all evils; it is through this craving that some have wandered away from the faith and pierced their hearts with many pangs.

1 TIMOTHY 6:9-10

CHAPTER 51

Jesus Praises the Prodigal Son and Prodigal Father

Luke 15:11-32

Let us eat and make merry; for this my son was dead, and is alive again; he was lost, and is found.

LUKE 15:23-24

GOD'S LOVE FOR SINFUL MANKIND

The story of the prodigal son concerns a delinquent young man. It also tells of his happy return to the family. Read the story in Luke's gospel (15:11-32). Here we have a narrative that lends itself to many different applications. The common interpretation is more than sufficient.

The prodigal son is sinful mankind. The father is God. The people with whom he wasted his money represent the sinful world. Eating with the pigs is a sign of the degradation of sin. The elder brother in the story is the self-righteous Christian who really does not grasp the meaning of the mercy of God. And, we should remember, "prodigal" means wasteful.

In a way, the story should be called the prodigal father because of the boundless love and mercy he shows his son. In a sense, he has so much love that it seems almost wasted. But this is only a way of speaking. One thing is certain, the father never ceases to love his son. Every day the son is gone, the father goes out to look for him.

When the son returns home, the father doesn't even wait for any kind of explanation. He doesn't demand a confession of guilt from the son. The father surrounds his son with signs of affection. Embracing the son who was dead and is now alive, he gives him a new robe, a chain, and a ring. He kills the best animal and orders a banquet. Let the musicians sing and the people dance. My son is home!

The Elder Brother's Attitude

Only one element mars this scene of joy. The elder brother refuses to take part. After all, he has been the faithful son. He did not waste his inheritance. He stayed home and worked. His money did not go down the drain for gambling, wild women, and nights out on the town. He avoided scandal. There was no need for his father to be ashamed of his conduct. How could his father give approval to his younger brother by all this celebrating?

Of course, the younger son should be forgiven. But let him first know his place. Punish him first. Let him serve time before he is given official forgiveness. The penalty will help him realize the depth of his faults and sins. Giving him a party like this will only serve to spoil him. He will never realize how serious was the shame he brought on the family.

What made the elder brother all the more peeved was that the father had never given such a party for him. It was almost as though infidelity was rewarded and fidelity was ignored. The elder brother had never failed his father, and in the logic of rewards and punishments, he deserved such a celebration.

Which Brother Is More Christian?

I have sometimes asked people which brother they would prefer to have as a friend. The majority have always said they would choose the elder brother. This was their first reaction. Partly, I think, they felt this was the expected answer to give a priest. After all, shouldn't I be on the side of the "good guys"? The elder brother was the just man. He was the correct one. Shouldn't he be chosen?

Then I press the question further. Which brother seems more human? Which one ultimately is more Christian? On second reflection, people usually say they would prefer the younger man as a friend. He had human weaknesses, but he also had the humility to want to confess his sin to his father and return home as a servant in the house.

Then I ask them which one rejected salvation. At first, it seems that neither one did. The elder brother was a morally correct man, and so seems to be already saved. The younger one has repented of his sins and so is also saved. But then the story says that the elder brother refused to go into his father's house. The father's house is a symbol of the Church. The Church is the community of those who enter the way of salvation. To consciously refuse to belong to this community is to run the risk of rejecting salvation.

The "Respectable" People and the "Sinners"

The really sad part of this story is that the apparently just man has deliberately excluded himself from full participation in the community of faith. The elder brother, who on the surface of things is a man who practices his religion, has, in fact, quietly moved to the margin of his father's house. His idea of religion is too narrow. He is unable to accept the incredibly wide mercy of God. His God is too small!

People like the elder brother are not absent from the Church today. We have some apparently just parishioners sitting in the pews of our churches, self-righteously looking down on sinners. They abhor both the sinner and the socially unacceptable. But this is in opposition to the mercy shown by the father in the parable. This attitude is out of step with Christ's own example of associating with outcasts and sinners. Today, we don't talk so much about sinners as we do about the socially unacceptable. Eating with them would spoil our status. Are we sure that Jesus, who associated with sinners and outcasts in his time, would not eat with these "sinners" today?

We are not talking about a matter of restaurants. We are saying that Jesus has a sense of human compassion far wider than the ordinary. To him, every human being is a pearl of great price — even if that person lives in the twilight zone of society. Jesus associates with such people so that he can discover their special gift and help them see their human dignity. He communicates with them so that he might restore their hope, and ease their entrance into the kingdom of God.

To have this courage, we need the alertness and fidelity of God. It is no small matter to oppose the un-Christian ideas of those with whom we work and associate. Unfortunately, it is all too easy for the "saved Christian" to forget the poor, scorn anyone who is different, and ignore the consequences of prejudice.

REFLECTION

Jesus once dined in the house of Matthew, a tax collector. Many other tax collectors and sinners joined Jesus at the table. The Pharisees asked Christ's disciples, "Why does your teacher eat with tax collectors and sinners?" Jesus gave the answer, "Those who are well have no need of a physician, but those who are sick [do]" (Matthew 9:11-12).

Jesus made the mercy of the Lord shown in the forgiveness of sins a personal affair. Religion for him was not simply a slick pattern. It was more than learning a few abstract ideas in religion class or writing out a check for charity. He knew there were annoying and embarrassing aspects to religion. He did not flinch from these. He entered the human family. He knew full well how many of his brothers and sisters had taken the heritage of the earth and wasted it in sinful ways.

He came to tell them about the mercy of the Father. He brought the sacraments of reconciliation and love. He invited the sinners to eat the greatest banquet of all, the Eucharist. He did not pout outside the dinner hall, like the elder brother. He himself was the host at the meal. These are some of the lessons Jesus teaches through the story of the prodigal son.

FOR DIALOGUE

What examples could you share about people who ran away from home and got into lots of trouble? What happened? How did their parents handle the situation? If they returned home, what was the reception like?

What would you be like if a member of your family left home and made a mess of their lives? How close would you be to the behavior of the "prodigal" father of the parable? What might incline you to be like the elder brother of the story?

If you have been taught to avoid bad company, how could you imitate Christ's association with sinners? How could you save a sinner whom you never met? How strong must you be in such cases, so that you are not converted to a life of sin yourself?

PRAYER

Merciful Father, thank you for always sending us your love and welcome. We praise you for the redemptive work of Jesus, your Son, by which we can always receive forgiveness for our sins and begin again as your friends.

"Rejoice with me, for I have found my sheep which was lost.' Just so, I tell you, there will be more joy in heaven over one sinner who repents than over ninety-nine righteous persons who need no repentance."

LUKE 15:6-7

CHAPTER 52

Jesus Describes the Last Judgment

Matthew 24-25; Mark 13; Luke 21:7-38

"But in those days, after that tribulation, the sun will be darkened, and the moon will not give its light, and the stars will be falling from heaven, and the powers in the heavens will be shaken."

MARK 13:24-25

THE DESTRUCTION OF THE TEMPLE

Near the end of his life, Jesus described the destruction of the temple and of the city of Jerusalem. He also used these events as images of the final end of the world and the Second Coming of the Son of Man. The change from the Old Testament community to the New Testament one would be traumatic for those involved.

To picture such dramatic change, Jesus employed apocalyptic language. This is a literary form that was used by the prophets when they foresaw catastrophe for God's people. Stars fall. The sun darkens. The moon fails to give its light. Earthquakes, floods, avalanches of rocks, wars and rumors of wars, family divisions, famine, plagues of insects are part of the "catastrophe language" that the literary form of apocalypse uses.

Jesus wanted to prepare his disciples for the pain and struggle that would accompany the end of the world they knew and the birth of the world they would face. Birth pangs would signal the emergence of the Christian Church. At the same time, these trials would happen again at the final judgment and the birth of a new heavens and a new earth. Jesus mixed these themes together letting one serve as a symbol of the other. (Read Mark 13:1-37.)

The Last Judgment Sermon

Jesus began his Last Judgment sermon during a visit to the splendid temple built by Herod. It was an engineering masterpiece as well as an artistic miracle. The disciples always marveled at its beauty and incredible stonework. Jesus used that moment to tell them the temple would be destroyed and not a stone would be left upon a stone. He also predicted that Jerusalem would be destroyed. He did not give them a date. It actually happened in A.D. 70 when the Roman General Titus invaded the city, ruined the temple, and laid waste Jerusalem.

Christ's words shocked and sobered them. Later they climbed the Mount of Olives that overlooked the city and the temple. They asked Jesus when such destruction would happen. He did not give them a date, but he did alert them to three signs that would forecast this tragedy: false doctrine, public chaos, and persecution. False prophets and Messiahs would appear and deceive even the elect. Natural calamities and pervasive wars would come next. Then there would be the persecution and martyrdom of true believers. Families would be torn apart. Social disturbances would be rampant.

Jesus was not happy about the forthcoming sadness. He loved the temple and the city. He loved his people. He wept over the city. "Jerusalem, Jerusalem... how often would I have gathered your children together as a hen gathers her brood under her wings but you would not!" (Matthew 23:37). There is a lovely chapel on the Mount of Olives today, called the "Dominus Flevit," (Where the Lord wept). The altar is in front of a picture window from which one can see the city and the temple. On the front of the altar is a mosaic of a hen protecting her chicks under her wings.

Jesus was insistent in not giving a precise timetable, unlike certain fundamentalist Christians and millenarians today. Jesus even says He does not know himself. Only the Father knows. "But of that day and hour no one knows, not even the angels of heaven, nor the Son, but the Father only" (Matthew 24:36). In his human nature Jesus received whatever he needed to know to save us. The exact time of the end of the world was not needed by him.

How should one prepare for such a calamitous event? The best preparation is to live each day in a fully Christian manner — vigilant, prayerful, and loving. When you think about it, the real end of the world as we know it comes for everyone about to die. Death is a personal end of life here — though not of life hereafter. How should one get ready for the end of one's personal world? The same way, by prayer, good behavior, love of others, and faith in God.

However, in the year 1000 (the first millennium) and again in the year 2000 (the second millennium), interest in the second coming and the last judgment arose again. In our final lesson in this book we will present the authentic Church teaching about the mystery of the Second Coming and refute some of the unacceptable theories about it. The truth is believed and affirmed in the Nicene Creed. How and when it will happen remains a mystery.

Christ's advice is still the best. Watch! Pray! Take heed! We will all die just as we have lived. So the best prescription is to live in faith, hope, love, trust, and surrender to God. Love conquers all, even death itself. Failure to live the Christian life means that the end is problematic and open to despair. Success means that the end is a birth, a new beginning, where, God willing, Jesus will gather us together with his saints.

REFLECTION

In describing the Last Judgment Jesus told the parable of the sheep and the goats. He painted a picture of the Son of Man coming in glory. The angels will accompany him, and he will sit upon his throne. He will gather before him every human being. He will separate them from one another like a shepherd dividing the sheep from the goats. The sheep go to his right and the goats to the left. The sheep are the saved, and the goats are the damned.

Jesus will invite the sheep to inherit the kingdom that the Father has prepared for those who loved Christ. Who is Christ? Jesus tells them. "I was hungry and you gave me food. I was thirsty and you gave me drink, a stranger and you welcomed me, naked and you clothed me, ill and you cared for me, in prison and you visited me." The people will ask Jesus when did this happen. Jesus will answer them that any time they did this even to the least human being, they did it to him. (Read Matthew 25:31-46.)

Mother Teresa interpreted this to mean that the humblest act of service we perform is a way of ministering to Jesus. She adds that we should learn how to do all our acts with great love for Jesus as well as for the person who is our beneficiary. Jesus chose ordinary acts as examples of what everyone can do to love people and also to love him. Both billionaires and the poorest of the poor are called to these simple ways of love. There is no need to manipulate or exploit others. Just love them in their everyday needs.

All these acts reach Jesus as well as the person loved. In a sense the one loved is Jesus in disguise. The goats in the parable missed the whole point of life. They failed to give even the most obvious acts of love so available to them. At the judgment they will lose God, "they will go away into eternal punishment, but the righteous into eternal life" (v. 46).

FOR DIALOGUE

In your experience how do people come to terms with the final judgment of God upon their lives? Why should people pay attention to the ultimate evaluation of their lives on earth? What is the truth of the old saying, "As you live, so shall you die"?

As you read Christ's Last Judgment sermon in Mark 13:1-37, what kind of feelings do the words arouse? Why did Jesus choose to speak of these matters to his disciples? Why did Jesus not give them the exact dates for the end of the temple and the city, as well as the end of the world?

What is the central message of Christ's parable of the sheep and the goats? What is so appealing about this parable? How can you begin to see Jesus in each person, loving them and loving him at the same time?

PRAYER

Lord,
When I have food, help me to remember the hungry.
When I have a warm home, help me to remember the homeless.
When I have work, help me to remember those without jobs.
By remembering help me to destroy my indifference
And arouse my compassion.

"MY BROTHER'S KEEPER" PRAYER

"Come, O blessed of my Father, inherit the kingdom prepared for you from the foundation of the world."

MATTHEW 25:34

CHAPTER 53

Jesus Begins His Passion

Matthew 26-27:1-32; Mark 14-15:1-20;
Luke 22-23:1-25; John 18-19:1-16

"The hour has come for the Son of Man to be glorified. Truly, truly,
I say to you, unless a grain of wheat falls into the earth and dies, it
remains alone; but if it dies, it bears much fruit."

JOHN 12:23-24

Holy Week begins with Passion Sunday (also called Palm Sunday), a holy time in which we contemplate the redemptive passion and death of Jesus Christ. Of all the words and acts of Jesus, none have the capacity to touch our hearts with love and gratitude more than those that occurred during his passion. The story of the Cross has converted hearts from sin to grace from apostolic times to the present day.

THE PALM SUNDAY PROCESSION

On Palm Sunday Jesus allowed himself to be the hero of an admiring throng for the first time. He was not looking for self-serving adulation. He was offering people the option for love, the option to receive him as their savior. Riding a donkey, a humble animal, he entered Jerusalem. The Passover crowds came out to praise him as a king. But their cheers were for a political liberator, not a spiritual savior.

The worried religious leaders asked him to tell the people to stop their applause and rapturous ovations. Jesus replied, "I tell you, if these were silent, the very stones would cry out" (Luke 19:40). Jesus completed his joyful entry into Jerusalem by going straight to the temple. He proceeded to remove from the temple the money changers and those who cheated the Passover pilgrims by selling the sacrificial animals at unfair prices. His attack on the corrupt religious leaders became one of the reasons they would seek to have him killed. "The chief priests and the scribes were seeking how to put him to death" (Luke 22:2). They found their solution in Judas.

The Lord's Supper

Then came the day of Unleavened Bread, on which the passover lamb had to be sacrificed. So Jesus sent Peter and John, saying, "Go and prepare the passover for us, that we may eat it" (Luke 22:7-8). Jesus and the twelve assembled in the upper room of a friend's house and sat on floor cushions around a festive table. Like a servant, Jesus had washed their feet as they entered the room. In this humble act he taught them to see their future ministry as one of humble service.

On the table they saw freshly baked loaves of unleavened bread, and a bowl of salt water to remind them of the tears of Israel during their slavery in Egypt. Salad bowls filled with endive and horseradish recalled the bitterness of their oppression. Dishes of an auburn-colored mix of crushed apples and dates surrounded with cinnamon sticks evoked memories of the bricks their ancestors made in the labor camps. Four cups of wine stood at each place setting. The roast lamb was the centerpiece, a remembrance of the first Passover lamb.

Jesus transformed this Passover meal into the first Eucharist. The words of institution of the Eucharist are found in the gospels of Matthew, Mark, and Luke as well as in 1 Corinthians 11:23-26. St. John used the scene to recall Christ's magnificent sermon on love. John reported Christ's teaching on the Eucharist in his chapter 6. After noting that one of the apostles would betray him and that another would deny him, Jesus changed some bread and wine into his body and blood at this supper.

Now as they were eating, Jesus took bread, and blessed, and broke it, and gave it to the disciples and said, "Take, eat; this is my body." And he took a cup, and when he had given thanks he gave it to them, saying, "Drink of it, all of you; for this is my blood of the covenant, which is poured out for many for the forgiveness of sins."

MATTHEW 26:26-28

The Agony in the Garden

Jesus led the final song of the Last Supper and brought Peter, James, and John with him to the garden of Gethsemane on the Mount of Olives. Jesus often used this garden retreat for nights of prayer (cf. Luke 22:39). The word Gethsemane means winepress. Just as grapes are crushed in a winepress, Jesus became crushed at the thought of what was about to happen to him. He asked his apostles to watch with him and pray. But drowsy with their meal, they slept. Jesus faced his agony alone. He prayed that he might not have to suffer, but he submitted himself to the Father's will. "Father, if thou art willing, remove this cup from me; nevertheless not my will, but thine" (Luke 22:42). To strengthen him, the Father sent an angel to comfort him. His prayer was so filled with agony and fervor that his sweat became like drops of blood. He went back to see his apostles and found them sleeping. They could not watch even one hour with him.

Betrayal and Denial

At that moment Judas led a group of soldiers into the garden. To identify Christ, he approached Jesus and kissed him. Jesus looked sadly at Judas and asked why he would betray him. It was Christ's last effort to save this poor man. Peter took a sword and cut off the ear of the high priest's servant. Jesus stopped Peter, warning him that to live by the sword is to die by the sword. Christ's kingdom is won by the power of love, not the love of power. Jesus was arrested and led to the house of the high priest. Judas had been paid thirty pieces of silver. He was now ashamed of what he had done. He threw the money back at the priests and elders saying that he had betrayed an innocent man. Then he went out and hanged himself.

Peter followed him at a distance and joined a group around a fire outside the high priest's house. People noticed Peter. A maid identified him as a follower of Jesus. Another person repeated the accusation. Someone else said that Peter's accent proved he was a Galilean. Each time, with greater ferocity and even curses, Peter swore, "I do not know the man!" (Matthew 26:74). At that moment soldiers led Jesus out of the house. He looked straight at Peter. The cock crowed. Peter remembered Christ's prophecy that he would deny him three times before the cock would crow. Peter felt the forgiving look of Jesus. He went away and wept bitterly.

The Trial of Jesus before the Sanhedrin

While Jesus was in the house of Caiphas, he was put on trial. The scribes and elders were there. They sought evidence, even false testimony, for putting him to death. Finally, two men came forward and said that Jesus claimed he could destroy the temple and rebuild it in three days. Caiphas asked Jesus to reply to the accusation. Jesus was silent. The high priest then said, "I order you to tell us under oath before the living God whether you are the Messiah, the Son of God." Jesus said to him in reply, "You have said so" (cf. Matthew 26:63). The high priest tore his robes and accused Jesus of blasphemy. He asked the opinion of the Sanhedrin. They said he deserved to die!

The right of execution belonged only to the Romans, so Jesus was turned over to the soldiers for the night. They spat in his face and struck him. Some slapped him and ridiculed him by asking him who had struck him. The following morning they took him to Pilate, the Roman governor.

Jesus before Pilate

On Good Friday morning, the religious leaders brought Jesus to Pilate's residence, the Fortress Antonia. They met with Pilate at the door of his house because it would be ritually unclean for them to enter the home of a Gentile. In their own court they had condemned Jesus on religious grounds of presumed blasphemy. In front of Pilate's court they changed the charge to a secular, political one. They falsely accused him of refusing to pay taxes to Caesar and of claiming to be a king.

The charge about kingship caught Pilate's attention. Roman governors did not want local people striving for sovereignty. He asked Jesus if he was the king of the Jews. Jesus replied that Pilate was using words put into his mouth by the accusers. Jesus added that his kingdom was a world of truth. The accusers pressed their case alleging that Jesus was another Galilean rebel. Hearing that Jesus was a Galilean, Pilate sent him to Herod who was in charge of Galilee. Conveniently, Herod was in town. Herod wanted Jesus to "amuse" him with some supernatural tricks. Jesus stood there in silence. He sent him back to Pilate.

The governor found no reason to condemn Jesus. He thought he would use the Passover Amnesty in which a prisoner could be released at the feast. He would give the crowd the choice of Jesus the innocent one, or Barabbas the convicted murderer and rebel. Before presenting the two men, he had Jesus scourged, believing this would gain the sympathy of the people. The soldiers not only beat Christ, but also crowned him with thorns and put a red robe on him, mocking him as a king. The people chose Barabbas and called for Christ's crucifixion.

Pilate caved into the popular will. Washing his hands of the case, he handed Jesus over to them to deal with as they wished. History has memorialized his moral failure in the creed with the words, "suffered under Pontius Pilate." Jesus now proceeded to the Cross.

REFLECTION

When the soldiers had scourged Jesus and crowned him with thorns, they knelt before the King of Glory. They bowed in mockery little knowing they bent with a gesture of reverence before the Master of the universe. The heartless prostrated before the King of hearts. They saw nothing more than a helpless man whom they could beat up and make fun of.

Jesus stood there, his body smarting with waves of pain, his head a blinding ache, all his natural sensitivities open to resentment at being treated both as a fool and a human rag doll. Yet incredibly his glory radiated there even more than during the excitement over the miracles of the bread, wine, and raising of Lazarus. No enthusiastic crowds sang his praises. But angels worshipped him and glorified the shimmering radiance coming through the beaten body. To our eyes of faith he is Lord of Lords even in this dreadful state. His *kenosis*, his self-emptying, is reaching its climax. Only then will resurrection, ascent, and seating at God's right hand follow.

FOR DIALOGUE

Which of these scenes from Christ's passion affects you most and why is this so? Why is the betrayal and suicide of Judas such a tragic story? By comparison why is the cowardice and denial and repentance of Peter actually a hope-filled narrative for us?

What is there about human nature that blinded the religious leaders from seeing the goodness of Jesus and his authentic messianic mission? Similarly, how could Pilate have handed Jesus over to death when he actually believed he was innocent?

What do the sufferings of Jesus have to say to people who bear pain, whether mental, physical, or emotional? How may we say that Christ's glory and majesty appear even more in his humiliation than in his miracles and other moments of triumph during his earthly ministry?

PRAYER

Jesus, in your own hour of grief you reached out to Judas, Peter, and even Pilate to invite them to conversion. Only Peter responded with tears of repentance. May we be alert to your loving presence, always inviting us to turn to you with repentance and conversion.

And they stripped him and put a scarlet robe upon him, and plaiting a crown of thorns they put it on his head, and put a reed in his right hand. And kneeling before him they mocked him, saying, "Hail, King of the Jews!" And they spat upon him, and took the reed and struck him on the head.

MATTHEW 27:28-30

CHAPTER 54

Jesus Goes to the Cross

Matthew 27:32-66; Mark 15:21-47;
Luke 23:26-56; John 19:16-42

They . . . put his own clothes on him. And they led him out to crucify
him. And they compelled a passer-by, Simon of Cyrene . . . to carry
his cross.

MARK 15:20-21

The Persians invented crucifixion. The Romans adopted it for the execution of non-Roman criminals, especially murderers and robbers. A trumpeter led the crucifixion procession to the execution mound. The sound of the trumpet both drew a crowd and admonished people to get out of the way of the march. Behind the trumpeter came a herald who carried a wooden poster bearing the name of the criminal and identifying the crime.

In this case the sign said, "This is Jesus of Nazareth, the King of the Jews." The INRI seen above Christ's head on crucifixes is an abbreviation of the Latin form of this accusation. The sign bore the inscription in Latin, the language of law; Greek, the language of philosophy; and Hebrew, the language of religion.

Two witnesses walked in the procession. They provided the possibility of having a second trial on the spot. A bystander could come forward and provide new evidence that might prove the innocence of the accused. The witnesses served as a kind of judge and jury. The accused walked behind the herald, carrying the T-bar of the cross. Jesus was so weakened with dehydration and pain from the scourging and crowning with thorns, that he was unable to carry the T-bar the full distance. Simon carried it in his place. The vertical post of the cross stood at the mound of execution outside the city walls. Four guards marched with the criminal. A centurion, usually mounted on a horse, came last.

The site of Christ's crucifixion was just a short distance outside the walls of Jerusalem. Scripture calls it Golgotha, the place of the skull (cf. Matthew 27:33). The Latin for Golgotha is *Calvarium* — Calvary. The name indicates that this was a place for beheadings as well as crucifixions. A legend says that Adam's skull was buried in the earth there and that the redemptive blood of Jesus (the new Adam) first touched the head of the old Adam to save him.

The execution mound was relatively slight in height. The vertical post was probably not more than ten feet high. Family members could be close to the victim to help him and comfort him. Christ's wrists were nailed to the T-bar and then he was raised onto the post where his feet were nailed. Normally death came by asphyxiation, caused by the inability to raise up one's self to inhale and exhale properly. Generally it took a week for the crucified to die. It is thought that Jesus died more quickly probably due to extensive beatings and excessive loss of blood. Just before Passover, crucified persons had their legs broken so that they would die and be buried before the feast began. Since Jesus had already died, there was a piercing of his side just to make sure.

THE SONG OF THE THORN BIRD

According to a legend, the thorn bird sings just once in its life. Leaving its nest, it searches for a thorn bush. Upon finding such a bush, it impales itself on the longest, sharpest thorn. At that moment it begins to sing. The bird out-carols the lark and the nightingale, and the world pauses to listen. God smiles with pleasure at the captivating melody. What is the message of this sacrificial music? Life's greatest achievement can be bought only at the price of great pain.

Christian faith has developed a meditation on Christ's time on the Cross, built around his seven utterances from the Cross as recorded by the gospels. These are known as the seven last "words" of Jesus. In a sense they are like the song of the thorn bird. The Word of God left the "nest" of divine love and glory to become incarnate in Jesus Christ. Jesus came to reconcile the world to God by his redemptive death. His ministry of preaching and healing and forming the apostles were part of that plan. Then, impaled on the wood of the cross, Jesus acted out his teachings. His last words constitute a song of love as well as an act that would redeem us from our sins and offer us a share in divine life.

To speak of his seven words as a song is not to sentimentalize what he did. Christ's final words are deeds of salvation. He preached forgiveness by the lakeside. At Calvary he gave it to others, most notably to the good thief. His word to John accomplished Mary's future security, and his word to Mary elevated her to being Mother of the Church. His word of surrender to the Father was the active gathering of his whole being to God.

Jesus spoke his seven last words in a biblical, oral culture that attributed the force of action to his utterances. He was not passive on the Cross. He composed a love song in seven parts. Far from being self-absorbed in his pain, Jesus provided his own commentary on the meaning of what he was doing — indeed, making the comments saving acts themselves. He also showed that the act of dying could be redemptive. Now, our own rendezvous with dying can be accomplished with similar dignity and — united with Jesus — be filled with saving power for others.

The seven last words of Jesus are scattered throughout the gospels. They are ordered by pious tradition, not by strict historical chronology. Luke and John differ on Christ's final utterance due to the purposes of each writer. Liturgical tradition favors John's account of Christ's last word because of its ritual, sacrificial quality.

This reflection section is devoted to a brief meditation on each of Christ's seven final words.

REFLECTION

When the apostles began preaching about Jesus, they started with the story of his passion, death, and resurrection, the essential narrative of how he redeemed us. The passion narratives in particular are the longest sections of the gospels. The seven utterances of Jesus from the cross offer us Christ's own interpretation of the meaning of what he was doing.

Father, forgive them, they know not what they do (Luke 23:34). The provocation for this saying of Jesus came from challenges presented to him by bystanders. They taunted him to save himself. The religious leaders said that he should save himself if he is really the Messiah of God. The soldiers jeered him, shouting that if he is the king of the Jews, he should save himself. The crowd challenged him, "If you are the Son of God, come down from the cross!" (Matthew 27:40). Such heartless words were meant to make Jesus forget his goal of saving and forgiving them and to think only of himself. He had taught them to love their enemies, to pray for those who persecute. Now in the midst of his own pain, he begged the Father to forgive them. They did not know what they were doing.

Amen, I say to you, today you will be with me in Paradise (Luke 34:43). Often the jail "cells" of that period were pits into which prisoners were lowered. Iron gratings covered them. Possibly Jesus was imprisoned with the two thieves crucified with him. They had a chance to watch him that night as well as see how he reacted to the scourging and crowning and choice of Barabbas. One thief was touched by Christ's nobility and peaceful surrender to God. The other was not. The second one also challenged Jesus to save them and himself. He even cursed Jesus for doing nothing. The "good" thief rebuked his partner, praising Christ's innocence and asking for salvation. It was like a "deathbed conversion." Jesus answered the thief's prayer and promised him Paradise that very day. As Archbishop Sheen loved to say, "He remained a thief to the end, for he stole heaven."

Woman, behold, your son. Then he said to the disciple, Behold, your mother (John 19:26-27). Mary and John stood by the Cross. Jesus had called Mary "Woman" at Cana, thus elevating her to a special role in the work of salvation. Again he calls her Woman and now elevated her to being Mother of the Church. (Here John symbolizes the church.) It was Pope Paul VI who had this insight into Christ's words to Mary when he gave her the title Mother of the Church. At the same time, Jesus made sure his mother was cared for, entrusting her to the care of John.

My God, my God, why have you forsaken me? (Matthew 27:46). The absolute nearness of death, coupled with the indignities of the passion plunged Jesus into the deepest aspects of the dying process. Even with his mother and closest friends beside him, he felt the sense of isolation and loneliness that closes in on a dying person. Above all he experienced the loss of God's presence. Like so many before him, he turned to that psalm of abandonment, Psalm 22 in which he cries out the question, "My God, why have you forsaken me?" The psalm helped those near him to feel his abandonment as well as his conviction that the Father will never actually leave him.

I thirst (John 19:28). The executioners brought with them a jug of soldier's wine, a rough fluid that helped them settle their nerves in their grisly task. They also shared it with the crucified persons to help dull their pain. The gospels say that there were two wine presentations to Jesus. The first one he refused, but the second one he drank. The soldiers used a sponge-tipped hyssop branch to present the wine. Hyssop was a herb used for healing. The scourging caused a great loss of blood and dehydration, hence the thirst was sharp and painful. Saints have seen in this word of Jesus his thirst for the salvation of souls. Jesus used his physical thirst as an occasion to express his spiritual desire to save us, basically saying, "Let me love you."

It is finished (John 19:30). Throughout his life Jesus participated in the various forms of sacrificial worship customary among his people. He witnessed the offering of the holocaust of sacrificial animals in the temple. He saw the offering of the loaves of bread and the sacred libation of wine poured out over the altar of sacrifice. He would have been present on the Day of Atonement when the priest symbolically laid the sins of the nation on the back of a goat and drove it out into the desert. This is the origin of the scapegoat. He participated in over thirty Passover meals, including the Last Supper. Jesus took all these acts of adoration of God, these sacrifices, and summed them up in himself. His sacrifice at Calvary fulfilled and replaced them. They crowned the act of reconciliation with the Father he came to accomplish. And so his last word in John's gospel is, "It is finished." The work of salvation has been accomplished. He said those words as he felt his own body to be God's lamb. At that moment, the high priest in the temple slew the last lamb and said, "It is finished."

At Calvary, the sacrifice really was finished.

Father into your hands, I commend my spirit (Luke 23:46). Mary had taught the child Jesus this night prayer to be said just before he went to sleep. What he learned as a child he used as his last prayer before he died. At his death the great veil of the temple was mysteriously torn in two. God's presence, hidden from all but the high priest, is now open for all the world to experience. The new covenant of Jesus is offered to all peoples to remove their sin and guilt and receive the life of the Holy Spirit.

FOR DIALOGUE

Which of Christ's seven words helps you appreciate how Jesus interpreted his suffering and death? How could his words inspire you to live a deeper Christian life? What is the link between Christ's words to Mary at Cana and at the Cross?

The good thief had a "deathbed conversion" at Calvary. What are some other such stories you could share about last-minute conversions? Why do such conversions make some believers uneasy?

In the fourth word, when even Jesus sensed what it is like to lose the presence of God, what might that mean for you? What lessons about forgiveness do you draw from Christ's first word?

Jesus crucified, how can I thank you for your loving sacrifice on my behalf? I praise you for your love. I pray that the mystery of the Cross will be a lasting source of grace and strength for me. Thank you.

The centurion ... said, "Certainly this man was innocent."

LUKE 23:47

CHAPTER 55

Jesus Rises from the Dead

Matthew 28; Mark 16; Luke 24; John 20-21

"Why do you seek the living among the dead? He is not here, but has risen."

LUKE 24:5-6

After Jesus died, Joseph of Arimathea, a secret disciple of Jesus, went to Pilate and asked for the body of Christ. Permission was given. Joseph and Nicodemus wrapped Christ's body in a clean shroud and placed it in a new tomb in the garden next to Calvary. The tomb belonged to Joseph. "Nicodemus also, who had at first come to him by night, came bringing a mixture of myrrh and aloes, about a hundred pounds' weight [to anoint the body]" (John 19:39).

The two men completed their work before sunset and closed the tomb by rolling a large, heavy, circular stone across the entrance. Good Friday came to a close. Jesus was dead and buried.

Meanwhile, the priests and Pharisees were concerned that Christ's disciples might steal the body and falsely claim that he rose from the dead. They went to Pilate and asked him to place guards at the tomb for three days. Pilate agreed with their request and ordered the tomb to be sealed and guarded.

THE STONE MOVED BY AN ANGEL

At dawn on Sunday, Mary Magdalene, and Mary the mother of James and Salome purchased spices and went to the tomb with the intention of completing the anointing of Christ's body. They wondered out loud, "Who will roll away the stone for us from the door of the tomb?" (Mark 16:3) Arriving at the grave, they experienced an earthquake as an angel moved the stone from the door of the tomb and then sat by the entrance.

The guards were terrified. The women were also frightened, but they entered the chamber and saw two angels dressed in white. One of the angels calmed them by saying, "Do not be afraid" (Matthew 28:5). They noticed the body was gone. Mary Magdalene said that someone must have taken away the body of the Lord.

An angel replied, "Why do you seek the living one among the dead? He is not here, but has risen. Remember how he told you, while he was still in

Galilee, that the Son of Man must be delivered into the hands of sinful men, and be crucified, and on the third day rise.... Go quickly and tell his disciples" (Luke 24:5-7; Matthew 28:7).

Mary Magdalene asked her friend to leave her alone in the garden for a time. As she lingered, weeping by the grave, a man came up to her. It was Jesus, but she did not recognize him. Jesus asked her why she was crying. She assumed he was the gardener, and she said that if he were the one who took away Christ's body, he should let her know where it was and she would take charge of it. Then Jesus simply said, "Mary." Recognizing him at last, she knelt at his feet and clasped them, saying, "Rabboni!" which means "Teacher" (cf. John 20:16).

THE FIRST TO SEE THE RISEN LORD

Jesus said to her, "Do not hold me, for I have not yet ascended to the Father; but go to my brethren" (John 20:17). She was the first to see the risen Lord.

Then Mary Magdalene and the other Mary ran to the house where the eleven apostles were hiding. Immediately, Mary Magdalene proclaimed the astounding news, "I have seen the Lord!" (John 20:18)

She told them that Jesus had risen from the dead. She is the first believer to announce the resurrection. Tradition calls her the "apostle to the apostles." The apostles refused to believe her, but sent Peter and John to check out her story.

Peter and John ran to the tomb. John looked in and saw the burial cloths, but he let Peter enter the tomb first. Following Peter into the chamber, John saw that the body was gone and immediately believed in Christ's resurrection.

The frightened guards went to the priests and told them what had happened. They were bribed to say that the disciples stole the body while they were asleep. The guards took the money and spread the story as they were told.

On Easter night, the risen Jesus came to the house of the apostles and appeared in their midst. He calmed them with the greeting, "Peace." They thought he was a ghost. Jesus showed them the scars in his hands and side and feet. He invited them to touch him and realize that he was not a ghost but had flesh and bones. He asked them if they had anything to eat. They gave him some roasted fish and he ate it in front of them.

PREACHING THE GOOD NEWS

He explained from the Scriptures that the Messiah was supposed to suffer, die and rise from the dead. Now they must preach the Good News of the kingdom of God, salvation from sins, and the graces of divine life. They must bring the gospel to the whole world.

Again he said "Peace" to them and conferred upon them the Holy Spirit and the power to forgive sins. "Receive the Holy Spirit. If you forgive the sins of any, they are forgiven; if you retain the sins of any, they are retained" (John 20:22-23).

A little later, two disciples, Cleopas and his companion, were walking from Jerusalem to Emmaus. As they were discussing the death of Jesus, he came along the road and greeted them, but they did not recognize him. Jesus asked them what was troubling them. Cleopas explained how depressed they were by the execution of Jesus. They had hoped he would liberate them from the Romans. They had heard a rumor that he was alive, but found that hard to believe.

Jesus explained from the Scriptures that the Messiah was supposed to suffer and die, and then rise from the dead and so enter into his glory.

Arriving at Emmaus, the pair urged the stranger to dine with them. During the breaking of the bread they recognized the risen Christ, at which moment he disappeared. Thrilled with this revelation, they hurried back to Jerusalem to share the good news, saying as they went, "Did not our hearts burn within us while he talked to us on the road, while he opened to us the scriptures?" (Luke 24:32).

DOUBTING THOMAS

The apostle Thomas was not with the others when Jesus had appeared to them. When they told him they had seen the Lord, he refused to believe them. He would only believe if he could actually see the nail marks and put his finger in them. A week later Thomas was with the apostles. Jesus came into the room, although the doors were locked. He gave them the word and gift of peace. Jesus invited Thomas to see the nail marks on his body and to touch them. Jesus asked Thomas to overcome his doubts and believe. Thomas believed and said, "My Lord and my God!" (John 20:28).

Jesus said to him, "Have you believed because you have seen me? Blessed are those who have not seen and yet believed" (John 20:29).

St. Paul summarized the numerous appearances of the risen Jesus in this powerful message: "For I delivered to you as of first importance what I also received, that Christ died for our sins in accordance with the scriptures, that he was buried, that he was raised on the third day in accordance with the scriptures, and that he appeared to Cephas, then to the twelve. Then he appeared to more than five hundred brethren at one time, most of whom are still alive, though some have fallen asleep. Then he appeared to James, then to all the apostles. Last of all, as to one untimely born, he appeared also to me. For I am the least of the apostles, unfit to be called an apostle, because

I persecuted the church of God. But by the grace of God I am what I am, and his grace toward me was not in vain. On the contrary, I worked harder than any of them, though it was not I, but the grace of God which is with me" (1 Corinthians 15: 3-10).

This is the gift and mystery we celebrate on Easter Sunday, on every Sunday of the year and in every Eucharist. Christ is risen! He is risen indeed!

REFLECTION

Dawn, Sunday morning.

Mary Magdalene came to the tomb and saw that the stone was rolled away. She encountered the risen Jesus in the garden and with joy came to believe in his remarkable resurrection. She reported this to the apostles who sent Peter and John to confirm it.

Peter and John ran to the tomb. John arrived first and waited for Peter. When Peter arrived, he entered the grave room. He saw the shroud rolled up on the shelf where Christ's body had been laid. The cloth, which had covered his head, was in a different place. The body was gone.

John saw this and believed. What led him to faith? Did he conclude the body would not have been stolen since robbers would scarcely have taken the time to unwrap the body and carry away a nude corpse? St. John Chrysostom points out the unlikelihood of theft. "If anyone removed the body, he would not have stripped it first. Nor would he have taken the trouble to roll up the head covering and put it in a place by itself" (Homily 85, 4).

Love is the real explanation of John's faith in the resurrection. Love is the best road to faith. John was the disciple whom Jesus loved — and who loved Jesus in return. John alone of the apostles stood at the cross. Jesus entrusted his mother to the care of John.

Later Jesus told Thomas that seeing his body in order to come to faith was not as great as believing without seeing. Possibly Jesus glanced at John while saying these words to Thomas. Love is stronger than death. The power of John's love for Jesus enabled him to believe in Christ's resurrection. John was the closest in love to Jesus. He was the fastest to look for him and the first apostle to believe in his resurrection. He believed without seeing.

FOR DIALOGUE

Scripture shows that the apostles were devastated by the death of Jesus and slow to believe in his resurrection. In imagining yourself in their shoes, how would you have reacted to Christ's death and resurrection? Why would Christ's death be so disappointing? Why might his resurrection be so unbelievable?

At the same time, they all came to appreciate the meaning of Christ's sufferings and death and come to faith in his resurrection. In your faith life, how has your faith developed in the gift and mystery of Christ's death and resurrection? What might you learn from the "doubting Thomas" narrative?

If it is love that brings us to faith, how is this apparent in the lives of Mary Magdalene and the apostle John? How does your love for Jesus help your faith in him to deepen? Is it also true that faith brings us to love? Are faith and love complementary virtues?

PRAYER

Risen Jesus, I hear your first risen word, "Peace." I am grateful for the gift of peace. Your peace reconciles me to you, to others, to myself. As your peace takes ever greater hold on my life, may I share that with others. I love you.

If Christ has not been raised, then our preaching is in vain and your faith is in vain.

1 CORINTHIANS 15:14

CHAPTER 56

Jesus Sends the Holy Spirit
to Us at Pentecost

John 16:1-15; Acts 1:1-4, 14; 2:1-47

When the day of Pentecost had come, they were all together in one place. And suddenly a sound came from heaven like the rush of a mighty wind, and it filled all the house where they were sitting. And there appeared to them tongues as of fire, distributed and resting on each one of them. And they were all filled with the Holy Spirit.

ACTS 2:1-4

THE JEWISH PENTECOST

In Jewish liturgy Pentecost was the feast that celebrated the giving of the covenant at Sinai. It recalled both God's covenant with Israel as well as the giving of the Ten Commandments. A mighty wind and fire swept the slopes of Sinai evoking the awesomeness of the occasion. The wind represented the breath of God as the source of all life. The fire symbolized God's glory that manifested his presence to his people. The Jewish Pentecost took place fifty days after Passover.

THE CHRISTIAN PENTECOST

Fifty days after the Christian Passover (Christ's death and resurrection) the Christian Pentecost occurred in the Upper Room. Led by Mary, the apostles and disciples, numbering 120 people, had completed nine days of prayer for the coming of the Spirit. The Upper Room became like a new Sinai. Once again the mighty breath of God and the fire of his presence swept through the communion of believers. The Holy Spirit confirmed them as the Christian community and manifested the Church. The Spirit filled them with enthusiasm, a term that means "the God within."

They began speaking in tongues (*glossalalia*), a language phenomenon that sometimes accompanies profound spiritual experiences. Armed with the fire of the Spirit, and with ecstatic speech on their lips, they flowed out of the

Upper Room into the square below where pilgrims from over fifteen nations had assembled for the religious observance.

The extraordinary joy of those who had just been filled with the Holy Spirit affected the pilgrims. In wonder, the crowd vibrated happily with the contagious enthusiasm and excitement of the Spirit-filled community. They identified with the language miracle. There was a fleeting moment when these representatives of the nations of the earth paused from their strife and profound community took place.

The artists of the Middle Ages loved to contrast the babbling and divided mob of Babel's Tower to the loving, linguistically united community in the square at Pentecost. The arrogance of Babel is replaced by the humility of Pentecost where God is all in all.

After the first glow of unity subsided, the skeptical soul reappeared. "And all were amazed and perplexed, saying to one another, 'What does this mean?' But others mocking said, 'They are filled with new wine'" (Acts 2:12-13).

Peter's Missionary Sermon

Jesus had made Peter head of the Church, a rock and shepherd of the new community. Peter now assumed his responsibility and raised his voice to explain to the assembly the meaning of what has happened. With a slight attempt at humor he noted that his people were not drunk. After all it was only nine o'clock in the morning.

Growing more serious, Peter cited the prophet Joel who predicted that in the final age of the world, God would pour out his Spirit upon all people. That prophecy has just been fulfilled in the Upper Room. Immediately, Peter turned their attention to Jesus Christ. He reminded them of how God worked mighty works and wonders through Jesus during his earthly ministry. Then, like an innocent lamb, he is led to death. But God has not let him remain in the bonds of death. Jesus rose from the dead fifty days ago at Easter.

Then with a touch of preacher's drama, Peter gestured toward the tomb of David, visible to all. Peter quoted a psalm verse in which David said, "You will not abandon my soul to the netherworld, nor will you suffer your faithful one to undergo corruption" (Psalm 16:10). Peter paused. Then he said that David's body had seen corruption. To whom then would his words apply? To the Holy One, the Messiah, the Jesus that Peter proclaimed. Christ's body did not see corruption. David was right. Jesus is the proof of his words.

Peter continued with the truth of Christ's Ascension. Again he quoted David. "The Lord said to my Lord, 'Sit at my right hand'" (Psalm 110:1). Clearly David did not ascend. But Jesus has ascended to heaven and has sent his Holy Spirit who has caused the marvels that astounded them that day. Jesus is thus LORD and Christ. As LORD he is divine. As Christ he is the Messiah they had been looking for.

Peter's sermon disturbed his listeners. "Now when they heard this they were cut to the heart" (Acts 2:37). He was not preaching a detached recitation of dry facts. He delivered a personal testimony designed to change the hearts of his audience. Peter was not interested in a neutral view of Jesus. His own soul pulsed with the glory of God. He was anxious that all the world should share his vision and joy. Good news in the heart calls for a compelling message on the lips.

Small wonder then that his listeners said they were pierced to the heart. Peter's talk had surfaced within them the fundamental thirst for God planted in every human heart. This was no whiling away the hour with curious discourse. People's destinies were at stake and the course of future history was the gamble of the hour. Thus the central question took shape. The cry was heard on all sides, "What shall we do?"

Peter called them to repentance and baptism and commitment to Christ. "Repent, and be baptized everyone of you in the name of Jesus Christ for the forgiveness of your sins; and you shall receive the gift of the Holy Spirit" (Acts 2:38). He urged and exhorted them to save themselves from that crooked and corrupt generation. About three thousand people were added to the Church that day.

The new communities that sprang up devoted themselves to the teaching of the apostles, to community life, to the breaking of the bread (the Eucharist), and to prayers. They sold their properties and divided the money among all according to each one's need. "They... ate their food with glad and generous hearts, praising God and having the goodwill of all the people. And day by day the Lord added to their number those who were being saved" (Acts 2:46-47).

REFLECTION

The Pentecost narrative is a revelation of the Holy Spirit. It is also the action of the Spirit revealing and manifesting the Church. While this is the formal introduction of the presence, person, and power of the Spirit in Scripture, it is necessary to point out that the Spirit has been living and active from the start of God's plan for salvation.

The Holy Spirit is involved in the plan of salvation from the beginning just as much as the Father and the Son. The Spirit is really

God. The Spirit is consubstantial with the Father and the Son and is inseparable from them (cf. CCC 689). The Spirit has the same "substance" or divine nature as they do. The Spirit has the same mission as the Son, in the cause of salvation. When the Father sends the Son He also sends the Spirit to save us from sin and give us divine life.

The word Spirit comes from the Hebrew *ruah*, which means breath, air, wind. The Spirit is God's breath, filling us with divine life, purifying our souls, sustaining our immortality until we love what God loves, do what God wants of us until this earthly part of us glows with divine fire.

Scripture calls the Spirit the *paraclete*, meaning our advocate and consoler. Jesus asked the Father to send us the Spirit to remind us of what Jesus taught and guide us into truth. On Easter night Jesus gave the Holy Spirit to the apostles, breathing into them the third Person of the Trinity. From that moment on the mission of Jesus and the Spirit becomes the mission of the Church. The revelation of the Holy Spirit at Pentecost is also the Spirit's public manifestation of the Church.

Tradition uses many images to illustrate the Spirit's actions:

1. Water, signifying the Spirit's saving action at baptism.
2. Oil and Seal, by which the Spirit anoints us at confirmation.
3. Fire, by which the Spirit transforms us into Christ.
4. Cloud, the shining glory that led Israel in the desert, dwelt on the Ark of the Covenant, overshadowed Mary at the Annunciation, and was present at Christ's baptism and transfiguration. The cloud image emphasizes how the Spirit helps us experience the effective Divine presence.

FOR DIALOGUE

What events in your life have been associated with the reception of the Holy Spirit? If asked to give a testimony to the Spirit's influence on your life, what might you say?

What is remarkable about the behavior of the apostles before and after receiving the Holy Spirit? What is impressive about the way Peter conducts himself after receiving the Spirit, especially in the light of his behavior in the gospels?

Why do we make an essential connection between the Holy Spirit and the Church? What was there about Peter's first sermon that produced such a reaction from the audience? Why did Scripture make a point about the formation of a Christian community as the first outcome of the Pentecost event?

PRAYER

Breathe on me breath of God.
My soul with grace refine,
that this earthly part of me,
may glow with life divine.

EDWIN HATCH

When they had prayed, the place in which they were gathered together was shaken; and they were all filled with the Holy Spirit and spoke the word of God with boldness.

ACTS 4:31

CHAPTER 57

Paul Preaches and Witnesses Jesus Christ to the World

Acts 9:1-30; 17:22-33; 1 Cor 1:10-31; 2:1-16

Whatever you do, in word or deed, do everything in the name of the Lord Jesus, giving thanks to God the Father through him.

COLOSSIANS 3:17, NRSV

St. Paul was born into a prominent Jewish family in Tarsus. The city was wealthy, cultured, and a thousand years old. It boasted a population of half a million at the time of Paul. So, Paul was a city man. That is why his writings do not have the rural comparisons found in the gospels. His epistles are filled with references to games in the stadium, business in the forum, and civic and military parades. He enjoyed Roman citizenship, learned to be a tentmaker, and mastered the Greek and Latin languages.

The final stage of his education took place in Jerusalem where he learned Hebrew and studied to become a Pharisee. He was a student of Gamaliel whose views were compassionate and moderate. This is how God prepared Paul for his world mission.

PAUL'S CONVERSION

He stormed onto the biblical stage as a persecutor of Christians. He was on the road to Damascus to arrest some Christians when he experienced a conversion that changed him completely. Struck to the ground by a light from heaven and touched by God, the angry Pharisee overnight became a militant Christian. He heard a voice saying, "Saul, Saul, why do you persecute me?" He said, "Who are you, Lord?" The reply came, "I am Jesus, whom you are persecuting; but rise and enter the city, and you will be told what you are to do" (Acts 9:4-6). His comrades brought him to Straight Street, where the Lord sent Ananias to baptize Paul and welcome him to the Christian community.

Paul then retired for a time into the Arabian desert. He needed to be alone with God in prayer to absorb the impact of Christ's call. It is quite possible that he had his other famed vision at this time that he describes in these words: "I will go onto visions and revelations of the Lord. I know a man in Christ who... was caught up to Paradise... and he heard things that cannot be told, which man may not utter" (2 Corinthians 12: 2, 4).

While Paul was enjoying such an ecstasy, he was rudely jolted by the reception of a "thorn in the flesh." He wrote, "And to keep me from being too elated by the abundance of revelations, a thorn was given me in the flesh, a messenger of Satan, to harass me, to keep me from being too elated [too proud]" (2 Corinthians 12:7). What was this thorn? Body sores? Eye infections? Sexual temptations? Incessant persecution and rejection? We will never know. What is clear is that it was severe enough to bother him fourteen years later when he wrote about it.

His Ministry as an Apostle Begins

Paul began his missionary work, preaching the gospel in a Damascus synagogue. Here he experienced his first success and first rejection. So angry did some of the listeners become that they threatened to kill him. To them he had betrayed the ancestral faith. He had to escape in a basket lowered over the city walls.

He decided to go to Jerusalem and meet Peter and the other apostles. He needed to be assured that his message was correct. He sought their approval and blessing. But given his former reputation as an enemy of Christians, he inspired fear and doubt in the Christian community. It took his friend Barnabas to calm the waters and convince the community that Paul's conversion was genuine.

So the giants of Christianity met each other. Paul, the wiry rabbinical student, and Peter, the rough-hewn fisherman. They spent fifteen days together. Peter shared with Paul the vivid details of the life and teachings of Jesus. He brought Paul to the place where Jesus saved the woman taken in adultery, and the rich man's house where the woman washed the feet of Jesus. They walked through the temple, and Paul heard of Christ's cleansing of God's house. They stood before the house of Caiphas, the palace of Pilate, and the pillar where Jesus was scourged. They walked the *Via Dolorosa* — the Way of the Cross — and knelt at Calvary. They prayed at the tomb from which Jesus rose from the dead.

In turn, Paul shared the account of his religious experiences on the Damascus Road and in the desert. This faith sharing was the beginning of a bond so firm that the Church celebrates their feast on the same day, June 29.

At the end of this two-week visit, one might think Paul was ready to conquer the world for Christ. Peter judged, however, that Paul needed more tempering. His fiery temperament might be too much for the fragile community. His boiling ardor could move things too fast. Paul's "hour" had not yet come. Peter asked Paul to return to Tarsus and await a call from the Church (cf. Acts 9:29-30). This was a difficult trial for Paul. A missionary with no mission, he would go home to a city where his family and friends and synagogue would reject him. The great preacher would pass his days making tents. He bore this with faith and obedience.

Four years later, the Church was ready to open a mission to the Gentiles at Antioch. Peter sent Barnabas to Tarsus to call Paul out of seclusion. Paul's "hour" had come (cf. Acts 11:25-26). From that time he would be called Paul instead of Saul (Acts 13:9). As the sea breezes filled the sails of his ship to Antioch, Paul stood and exulted, "I am convinced that neither death, nor life, nor angels, nor rulers, nor things present, nor things to come, nor powers, nor height, nor depth, nor anything else in creation will be able to separate us from the love of God in Christ Jesus our Lord" (Romans 8:38-39).

REFLECTION

Paul is so well known as an active evangelizer and missionary that it is easy to forget he spent time in prayer in the desert and four years in seclusion in Tarsus. Paul, the man of prayer and obedience, preceded the activist. The deeper the preparation, the more profound the result.

One of the first pastoral challenges he faced was the divide between the Jewish and Gentile converts. The Jewish converts retained their religious practices of circumcision and the dietary laws. They expected the Gentile converts to do the same. Paul had the insight to see that such customs were not essential for Christians. Faith in Jesus Christ and baptism were the paths into Christianity. Paul's teaching eventually won out. He challenged Peter on this matter at Antioch (Galatians 2:11). Then he won approval for his point of view at the Council of Jerusalem (Acts 15). Finally, he was able to teach that divisions between Jew and Gentile, Greek and barbarian, had been torn down. The dividing walls that separated men had been demolished by the peace of Jesus Christ (cf. Ephesians 2:11-22).

Paul developed a missionary method, part of which is still in use today. His first job was to organize a community. He moved on when he felt the community could stand on its own feet. He kept in touch with the community through letters and messengers. He always brought the gospel first to the Jewish community in the synagogues. Then he would turn to the Gentiles. After a time, the inevitable blowup would come. He had to trust that he would survive riots, stoning, prison, and exile.

He was an administrator as well as an evangelist. Many pastoral problems were new to him. In Corinth, alone, he had to find a Christian solution for interfaith relations, the end-of-the-world scare, sexual issues, dietary laws, women's fashions, and whether Christians should take other Christians to pagan courts. Many of his decisions have influenced Christian pastoral practice for centuries.

Like Peter, Paul also journeyed to Rome. They would both become martyrs for Christ. St. Luke wrote of Paul's arrival in Rome: "And so we came to Rome. The believers from there, when they heard of us, came as far as the Forum of Appius and Three Taverns to meet us. On seeing them, Paul thanked God and took courage. When we came into Rome, Paul was allowed to live by himself, with the soldier who was guarding him.... He lived there two whole years at his own expense and welcomed all who came to him, proclaiming the kingdom of God and teaching about the Lord Jesus Christ with all boldness and without hindrance" (Acts 28:14-16; 30-31, NRSV).

FOR DIALOGUE

What aspects of Paul's life and mission appeal to you? Why has Paul's influence been so pervasive in the history of the Church? Why is our Church always training missionaries and opening missions where people have yet to hear of Jesus and his saving work?

What makes Paul's temporary exile in Tarsus such a model for our obedience to the will of God? What kind of a companion do you think Paul would have been for you?

Paul died a martyr for Christ. What makes it possible for such an ultimate witness for Jesus? Share some personal stories in which you had to take a stand for Jesus in the face of a certain challenge.

O God, we praise you for the graces you gave to Paul the apostle. We thank you for giving him to our Church and for his extraordinary mission activities. Grant us the graces we need to have the heart and dedication of a missionary for Jesus.

My eager expectation and hope that I shall not be at all ashamed, but that with full courage now as always Christ will be honored in my body, whether by life or by death. For to me to live is Christ, and to die is gain.
PHILIPPIANS 1:20-21

CHAPTER 58

Glory and Praise to You, Lord Jesus Christ

Revelation 1:9-20; 4-5, 21

Then I saw a new heaven and a new earth.... I saw the holy city, new Jerusalem, coming down out of heaven from God.... I heard a great voice from the throne saying, "Behold, the dwelling of God is with the [human race]."

REVELATION 21:1-3

A MESSAGE OF HOPE AND COURAGE

The Bible ends with the book of Revelation, also called the Apocalypse, the Greek word for revelation. The author of this book wrote it to give hope and courage to the infant Christian community facing the threats and persecutions coming from imperial Rome. The book contains applications at three levels: first to the early Church, second to the Church in all ages of history, third to the Church at the end of time.

Its message contains violent images of the terrors the Church must face. These are found in the passages about the four horsemen of suffering and death, the seven trumpets of doom, and the seven bowls of wrath. These tribulations are accompanied by the antichrist, the scarlet woman, dragons and beasts, and a final battle between good and evil at Armageddon.

So vivid are these pictures that readers often fail to note that far more attention is paid to Christ in glory in the numerous scenes of the heavenly liturgy. If you were to see portraits of the 22 chapters in an art gallery, you would find all the brutal scenes tucked in between majestic canvases of Jesus in glory. Though it is unreal to avoid the impact of evil upon believers, it is equally illusory to forget the victory Jesus obtained for us in his redemptive death and resurrection.

This guide to the Bible ends with a picture of Christ in triumph as portrayed in the heavenly liturgies of the book of Revelation. Its nineteenth chapter is an excellent example of the Son of God glorified. The best way to imagine the opening of chapter 19 is to envision a great stage with an enormous choir singing rapturous praises to God for the absolute victory over evil. "Alleluia! Salvation, glory and might belong to our God.... Let us rejoice and be glad and give him glory" (Revelation 19 1,7).

Love is the Dominant Theme

Thousands of verses in the Bible tell the dreary story of human sinfulness. Happily, thousands more contain a tapestry of praise songs that adore God for the gift of salvation. What virtue dominates these full-throated acclamations of God? Love, and love alone.

St. Augustine writes, "Anyone who has learned to love the new life has learned to sing a new song.... We cannot love unless someone has loved us first. The source of our love for God can only be found in the fact that God has loved us first. This love is not something we generate ourselves. It comes to us from the Holy Spirit who has been given to us. God offers us a short route to the possession of himself. God cries out, 'Love me and you will have me, for you will be unable to love me if you did not already have me'" (Sermon 34).

A love of music is not enough. We must have the music of love, of lives responding to the love received from God. The hymns we hear in Revelation 19 are songs rising from Christian witnesses whose lives identified with the Lamb slain and risen. Each singer is a case study in the paschal mystery. The music of the redeemed is more than an esthetic experience. It is the outcome of an ascetical life, the way of the Cross that leads to Easter.

"Then I saw the heavens opened and there was a white horse. Its rider was called Faithful and True.... He has a name written on his cloak and on his thigh, 'King of kings and Lord of lords'" (verses 11, 16). Many will be familiar with these titles of Christ as set to the music of Handel's "Messiah" in the Halleluiah Chorus.

The community of the redeemed join in these hymns of praise. Men and women from every nation, race, people, and tongue have received the loving mark of Christ on their foreheads (cf. Revelation 7:9-17). They wear a white robe, a symbol of spiritual victory, and carry a palm branch, a sign of spiritual triumph. They take no credit for this outcome. They sing, "Salvation belongs to our God who is seated on the throne, and to the Lamb" (Revelation 7:10, NRSV).

Just before his Ascension, Jesus met with his apostles on a mountaintop. Despite their small number and their unpromising talents, Jesus commanded them to bring the gospel to the whole world. The scene in Revelation of the enormous army of the redeemed shows the extraordinary outcome of the mission of the apostles. In human terms, it seemed impossible. With the power of Jesus, it was indeed possible.

Two thousand years later, we see the gospel is preached and witnessed in virtually every nation on earth. Millions accept it. Many do not. Pope John Paul II lived the call to reach almost every country on earth with the gospel. He wrote, "The number of those who do not know Christ and do not belong to the church is constantly on the increase. Indeed, since the end of the Council, it has almost doubled. When we consider this immense portion of humanity which is loved by the Father for whom he sent his Son, the urgency of the Church's mission is obvious.... Peoples everywhere, open your doors to Christ!" (*The Mission of the Redeemer*, 3).

The many scenes of heaven in the book of Revelation remind us of our destiny. It is a place where the redeemed will not hunger or thirst anymore. "The Lamb who is at the center of the throne will be their shepherd, and he will guide them to springs of the water of life, and God will wipe away every tear from their eyes" (Revelation 7:17, NRSV).

REFLECTION

One of the most interesting teachings of the book of Revelation is the transformation of creation into a new heaven and a new earth. The violent scenes of destruction are less a description of the end of the world and more the birth pangs of a new creation. The Second Vatican Council document *Gaudium et Spes* (The Church in the Modern World) has this to say:

We do not know the time when the earth and humanity will reach their completion, nor do we know the way in which the universe will be transformed. The world as we see it, disfigured by sin, is passing away. But we are assured that God is preparing a new dwelling place and a new earth....

We are warned that a man gains nothing if he wins the whole world at the cost of himself. Yet our hope in a new earth should not weaken, but rather stimulate our concern for developing this earth, for on it there is growing up the body of a new human family, a body even now able to provide some foreshadowing of the new age.

Hence, though earthly progress is to be carefully distinguished from the growth of Christ's kingdom, yet insofar as it can help toward the better ordering of human society it is of great importance to the kingdom of God.
GAUDIUM ET SPES, 39

Why do you think people tend to dwell on the trials and tribulations described in the book of Revelation rather than its abundant attention to Christ in glory in the heavenly liturgies? Why is it more useful for our faith to give our primary attention to Jesus victorious over evil?

At the same time, what is the spiritual value in reflecting on the recurrent sufferings and persecution endured by the members of the Church? How would you connect the Church's sufferings with those of Christ's passion and death?

The dramatic catastrophes described in the book of Revelation never destroy more than a third of the earth. At the end of time the world as we know it comes to an end. But, as *Gaudium et Spes* and the book of Revelation teach, this world will be transformed into a new creation. What do you think of this? How does it compare with your imagined end of time? Why is it a more hope-filled understanding of the mercy and love of God?

PRAYER

Christ in glory, we join the angels and saints in their songs of praise for your redemptive love for us. We see a river of life-giving water flowing from your throne into all creation. We hear your voice promising that you will come to us again. Amen! Come, Lord Jesus!

"Let us rejoice and exult and give him the glory,
for the marriage of the Lamb has come,
and his bride has made herself ready...."
"Blessed are those who are invited to the marriage supper of
the Lamb."

REVELATION 19:7, 9